THE INVENTION OF AMSTERDAM

The
INVENTION
of
AMSTERDAM

A History of Europe's Greatest City in Ten Walks

Ben Coates

SCRIBE

Melbourne | London | Minneapolis

Scribe Publications
18–20 Edward St, Brunswick, Victoria 3056, Australia
2 John St, London WC1N 2ES, United Kingdom
3754 Pleasant Ave, Suite 100, Minneapolis, Minnesota
55409, USA

Published by Scribe 2025

Typeset in Sabon by the publisher

Printed and bound in the UK by CPI Group (UK) Ltd,
Croydon CR0 4YY

Scribe is committed to the sustainable use of natural resources
and the use of paper products made responsibly from those
resources.

978 1 915590 35 0 (UK edition)
978 1 964992 09 9 (US edition)
978 1 761386 19 0 (ebook)

Catalogue records for this book are available from the
National Library of Australia and the British Library.

scribepublications.com.au
scribepublications.co.uk
scribepublications.com

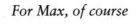

For Max, of course

CONTENTS

INTRODUCTION

Miracle City

Welcome to Amsterdam. It's a Thursday evening in June, one of those special days — relatively rare in this part of the world — when the temperatures feel more Mediterranean than Baltic, the streets are bathed in honey-coloured sunlight, and the whole city seems to have stopped work early and headed outside. I've just finished work myself, in a sturdy office building by the historic Herengracht canal, and have come outside for a walk along the water. You can probably picture the scene already, even if you've never been here yourself: a pretty waterway lined with brick-paved streets, a string of arched little bridges stretching into the distance, and a long row of gorgeous old townhouses lined up along the water like books on a shelf. It all looks pristine and historic; so perfectly preserved that you half expect Rembrandt to appear from round a corner at any moment with a paintbrush and easel in hand.

I walk north along the canal, crossing the tramlines of the

Raadhuisstraat* and glancing left at the soaring tower of the Westerkerk, which looks as if it could be a decoration on a wedding cake. Beside it snakes the tail end of a long queue of tourists waiting to see Anne Frank's annex, guidebooks and cameras in hand. This being Amsterdam, there are few cars on the road, but there's a constant flow of pedestrians passing by on the pavements, boats gurgling along the pea-green canal, and, of course, dozens and dozens of bicycles, weaving effortlessly in and out of one another like fish in a stream.

Amsterdam's canals and streets are (in this part of the city, at least) shaped something like a spider's web, radiating concentrically from Dam Square. Reaching the junction with the Leliegracht, I turn sharply right down a small interconnecting street that threads between the tall buildings towards the next canal over — the Singel. At its end, the alleyway opens out onto a lovely bridge, the Torensluis, which is cobbled with fist-sized grey stones and shaped like an hourglass toppled across the canal. Atop the bridge is a car-sized bust of the great Dutch writer Multatuli, staring severely down at the boats passing below, and around him are dozens of tightly packed cane chairs forming a café terrace. Although the Dutch weather often discourages it, Amsterdammers were drinking and dining al fresco long before pandemics made it cool. I pull a cane chair up to a table on the bumpy cobbles, wobbling like a cow on an ice

---

* By way of introduction to Dutch place names: a *straat* is a street, a *laan* is a lane, and a *weg* is a way; a *gracht* is a canal. A *kerk* is obviously a church, a *kade* is a key and a *bocht* is a bend. In Amsterdam, the River Amstel once divided the city into 'old' and 'new' parts (which were both pretty old), so you'll sometimes see street names beginning with *Oudezijds* (Old-side) or *Nieuwezijds* (New-side) to reflect this.

rink, and order a beer — Belgian, of course. I feel guilty for a moment for not supporting my adopted home country by ordering something Dutch, then cheerfully overcompensate by ordering quintessentially Dutch bar snacks: a small platter of greasy *bitterballen*, deep-fried meat balls that stretch the definition of 'meat' to its absolute limits.

Munching my crispy 'meat', I glance around at my fellow drinkers and diners and see that they encompass a broad cross-section of modern city life: an older man with little round spectacles carefully reading the newspaper, *de Volkskrant;* three glamorous young women ordering small portions of coleslaw and nothing else; a tattooed English guy and his girlfriend discussing how to pronounce *Hoegaarden* (no, guys, not like that; it's not an open-air brothel); and a pair of young men in suits, laughing and speaking Swahili. Everyone has rotated their chairs to face the warm early evening sun, and everyone looks happy. In the distance, a crane mounted on a barge swings a pallet of bricks low over the water, narrowly missing the DHL parcel delivery boat that slips underneath like a giant banana floating downstream. A church bell tinkles in the distance, its music mingling prettily with the sound of a far-off tram bell, clanking angrily at some rule-breaking cyclist. The city feels simultaneously very laid-back and very alive.

I finish my beer and swiftly order another. The worries of work and family life drain away like warm water from a bath and I briefly feel that for all the talk of penicillin and the steam engine and the pneumatic tyre, this, actually, might be Western civilisation's pinnacle of accomplishment: a beautiful city where bicycles outnumber cars, kids can play safely in the streets, old buildings are bathed in golden sunlight, and an attentive waiter keeps asking if I want more beer or bar snacks. Amsterdam is, I think, Paris without the noisy traffic. London without the inequality. Venice with bicycles. If the whole world was like this city, then, well, that would be absolutely fine with me.

I first came to Amsterdam more than twenty years ago now, as a child on holiday with my parents and sister. As a young teenager, the city's myriad delights were largely lost on me — somewhere in my parents' house in England, there's still a yellow Kodak envelope of photos which show me looking riled at the Rijksmuseum, annoyed at Anne Frank's house, cross on a canal tour, and vexed by the Van Gogh Museum. Later, in my early twenties, I came back a couple of times and enjoyed myself, despite behaving like the cliché of a British tourist in Europe: eating Belgian waffles and American hamburgers, smoking weed, and, if memory serves, offending an elderly Dutchman by asking him why the French flag was flying everywhere. (It wasn't; the Dutch and French flags just look similar). Then, about twelve years ago, I found myself here again, after a cancelled flight left me stranded in an Amsterdam thickly carpeted with snow. With nothing to do and nowhere to go, I called a Dutch acquaintance and she invited me round for dinner. As the saying goes, the rest is history. Within just a few weeks, I was living the life of an honorary Dutchman: spending summer evenings like this swimming in the Amstel and then drinking cheap rosé on someone's balcony, and winter evenings talking in grotty brown bars until the sun came up. Within a few years, I'd gained, more or less by accident, a cottage in the countryside south of the city, a Dutch wife, Dutch children, a half-Dutch dog, a Dutch job in that office on the Herengracht canal and even a Dutch passport. I cycled almost everywhere, and subsisted on a diet that was approximately 50 per cent cheese and 50 per cent beer. I'd learned to speak Dutch, turning phlegmy coughs into vaguely pronounceable words with the reckless enthusiasm of a man who was all out of cough syrup. I even owned a pair of yellow clogs, which I wore to walk the dog in the rain.

As I explored Amsterdam, I quickly realised it wasn't — and isn't — perfect. Like all big cities, the postcard imagery can hide a multitude of sins: drug abuse and gang crime, racism and populism, high house prices and declining public services, the crowding out of locals by noisy tourists only interested in having a good time. However, like a lover learning to adore someone's scars and blemishes, I soon also learned to embrace the city's contradictions: recognising its complexities and flaws as being an essential part of its charm. There was, I came to realise, great joy in the fact that Amsterdam was (and is) both orderly and anarchic, historic and modern, perfectly preserved and constantly changing, achingly hip and charmingly old-fashioned. This is a place where you could go clubbing until dawn in your underwear but might still, if you forgot to wash your windows, get tutted at by a neighbour who thinks anyone who moved here after 1980 is an outsider. I loved the way the city felt both compact and enormous: with around 900,000 people,[1] Amsterdam is bigger than Frankfurt or San Francisco, and a bit smaller than Birmingham. By Dutch standards, it counts as a mega metropolis, but it somehow retains the feeling of being a large village, where if you walk just a few minutes across town you're quite likely to bump into someone you know. I loved the endless variety of delightful cafés, bars, restaurants, and bookshops, and the lively cultural scene. I loved the no-nonsense attitude of the people, who were overwhelmingly kind and friendly but would also, if you put on weight, not hesitate to diplomatically point out: 'You've got fat.' I loved the way streets were safe at midnight, but you could also get away with doing things that might get you arrested in Rome or Boston. I loved that on summer evenings like this, the wide sky and reflective properties of the omnipresent water make the light as bright and clear as on a mountaintop. And perhaps most importantly, I loved — and still love — the way Amsterdam is fun in a way some historic cities are not, combining high culture and hedonism in an irresistibly heady cocktail. There aren't many places in the world in which you can admire world-class collections of Rembrandts and van Goghs in the morning, go to the beach in the afternoon, have dinner in a hipster converted warehouse brewery, and then (if you so wish) visit a 5D sex club on the way home. Like all cities, Amsterdam can be infuriating sometimes. And it's wonderful.

I started walking around Amsterdam after I broke my leg. I was running through the countryside south of the city when it happened, loping across a grassy field towards a scenic windmill with my dog galloping at my side. Feeling athletic and full of the joys of spring, I vaulted majestically over a steel gate at speed, then landed with one leg folded un-majestically underneath me. There was a loud crack, like the sound of a snapping breadstick. Months on crutches ensued, during which the break stubbornly refused to heal, followed by painful surgery that left the inside of my leg looking like the Eiffel Tower, with more metal than bone.

For a couple of months, I mostly stewed at home, trying to improve my Dutch by watching Danish thrillers with Dutch subtitles, which was about as confusing as it sounds. Then, with my leg still in a heavy blue plaster cast, a doctor recommended that I should start taking regular walks with a pair of crutches. And so began a new routine: once or twice a week, I'd take a tram or an Uber to a different part of Amsterdam and go for a walk, partly as a way of building my strength and partly as a way of alleviating my boredom. At first, my expeditions were painfully slow: with a crutch under each arm, I could just about hobble a hundred metres along a canal and back before collapsing on someone's doorstep, wheezing and sweating as if I'd just run a marathon. In time, though, as the scars healed and my strength grew, I replaced the crutches with a wooden walking stick and began venturing a little further: first one canal over, then two, then to the church at the end of the street, then to an exhibition at the Museumplein, and then to that nice bar on the edge of the Jordaan. Gradually, as my strength grew further, I embarked on what felt at the time like truly epic adventures: out through the lively neighbourhood of de Pijp or the Western Docklands, along the old wharves and warehouses north of the River IJ*, or along the River Amstel into the surrounding countryside.

In some ways, walking slowly through Amsterdam was an odd way to explore the city. This is famously a city of bicycles, with two underground bike parking sheds at the

---

* That's not a typo — in the Dutch language 'IJ' is a diphthong, always capitalised and pronounced 'eye'.

central train station, which together contain eleven thousand spaces[2] (and reportedly cost more than €65 million to build)[3] yet still often seem full. When I first began walking the city, I was frustrated at being forced to explore slowly on two feet rather than quickly on two wheels. In time, though, I realised that central Amsterdam is not just a cyclist's paradise, but a pedestrian's one too. Some cities, like Moscow and Berlin, feel as if they were designed for parades and troop movements, but Amsterdam feels designed for strolling. It has a centre that you can walk across in an hour, flat terrain, a simple layout, largely car-free streets, and a nice café or bar on almost every corner for the benefit of those (like me) who find it hard to go more than thirty minutes without a coffee and a cookie. Two wheels are great fun, but two legs can be just as good.

Moving slowly through the city, I also found myself suddenly noticing things I'd previously rushed past. I'd spent years traversing this city in all directions and at all times of day and night, but always at high speed. Now, though, in need of regular stops to rest my leg, I found myself carefully studying buildings I'd zoomed past hundreds of times before, poking my head through open doorways and nosing through courtyards and churches. As my walks got longer, I also took to carrying a book with me. When my leg throbbed too much, I'd sit on a bench or canal wall for a while and read about the history of places I was walking through. The city, once a playground to me, became a classroom.

After a few months of almost daily walking, reading, and scribbling notes, I decided to formalise things and explore properly. The result was a series of ten walks, starting in the heart of the city in Dam Square and spreading out from there like the ripples from a pebble dropped in a canal. My walks varied in length from just a mile or two to about ten miles; with the earliest, shortest ones focused on the oldest, most central parts of the city, and the later, longer ones spanning the outlying areas developed in the 1800s, 1900s and beyond. This book is, quite simply, the story of those walks and the things that I learned on them.

It's perhaps important to acknowledge up front that the ground I covered during my walks was not off the beaten track, either figuratively or literally. Amsterdam and its glory years can only be considered 'unknown' or 'unexplored' in the same way that Tenerife might be described as a 'secret island' or the Rolling Stones as an 'undiscovered new band'. However, as I walked and talked and read my way around the city, it also became clear to me that there's a lot more to Amsterdam than meets the eye. In the English-speaking world, some elements of the story (such as the life of Rembrandt) have been told before. However, other aspects of the city's history are barely known. It's still bafflingly easy to find magisterial histories of European civilisation that inexplicably don't include the word 'Amsterdam' at all — or, indeed, magisterial histories of Amsterdam that don't include words like 'slavery' or 'colonialism', let alone 'Bijlmer' or 'Sloterplas'. Too often, this city is still viewed in terms of breezy clichés; or as a place where history started in 1600 and ended in 1700. Amsterdam is portrayed as a kind of peaceful, tolerant museum piece rather than a living, breathing, complicated place, with grand churches and beautiful art galleries but also grimy bus stations, post-industrial wastelands, and low-income housing. This city's history is (like most places' histories) a complicated patchwork of triumphs and failures, golden eras and dark times, victories and defeats. Amsterdam has reinvented itself repeatedly.

This, then, became the immodest goal of my walks, and this book: to give a balanced overview of how Amsterdam is today. It recounts the story of how a muddy fishing and farming village transformed into a world-beating metropolis. It explains how Amsterdammers helped create world-beating art and architecture, how Rembrandt was inspired by walks along the Amstel and how Spinoza grew up in the city's Jewish Quarter. It explains how Amsterdam was, for a good while, one of the wealthiest and most dynamic cities in the world; becoming the place that invented the limited company and the stock exchange, introduced products like coffee and porcelain to Europe; pioneered surgery, printing, mapmaking, and microscopy; and ran an empire stretching from Brazil to Borneo to boot. But it is also a story of invention and reinvention: explaining how Amsterdam rose to great prominence in its Golden Age, then fell from glory, then rose to riches again in a Second Golden Age, then was wrecked and humiliated in the mid-20th century, and then rose yet again; like a boxer in a Stallone movie who just can't be kept down. In the course of writing, I visited blockbusters like the Rijksmuseum, Vondelpark, and Anne Frank House, but also less touristy spots such as KNSM, Tuindorp Oostzaan, IJburg, and Bijlmer. This book explores the city's many glories and delights, but also looks at some of the challenges Amsterdam will face in the future, including a looming sea-level rise, which is pretty alarming for a city already several metres below sea level. But anyway, that's enough of all that for now. It's a beautiful evening, and all my bar snacks are finished now. Let's go for a walk and look around together.

CHAPTER ONE

Pride, the Prinsengracht, and the Old City Centre

*The founding of Amsterdam
and how it won its freedom*

Pride in Amsterdam is one hell of a party. By noon, the streets along the Prinsengracht canal are already packed with people — half a million of them, according to news reports, thronging the narrow streets, squeezed onto bridges and hanging from the windows of the tall canal houses that line the route of the waterborne parade. There are rainbow-coloured flags and balloons everywhere, and deafening disco music echoes through the surrounding alleyways. Down on the canal itself, a succession of boats surges by, each carrying dozens of people dancing and waving, most of them wearing neon or rainbow-coloured clothes, or wearing sparkly wigs, or wearing almost nothing at all. I've made a token effort to fit in by wearing a pink hoody, but feel so boringly underdressed that I might as well have donned a funeral suit. A man with rainbow-coloured angel wings on his back blows me a kiss and then does a little butt-shaking dance for the benefit of a tiny passing baby, only a couple of months old, who is wearing ear plugs and has a rainbow flag painted across his face. Nearby, a middle-aged man removes a T-shirt printed with the slogan 'GAY AS FUCK' to reveal a silver chain that links his nipples together before heading down into his underpants.

In many ways, Pride is a terribly clichéd place to begin an exploration of Amsterdam. When I began getting to know the Netherlands properly more than a decade ago, I was immediately struck by the way the country is mischaracterised internationally. Endless attention is given to the liberal, hedonistic side of Dutch culture and none at all to the fact that the Netherlands often feels quite conservative: a place where the perpetual risk of flooding and old religious values mean a tidy, small-c conservatism is the default setting. In many smaller Dutch towns and villages, you're about as likely to find a gay bar as you are a ski resort. However, it's also clear that LGBTQ+ rights have long been an area in which the Dutch have particular expertise. Surveys have found that 92 per cent of Dutch people say homosexuality 'should be accepted', compared to 72 per cent of Americans, 86 per cent of Brits and Germans, and 47 per cent of Poles.[1] It's also notable that even far-right politicians in the Netherlands go out of their way to stress their support for LGBT rights — intolerance of Islam is often framed as Islam being incompatible with equal rights for LGBT people.[*] And even within the Netherlands, Amsterdam is particularly

---

[*]   Surveys have found that while only 36 per cent of Americans with right-wing political views support gay marriage, in the Netherlands the equivalent figure is 85 per cent — roughly the same level as on the political left. (Pew World Values Survey, 2020)

gay-friendly. The first gay bar in Amsterdam opened in the 1920s, and the city's main LGBT advocacy group (COC) claims to be the oldest such organisation in the world. Same-sex marriages have been legal here since 2001, and the first Pride parade took place in 1996.[2] In 2022, between 12 and 16 per cent of all Amsterdam residents said they were gay, lesbian, or bisexual,[3] and (relative to its population) there are nearly three times more married gay people in Amsterdam than there are in Rotterdam.[4] Thanks to this history, Pride today feels like the embodiment of two of the things which make Amsterdam so unique: its freewheeling, slightly anarchic spirit; and its tolerance of minorities. It also, for me, embodies some of the joyous contradictions at the heart of the city's charm. Pride is a raucous, rowdy, sexy, hedonistic party that has been carefully planned by the authorities months in advance, which will all have been neatly tidied away within a few hours.**

As I watch from the canal bank, another colourful boat sails past: the official vessel representing the Dutch military, loaded with soldiers, sailors, and aviators dancing to Gloria Gaynor. Suddenly, a command rings out and the whole boat abruptly snaps to attention, salutes, then holds their pose rigidly for a few seconds, before another order rings out and they all start dancing again. The spectators on the canal bank go wild. The Netherlands was the first country in the world to lift a ban on homosexuals in its armed forces, in 1974 — more than thirty-five years before the US military scrapped 'Don't Ask, Don't Tell' in 2011. However, this will be the first year

---

** The event has changed names several times, including from Gay Pride to LGBT Pride to Pride. I have used the simplest, most recent name throughout.

that the head of the Dutch armed forces, Onno Eichelsheim, actually takes part in Pride. I see him now, grinning at the centre of the boat, resplendent in a dark uniform glittering with golden badges. 'I want to show that I stand behind my people,' he later says.

I could happily stay and watch the parade for hours, but I've set myself a goal of limping in a loop through the old city centre for exercise today, and so I set out to do that, intending to pop back to check in on the party later. Leaving the Prinsengracht, I walk along a pretty side street leading towards the Keizersgracht — the next ring in the concentric pattern of canals that radiates outwards from the Dam. Just a few steps from the main parade route, the city is already a lot quieter, although there's still a carnival atmosphere, with most shops and bars flying rainbow flags, and hundreds of revellers in the streets. One enterprising young man is selling cans of beer from the front of a *bakfiets* (cargo bike) and another is doing a roaring trade in plastic cups of orange Aperol. I stop at a pop-up bar in a restaurant doorway and order a mojito.

'I don't actually know how to make a mojito,' the lanky barman confesses in Dutch, brushing his long orange wig away from his face, 'but I think I can figure it out.' A minute later, I receive a large plastic cup of rum and ice with a sprig of mint on top, which I guzzle happily as I walk on. I pass a young man wearing a pair of tight white trousers who is inviting strangers to sign them with a thick black pen, like a kid collecting autographs on a plaster cast. A police officer passes by and grabs the pen, scrawls her name across his buttocks, then blows him a kiss before walking away.

Many cities have their own foundational myth. Athens was, we're told, named after Athena, goddess of wisdom, who planted an olive tree there. Alexandria was born when Alexander the Great dreamed of a beautiful naval city; Antwerp when a local hero defeated a giant guarding the River Scheldt; and Rome by Romulus and Remus, brothers raised by a she-wolf. In the case of Amsterdam, however, the story is a little more prosaic. Several versions of the city's founding myth exist, but my favourite claims that the city was born when two men and a dog went fishing in a small boat on the Zuiderzee, an offshoot of the North Sea tucked in behind present-day Amsterdam. All was going well until a storm hit, the boat began rocking wildly, and the poor dog became terribly seasick. Feeling sorry for him, the sailors steered their boat towards the nearest spot of dry land, upon which the dog leaped out of the boat and promptly threw up. Amsterdam was then founded, naturally, on the very spot where the pooch's puke had landed — an early tribute, perhaps, to all those stag party tourists who still regularly Jackson Pollock the canal sides after enjoying too many Heinekens.

The story of the vomiting dog is almost certainly a myth, but historians agree that Amsterdam was born as a small fishing, farming, and trading community, located at a convenient watery crossroads where the River Amstel flowed into the larger River IJ. ('Ame' means water and a 'stelle' is a protected or safe place.) In the 13th century, the locals built a dam bridging the Amstel, roughly where Dam Square is now, creating a little harbour where people could easily load or unload their boats. Interestingly, this implies that compared with many other cities in Europe, Amsterdam is a relatively recent invention. At the time of the Dutch capital's first recorded history, in 1275, the Tower of London's main building had already been standing for more than a century, and Paris's Notre Dame Cathedral was already largely complete. Yet Amsterdam in the late 13th century was what we'd now call a hamlet or village, a small cluster of wooden houses and outbuildings. It would have looked less like London or Paris and more like somewhere Shrek might live.*

Why, though, did Amsterdam get started so much later than some other cities? The answer lies largely in Dutch geography. Fly into or out of Schiphol Airport today and, if the clouds are sparse enough, you'll see one of the wettest landscapes in Europe: an endless soggy expanse of canals, rivers, drainage ditches, and lakes, cobwebbing the flat green landscape like the shiny lines printed on a circuit board. Barely fifteen miles west of Amsterdam lies the North Sea, and less than ten miles to the east are the vast lakes of the IJmeer, the Markermeer, and IJsselmeer (which used to be the Zuiderzee). The whole region has the consistency of a wedding cake that has been dropped in a puddle.

Given this, it's little surprise that the earliest Amsterdammers lived simply, in turf or wooden houses which were constructed on top of heaps of mud, branches, and animal skins. The whole region was, as Thomas Macaulay wrote in the 19th century, 'a desolate marsh overhung by fogs and exhaling diseases, a marsh where there was neither wood nor stone, neither firm earth nor drinkable water'.[5] The

---

* The country we now know as 'the Netherlands' has been known by different names at various times in its history, including 'the Dutch Republic' and 'the Batavian Republic'. To keep things simple, I call it 'the Netherlands' throughout.

region's fortunes began to improve with the arrival of the Romans in the 1st century BC. Roman settlements in places like Utrecht, Nijmegen, and Maastricht grew into sizeable towns, with handsome mosaiced villas, temples, bathhouses, and even homes with central heating. To the north, though, things were rather different. Flevum, near Velsen, on the coast to the west of modern Amsterdam, became an important military base for the Romans; probably used as a launchpad for the invasion of Britain. But around Amsterdam itself, the swampy terrain and strong resistance from local tribes meant there was little in the way of permanent Roman settlement.

Archaeologists have found a few Roman coins when digging tunnels under the River IJ but otherwise there's little evidence that the Romans had much presence in Amsterdam itself. The famous *Tabula Peutingeriana* — a sort of Roman road atlas of important cities and stopping places — doesn't include anywhere north of Katwijk, a good distance south of modern Amsterdam. For people used to Mediterranean climes, it just wasn't that appealing here. In his *Germania* (AD 98) the great chronicler Tacitus described the northern Netherlands as 'wild in its scenery, harsh in its climate, and grim to inhabit and behold'. The local people, Tacitus said, 'love idleness' — something many Dutch people from outside Amsterdam will tell you still applies to the locals today.

Overstretched and beset by incursions from tribes, the Romans began to pull out of the Low Countries in the 3rd century AD. Infrastructure crumbled and towns like Utrecht faded into insignificance. The Roman exit did have one important effect, though. As Roman roads fell into disrepair, rivers like the Amstel and Rhine became increasingly important as trade routes, enabling goods and people to be moved smoothly and cheaply from one place to another. By about the 11th century, trade began to pick up again and the population of the Low Countries began to grow, with people moving into places like Abcoude and Sloten, which now form suburbs of modern Amsterdam. As the population grew, food sometimes ran short, and so, in about the 11th century, people began the process of reclaiming land; building dikes, digging drainage ditches, and damming rivers to help drain water out of marshland. Along the River Amstel to the south of the modern city, clusters of farmers and craftsmen raised pigs, grew crops, and made iron tools and weapons. Ouderkerk aan de Amstel, south of Amsterdam, grew into a small town, with fisherman and traders heading downriver to where the Amstel met the IJ. And then came the Amstel-dam itself, built near the junction of the Amstel and IJ rivers, a knot of civilisation in a Y-shaped blue string. A harbour appeared behind the dam. Traders came by boat to buy and sell fish and other goods. More dikes sprang up, increasing the area of dry land to be built on. And the little town on the Amstel-dam grew and grew.

With my cup of rum still in hand, I continue walking east towards Dam Square, along a narrow street that is enclosed by two high rows of houses like a tectonic rift. I'm already deep into the touristic zone that many 'real' Amsterdammers rarely visit.

'I don't cross the Prinsengracht. Ever,' one local friend told me, 'unless there's some kind of emergency.'

At the end of the street, the Nieuwe Kerk (New Church) rises sharply before me like a cliff face. Up close, the church is soot-stained but impressive; a hulking mass of stone and stained glass made delicate by the inclusion of hundreds of Gothic archways, statues, and spires. Only in Europe, I think, could a church more than 500 years old still be called 'New'. I loop left round the back of the church like a pilgrim circling a prayer wheel. In other countries, great cathedrals like this often stand clear of everything else, surrounded by an empty square or grassy plaza, but in this busy little country — nearly twice as densely populated as Britain[6] — everything is packed in tightly, and on this side of the building only a few metres separate the church from its neighbours. Frisbee a *stroopwafel* from the window of a nearby café and you'd risk breaking a stained-glass window. I pause for a takeaway coffee and sit for a moment in the sun while it's made. Next to me are two Muslim women in headscarves discussing the best location for viewing the Pride parade. We're perhaps half a mile from the parade itself now, but the music in the distance is at times so loud that the crockery on the café tables trembles as if there's an approaching dinosaur.

'I just love seeing all the old guys wearing chains and stuff, as if it's completely normal!' one of the women says.

Coffee in hand, I round a corner and am confronted by one of the city's most famous landmarks: the Royal Palace on Dam Square; a majestic pile of sand-coloured stone with a greenish clock tower on top and a wide balcony. A few steps further and I emerge onto Dam Square itself, the epicentre of the city, sprawling in front of the Palace like an apron.* I pause for a moment and soak up the panorama. To the west, where I've just walked from, are the grimy Nieuwe Kerk and

---

*   Amsterdammers often refer to Dam Square as just 'the Dam', while foreigners tend to use the longer name. In this book, I use both.

Palace; and to the east, a wide plaza dominated by a gleaming white war memorial, all ringed by grand shops, banks, and apartment buildings. The square is crowded with selfie-taking tourists, hotdog sellers, and an uncountable number of young Englishmen who look as if they need a spell in rehab.

At this point in the narrative, I should probably wax lyrical about how beautiful Dam Square is. Yet if we're being honest, the Dam is actually a fairly forgettable place. Yes, the Nieuwe Kerk is beautiful, but in a glum sort of way. It looks as if it could do with a good clean. The Royal Palace next door, meanwhile, is grand in scale but also quite austere and generically north European. One historian accurately described it as a palace that is 'pretending to be a large post office'.[7] Many of the other buildings around it look sturdy rather than stunning. The contrast with somewhere like the Grand Place in Brussels, 130 miles to the south and bursting with baroque gold leaf, is stark. Yet there is, I suppose, something quintessentially Dutch (and even quite charming) about the humility of it all. For the main square to be pleasant but forgettable feels entirely fitting for a country where a cheese roll is considered a decent business lunch and the prime minister's motorcade is a bicycle.

Crossing the square, I pass Madame Tussauds and begin walking down the Kalverstraat; a slender shopping street that dangles off the southern edge of Dam Square like the tail of a tadpole. The Kalverstraat is ostensibly one of the most important commercial thoroughfares in the Netherlands — on the Dutch version of Monopoly, it occupies the space taken by Mayfair in the English version. However, like Dam Square itself, it is a little underwhelming. The Kalverstraat is only about ten paces wide, and the buildings on either side are an odd mishmash of different styles and eras; not exactly ugly but not too beautiful either. It's no Champs-Élysées. Rubbish bags sit piled next to shop doorways waiting to be collected, and the only real sight worth noting is a big Lego rainbow in the window of the Lego shop. Outside the Body Shop, an advertising board encourages shoppers to 'grab hemp by the handful' — something that I'm sure many of them have already been doing, anyway. There are some hidden treasures, though. Passing number 78, I glance up and notice a nice little statuette of a luxuriantly moustachioed man in baggy blue trousers, perched imperiously above a shop entrance. In the days when literacy was low, *gevelstenen* like this helped identify who lived or worked inside — look around town and you'll see ones decorated with trees and castles, accordion players and prophets, hippos and dragons. Often in Amsterdam, the best view is to be found up above street level, where colourful plaques, statues, and engravings abound.

Rather improbably, some of the very first houses in Amsterdam were likely to have been built where the Kalverstraat now stands. The original street level would have been a few metres lower than it is today, and if you lifted up the concrete tiles under the feet of the shoppers and began digging, you'd probably soon reach a layer of wood, animal hides, and other junk that constituted some of the earliest foundations of the city.

The first written mention of Amsterdam famously came in 1275, when one of the region's rulers, Count Floris V, issued a document granting the people living in this area the freedom to navigate the rivers of Holland without paying tolls. Go to the city archives on the right day and you can still see the so-called *Tolprivilege*: a wrinkled document that looks like it's

been soaked in a bowl of tea, scrawled with text declaring
the creation of a nice tax cut for '*homines manentes apud
Amestelledamme*' — 'people living near the Amstel dam'. For
historians, this counts as the closest thing Amsterdam has to
a birth certificate. The toll exemptions were a real gift for a
small town in a soggy location. Amsterdammers could now
buy or sell goods across a wide area without paying taxes
on their journey. Trade flooded in, and within a few years
Amsterdam was importing and exporting goods, including
wine, beer, salt, honey, herring, lumber, and livestock. The
city lay, then as now, at the crossroads of northern Europe: an
easy journey downriver from France or Germany; relatively
close to Hamburg, London, Cologne, Antwerp, Lille, Bruges,
and Brussels; and conveniently near to the point where ships
passing between the Baltic, North Sea, Channel, Rhine,
and Maas had to pass. If someone wanted to ship a load of
German wines to London, or a boatful of timber from Sweden
to northern France, or some Russian amber to Flanders, it
would have to pass either through or close by here. Other
great trading cities — Lisbon, Seville, Venice — specialised in
valuable, relatively lightweight goods like silks. But the Dutch
in the early days did the opposite, focusing on the transport
of big, cheap, heavy goods, which they could move around on
their rivers at remarkably low cost. The bishop of Avranches
once expressed amazement at how low shipping costs meant
that the price of Swedish products was the same in Amsterdam
as in Sweden. Amsterdam's watery geography had once been
its greatest weakness, but was now its trump card.

As the city's prosperity grew, new streets, walls, and
canals gave it a new shape. In the early days, goods arriving
in Amsterdam by sea would have pulled up somewhere

close to the current train station, where the river mouth was shielded by a long row of wooden stakes sticking out of the water like dragon's teeth. There were also big wooden booms that swung shut every evening, closing the harbour at night. Larger ships arriving from elsewhere in Europe would have moored just beyond the stakes and offloaded onto smaller boats, which then shuttled inland towards the Dam. Upon reaching the centre, cargoes were then transferred onto carts, wheelbarrows, smaller boats or — if it was snowy — sleighs, which were dragged through the town and sometimes caused chaos when they hurtled out of control down the slopes of bridges.

Between 1300 and 1400, Amsterdam's population more than tripled, from about one thousand to roughly four thousand people.[8] One can almost imagine the surprise of a befuddled farmer, paying a rare visit to the city after years away, and being astonished by the sight of Danes, Germans, Swedes, and Scots buying and selling all kinds of goods, where just a decade or two previously there had been nothing but mud, fishing equipment, and livestock. Foreign visitors were amazed. An Italian called Lodovico Guicciardini described the city as having 'one of the goodliest havens in the world ... [with] sometimes at one instant five hundred ... ships riding in the port'.[9] Amsterdam was, he said, 'so rich that [if] a fleet of sails, laden with all kinds of merchandise arrives there, the Citizens within five or six days will buy up all their wares'. Amsterdam was from the outset an outward-looking city, which understood that its success depended on being open to the wider world. 'The cow's udder cannot enrich the city's life,' the great poet Vondel wrote, 'but sea trade builds it up, and makes it truly thrive.'[10]

Resisting the urge to buy a Lego windmill, I walk further along the Kalverstraat, weaving my way through crowds of mid-morning shoppers. With my happy glow from the rum already wearing off, I'm getting hungry and so stop to buy a favourite Dutch dish: a *broodje rookworst*; a sort of chunky hotdog containing an enormous half-horseshoe of fatty sausage, slathered with mustard. I stand in the street for a minute gobbling hungrily, spilling mustard on my shoes and telling myself my diet will start tomorrow. How Dutch people manage to remain so slim while eating so much cheese, sausage, and fried food is one of life's great mysteries. This is, perhaps, the only country in the world where retailers could routinely get away with calling a baguette filled with eggs, ham, and cheese a '*broodje gezond*', or 'healthy roll'.*

I walk a few hundred metres further and the Kalverstraat opens out into a square; the Spui, which is much smaller than the Dam, but arguably prettier. After the modern chaos of the Kalverstraat, the Spui feels almost like a little slice of Paris: leafy and tranquil and lined with cafés and bookstores. At one end of the square I find a modest local landmark, the Jonk Volendammer herring stall: a fishmonger's specialising in noxious pickled fish. Herring stands like this are a great Dutch institution, and an excellent place for a snack if you want to become or remain single.

Turning north, I cross the Spui and head up a little alleyway to where there's a dark wooden door set in a high brick wall. It's locked, but after a minute or two a woman comes out, and I duck through it just before it slams shut

---

*   The Netherlands has more McDonald's 'restaurants' than Finland, Ireland, and Belgium combined.

again. Inside is a well-known attraction that I've never been to before. I could be forgiven for not having seen it, though, as the whole point is that it's somewhat hidden, walled off from the outside world.

The Begijnhof is a historic place of refuge, first mentioned in city records in the 1300s. *Begijnen* were deeply religious Catholic women who behaved somewhat like nuns but didn't want to live in a convent under strict vows, and so settled here instead, in a kind of sheltered accommodation reserved for devout Catholic ladies. They lived there more or less for free and received medical care, peat to burn, and food. It must have been very peaceful, not least because the Begijnhof used to be almost completely surrounded by water, only reachable by bridge.

Today, the religious significance of the Begijnhof itself has faded, since the last official *Begijn* passed away in the 1970s. But it remains a place of refuge and tranquillity, where only women — about a hundred of them in total — are allowed to live. Walking further past the gate, I emerge into a beautiful courtyard, hemmed in on all sides by pretty little terraced houses. At the centre lies a triangular lawn of immaculate emerald grass, surrounded by beautiful tall trees, and a stout brick church. I remember reading somewhere that the neatly mown lawn was originally used to dry laundry, and that the courtyard remains roughly a metre lower than the rest of the city centre, still at the original street level. It feels almost as if an idyllic English village has somehow been airlifted here and dropped intact in the heart of Amsterdam. Most remarkable of all is the silence: standing near the front door of the church and closing my eyes, I can hear the occasional jangle of a tram bell or car horn, but otherwise it's almost completely silent. It's hard to believe I'm only a few yards from the main shopping street in one of the busiest cities in Europe.

Today it may seem odd to think of central Amsterdam as a place of religious sanctuary — internationally, the city has a reputation as a place where commandments are broken rather than obeyed. However, religion and pilgrimage also played an important role in the early growth of Amsterdam. In 1345, in fact, a miracle took place on the Kalverstraat. The story goes that a dying man, unable to eat, threw (or perhaps vomited) a wafer into a fire, probably at the location where the Amsterdam Dungeon stands today. The next morning, a cleaner found the wafer still intact, and a priest threw it in the fire again, but the same thing happened again: the dying man's snack survived the flames unscathed. As myths go, a fireproof biscuit might not sound much more impressive than a puking dog, but in the 14th century such a tale was enough to get the townspeople pretty excited. The Catholic Church heralded a miracle, and pilgrims were soon flocking to the Kalverstraat in large numbers. A chapel was built on the site where the non-burning had happened — the building is sadly long gone, but you can still see a big pillar from it standing on the Rokin, in front of Starbucks. Other miracles followed the one with the wafer, and pilgrims were soon travelling from across Europe to see the place a sick woman managed to walk around a church or a man was saved from drowning. Pilgrims included Maximilian I, later Holy Roman Emperor, whose visit helped raise the profile of the holy sites further. (Amsterdam repaid Maximilian by supporting his military adventures, after which he let the city use his crown symbol — you can still see it on

the city's coat of arms, and atop the tower of the Westerkerk.*)
The keenest pilgrims arrived on foot, having walked here
along the Heilige Weg, or Holy Way — a street called
Heiligeweg still exists today. (Also still around: an alleyway
near the Rokin called *Gebed Zonder End*, or 'prayer without
end'.) Eventually, by the 16th century, perhaps a fifth of the
city's land would be given over to churches, monasteries, and
their gardens, breweries, and orchards. A city now known for
its hedonistic godlessness was, for a long time, a profoundly
religious place.

Walking in a circle through the Begijnhof garden, I spot
another sight that I've read about many times but somehow
never found the time to visit before. The so-called *Houten
Huis*, or Wooden House, stands at Begijnhof 34 and is one
of the oldest buildings in Amsterdam, dating from the late
1400s or early 1500s, which makes it, among other things,
more than three centuries older than most of Westminster's
Houses of Parliament.** Walking closer, I see that the name
is a little misleading: the house clearly isn't entirely made of
wood. But it is a large, surprisingly imposing structure, with a
pointy triangular roof and a sheer wooden façade painted as
black as coal, inlaid with five rows of neat white windows. It
looks like somewhere Harry Potter might go to buy a wand.

At the time the wooden house was built, Amsterdam
was growing fast — by 1560, it would already have 27,000

---

*   Another symbol you'll see around town: the XXX symbol of
    St Andrew, an apostle and fisherman who was martyred on an
    X-shaped cross. When Amsterdam was a fishing port, all ships
    from here paid tribute by flying the XXX flag.

** The exact age of the *Houten Huis* is disputed; for years it was thought
    to be from the 1450s but more recent research dates it to the 1520s.
    Either way, it's still the oldest house in Amsterdam.

inhabitants.[11] However, it was still a scruffy and disorganised place. A visitor wouldn't have had to walk far to encounter livestock roaming freely and manure underfoot. There was rubbish in the rivers and the air was often thick with soot from cooking fires. Thousands of people lived in very cramped conditions. Given the crowding and poor hygiene, outbreaks of deadly disease were frequent. 'Sickness contrasted more strongly with health,' wrote Johan Huizinga. 'The cutting cold and the dreaded darkness of winter were more concrete evils.'[12] Terrible fires were common: in the spring of 1421, a single conflagration destroyed a third of the homes in the city. Flooding also remained a constant threat. 'Amsterdam is in permanent peril of inundation', one early visitor wrote, 'and its preservation is the result of the constant exercise of no small attention and skill in the regulation of the various waters amidst which it stands.'[13] Houses would sometimes sink downwards into the boggy ground, and parts of the city were muddier than a music festival.

Against that backdrop, it's perhaps not surprising that as time passed, Amsterdam's leaders began making concerted efforts to tidy things up a bit. Given the primitive state of building equipment and the bogginess of the ground, adding new houses or canals required an extraordinary effort. Famously, the soft ground meant that new buildings often had to be built on top of long wooden poles pushed deep into the ground. Erasmus once said that Amsterdam was 'a city where the inhabitants are like rooks living in trees',[14] while Caspar Barlaeus noted the oddity that 'decaying pines support the most prosperous Mercantile centre in Europe'.[15] Amsterdam's central train station (built in the late 1800s) would famously be propped up by more than eight thousand wooden poles, teetering like an elephant on a bed of nails. The cost of building could, therefore, be huge, which encouraged people to build houses that were tall and skinny, with a small footprint, supported by as few pilings as possible. However, for early Amsterdammers, investing in construction was already proving very worthwhile. By digging more canals and harbours, they could generate more income, which meant they had more to invest in canals and harbours, which meant even more income. And as incomes rose, Amsterdam began to acquire the trappings of a real town, with churches and some beautiful homes. Foreign travellers who arrived in the city were often delighted by what they saw. Vicente Álvarez toured Holland in 1549, for example, and was amazed by the amount of food consumed here, the cleanliness of the houses, and the signs of wealth that were everywhere. 'Almost everyone knew how to read and write,' he recorded in amazement, 'even women.'[16]

Leaving the blissful courtyard of the Begijnhof, I head back to the Spui, pausing to take a photograph of the famous statue *Het Lieverdje*, whose cute appearance (a smiling boy in shorts) belies its history as a meeting place for anti-government protests. The name comes from an article in *Het Parool* by Henri Knap in 1947, in which he described a young tearaway who rescued a drowning dog as a *'lieverdje'* (little darling). Heading east, I walk on to the Rokin; a wide road with trams running down the middle and a truncated canal on one side. Centuries ago, this area would have been a busy harbour, packed with ships bringing goods from around the world. Nowadays, the waterway has been partly built over and the main transport interchange is a metro station. The station only opened a few years ago and I've never been inside, so I descend the escalators and discover a real treasure trove: some 9,500 archaeological finds unearthed during the building of Amsterdam's new North-South metro line in the 2010s, now on permanent display between the escalators leading to the platforms. I ride up and down three times, peering over the handrail at neatly arranged rows of blue-and-white pottery, weapons, glassware, coins, street signs, and musical instruments. In total, some 700,000 artefacts were discovered during the metro line's construction, dating from 119,000 BC to 2005, including everything from fish fossils to a 15th-century pair of shoes and a samurai sword.

I leave the metro and emerge blinking into the sunlight next to a big statue of Queen Wilhelmina on horseback, staring beatifically down at a group of Spanish teens who are rolling a fat joint in the sunshine. I walk down the narrow Langebrugsteeg, past a string of jewellery shops and a nice bakery. A group of English men are leaning drunkenly on a window decorated with the words 'Discover Cider'. It looks as if they already have.

At the end of the street, I turn left onto the Oudezijds Voorburgwal. Despite having a name that could choke an Englishman, this is one of the prettiest streets in central Amsterdam: a ribbon of attractive red brick threading alongside a gorgeous canal. 'The Velvet Canal', it used to be called, because of the wealth of the people who lived here and the expensive clothes they wore. I'm quite a long way from the Pride event now but the atmosphere is still festive, and the canal is busy with boats, many of them flying rainbow flags and mixing cocktails on board. In front of the University of Amsterdam building, a group of young men sits on the waterfront playing very loud dance music through a Bluetooth speaker. An old lady walks past frowning and I think she's about to scold them, but instead she raises two index fingers and does a little dance as she passes.

'Whoop, whoop!' she cries, as the lads all cheer.

Walking north along the Oudezijds the scenery is at first quintessentially old Amsterdam: beautiful and sedate, with slender old homes, big trees, bikes resting everywhere, and worn red bricks underfoot. Near the junction with the Oude Doelenstraat, however, there's an abrupt change. The Red Light District is nearby, and suddenly the streets get busier and trashier; packed with young tourists and lined with vape shops, tattoo shops, noodle shops, and dildo shops. The graceful canalside buildings host numerous drug-vending 'coffee' shops, including several branches of the famous (or infamous) Bulldog Café. The street reeks so strongly of cannabis that I suspect you can smell it from Brussels.

About twenty minutes after leaving the Spui, I arrive at my next destination; one of the nicest cafés in Amsterdam. De Koffieschenkerij is a little oasis tucked right under the wing of the Oude Kerk, the huge church that claims to be the oldest building in Amsterdam. This spot isn't exactly off the beaten track — the streets surrounding the café must be some of the most touristy in Europe. But somehow, the Koffieschenkerij still manages to retain the air of a cottage garden, with uneven brick floors, creepers on the wall, and red shutters on the windows. I've always thought cafés like this occupy a central place in Dutch society, playing a communal role similar to that played by pubs in Britain. One gets the sense that for many Dutch people, it doesn't matter what pandemic or crisis or war wracks the world as long as they can still sit in the sun somewhere with a small cup of strong coffee and a slice of apple pie.

After drinking another coffee, I leave the café and head through a neighbouring doorway, passing through a tunnel-like whitewashed entrance into the Oude Kerk itself. I've been here many times before, but it's still an impressive place: a cavernous space with a high, red-painted ceiling held up by a forest of thick stone pillars. At one end, there's an organ with dozens of shining vertical pipes that make it look like a silver piece of artillery. The ceiling reminds me of the upturned hull of a ship, and I remember reading somewhere that the church's builders used shipbuilding techniques to construct it.

The Oude Kerk began life back when Amsterdam was little more than a village, as a small wooden chapel constructed atop a lump of drier land where the Amstel dumped its sediment before flowing into the IJ. Some of Amsterdam's sailors probably moored right outside the church before heading off to sea, and by about 1300 a stone chapel had been built, dedicated to Saint Nicholas, the patron saint of sailors. In years gone by, the Oude Kerk would have been a real hub of the community; a place where women came to do their washing, children studied or played, businessman cut deals, and nervous soldiers climbed the tower looking out for approaching enemies. Today, it's much quieter. Wandering in the gloom, I browse the gravestones set in the church floor. There are about ten thousand people buried here, stacked on top of one another like cards in a deck. After a while, I spot one grave I have been keeping an eye out for: a simple black stone engraved unfussily with the words 'SASKIA 19 JUNI 1642'. Although it's not much to look at, this is one of the most famous graves in the city; the final resting place of Saskia van Uylenburgh, better known as the wife of Rembrandt, who died in her thirties.

I've grown used to the idea that a great church like this one should be stuffed to bursting with candlesticks and tapestries, big Bibles and coloured glass, paintings and statues. Here in the Oude Kerk, though, the walls are bare and the alcoves empty. The huge windows are mostly plain transparent glass, and it feels as if a team of builders has just stripped the place bare ahead of a major renovation. Near the organ, one large alcove contains a statue of a man in a ruffled collar, looking grand and statesmanlike, except for the fact that he is missing a head, like a prop from a Hollywood horror movie.

'You know what they say, honey,' I hear a passing American tourist exclaim, to an audible groan from his long-suffering wife, 'come to Amsterdam and get off your head!'

The nakedness of the church is not unusual in these parts, and points to another reason why Amsterdam lagged behind many other cities in Europe in its early days: it spent much of the 1500s at war. In the early 16th century, most of what is now the Netherlands and Belgium were under Spanish control. This was an arrangement that might have worked well were it not for the minor matter of the Reformation, during which the church in Western Europe cleaved into Protestant and Catholic wings. In the words of the historian Martin Rady: '[King] Charles [of Spain] was a devout Catholic who felt that both the office of Emperor and the example of his predecessors obliged him to defend the faith whatever the cost.'[17] As much of the northern Netherlands began to turn Protestant, Charles and his subjects began fighting like cats in a sack.

In Amsterdam, the Reformation at first caused no great

upheaval. Catholic city leaders were more interested in the bottom line than in the Ten Commandments, and at first people seeking to convert from Catholicism to Protestantism were not treated too harshly. In 1522, for example, an Amsterdammer who had 'sworn against God' was merely ordered to go on a pilgrimage to get his beliefs in order.[18] However, as dissident beliefs spread, the authorities' tolerance waned. When in the 1530s a handful of Anabaptists (particularly radical adherents of Protestantism) ran naked through Amsterdam shouting 'the day of the Lord has come',[19] some of them were quickly sentenced to death. Executed on Dam Square, they had 'the heart removed and thrust into their faces' and 'their parts ... hung outside the gates'.[20] In 1540, three women were even tied in sacks and drowned in barrels for their beliefs, not too far from where the front doors of H&M are today.

For a while the crackdown worked, and most Amsterdammers remained Catholic. However, like parents trying to discourage kids from smoking and drinking, the Spanish rulers of the Netherlands soon found that taking a hard line against rebels backfired. By 1562, the authorities were fretting that 'everyday heresies are committed and heretical gatherings held all over the town'.[21] Then, in 1566, came the famous Iconoclastic Fury, or *Beeldenstorm*, when pissed-off Protestants destroyed statues, paintings, and other religious imagery across the Low Countries. In Amsterdam, there was a near-riot at the Oude Kerk, with protestors interrupting a baptism, chanting slogans and smashing statues and windows. 'Nimbly, indefatigably, audaciously the destroyers worked,' one 19th-century historian reported, 'bringing into requisition bludgeons, sledgehammers, ladders, pulleys, ropes and levers all of which they had carried concealed under their clothes.'[22]

The authorities quickly suppressed the riot, but the damage had been done, and the walls of the church would forever remain in what Alexandre Le Riche de La Poupelinière called a state of 'sad nudity'.[23] A city that had previously been a safe haven was now on the frontline of a bitter religious war.

I leave the Oude Kerk and walk a swift circle around the building, just as I did at the Nieuwe Kerk earlier. As always in this crowded city, the buildings around the church are a fascinating exercise in contrasts. Perhaps four metres separate the church from its nearest neighbours: half a dozen red-lit windows where sex workers with enormous breasts stand pouting at potential customers. Several of them tap on the windows as I pass, blow kisses, and frown with exaggerated disappointment when I just give a cheery wave and keep on walking. I pause to check my phone and a young man with curly hair and a Middle-Eastern accent comes rushing up to me, breathing fast, and asks: 'Please, please, where is Red Light District?' I happily point him towards the nearest red light and he bustles off in a cloud of pheromones.

Only a few hundred feet later comes my next destination, another church, this time not Old or New but dedicated to *Ons' Lieve Heer Op Solder*, or Our Dear Lord in the Attic. Entering from the street, it doesn't look like much: a glass door, a gleaming reception desk and a gift shop selling postcards and fridge magnets. I could easily be arriving at a mid-price corporate hotel. Heading down a staircase and then up into a neighbouring building, however, I'm confronted by something rather special. A rickety maze of narrow staircases and creaking wooden floors leads up and up through a series of rooms filled with big fireplaces and heavy furniture and paintings. And then, on the top floor of this creaky old home comes the surprise: a beautiful chapel, complete with altar, organ, pews and all the usual churchy trimmings, but scaled down to a fraction of the normal size, squeezed between the rafters. It feels like finding a football stadium in someone's spare bedroom.

Such hidden places of worship were once common in Amsterdam. Following the 1566 destruction of the churches during the Iconoclastic Fury, a vengeful King of Spain sent an army north to regain control. Much bloodshed ensued. Travelling through the Dutch countryside, one observer reported that 'all trees on the road ... are everywhere full of innocent people [hanging]. All marketplaces are blazing with the fires in which simple folk are burned alive [and] the canals are filled with dead corpses.'[24] In 1567 regular executions began to be staged on the Dam, with celebratory banquets held by the authorities after each beheading or hanging. In 1572, one priest wrote that the town was now known as 'not Amstelredam but Murderdam'.[25]

Despite these horrors, however, things in Amsterdam were never quite as bad as in some other places. This was for the simple reason that while parts of the Netherlands fought tooth and nail against their Spanish overlords, the city of Amsterdam remained officially loyal to them. To a modern reader, accustomed to thinking of Amsterdam as a free-thinking and libertarian place, the city's decision to side with the Spanish might seem like an odd one. However, as the conflict raged, Amsterdammers found good commercial reasons to stay friendly with the Spanish, selling them supplies, buying their exports, and even lending them money

— the 16th-century equivalent, perhaps, of a modern nation that declares its strong opposition to a totalitarian regime, but is also happy to receive its laptops and smart phones.

In early 1578 there was an attempted coup, triggered when a group of Calvinists — a devout subset of Protestants, who believed in simple worship — went to the town hall and told the council they were all under arrest. In the wake of this uprising, the city's leaders reluctantly made a deal with the rebels and Amsterdam effectively switched sides, with Protestants taking over the reins of the city government from the Catholics and Amsterdam officially joining the alliance against Spain. Historians call this shift in allegiance 'The Alteration', which makes it sound like a Netflix sci-fi miniseries. 'A revolution without bloodshed', one writer called it.[26] Buildings belonging to the Catholic Church were converted into things like orphanages and schools and the Oude Kerk was adorned with a new brass gate bearing the snappy slogan 'The abuse of God's church practiced here of late, was driven out again in seventy and eight'. In the grand scheme of things, the switch in Amsterdam's loyalties didn't deal a death blow to the Spanish cause. It was, however, reflective of a broader trend. In 1579, after years of conflict, a band of seven Protestant-dominated northern provinces joined together to form the Union of Utrecht; agreeing on what amounted to a sort of Dutch version of the Declaration of Independence. It was a major step towards the formation of an independent state in the northern Netherlands — known as the Dutch Republic — and Amsterdam was its economic heart.

Sadly, the creation of the Dutch Republic didn't mean the end of the war, which would rumble on in a stop-start fashion for decades. However, the waning of the conflict towards the end of the 16th century did have two major effects on the future of Amsterdam. The first big legacy of the conflict was the political structure of the Dutch Republic, and the role of Amsterdam within it. In the late 1500s, most countries in Europe were still essentially feudal, with a monarch and a merry band of priests, princes, or nobles running the show. The new Dutch Republic created via the Union of Utrecht was, however, exactly what it said on the tin: a Republic, in which power was exercised by what Gustav Renier called 'a commonwealth of merchants'.[27] It was headed by a *stadtholder* who looked quite like a modern Prime Minister or president, and let powerful towns and cities competitively guard their rights and freedoms. Many observers thought the new state was an oddity bound to fail. 'How could a motley collection of tradesmen, salt dealers, fishermen and tallow chandlers hope to govern themselves?' one writer wondered.[28] However, the Dutch Republic's rulers realised that a liberal, competitive approach to trade was the best way to make their country rich, and to decisively slam the door against Spanish interference. In an era when most countries were run as royal playthings, the Dutch Republic was, by the late 1500s, remarkably free-thinking and business-minded, and inclined to let big cities do as they pleased. It was a critical step towards Amsterdam becoming one of the richest places in the world.

Another big shift resulting from the war with the Spanish was the demise of some of Amsterdam's leading rivals. Most notable among these was the city of Antwerp, which lies about 100 miles southwest of Amsterdam, in present-day Belgium. Antwerp was, for much of the 1500s, one of the richest cities in Europe; a trading powerhouse almost unrivalled on the world stage. 'Commerce was its identity', Michael Pye wrote, 'the energy which held it together'.[29] In 1585, however, Antwerp was conquered by Spanish troops. The northern provinces responded by blockading the River Scheldt, making it impossible to reach Antwerp by sea. It was a decisive moment: almost overnight, Antwerp went from being one of Europe's major trading centres to a relative backwater. As Antwerp withered, perhaps 80,000 people — Flemish Protestants, merchants, investors, and artists — flooded north in search of safety and freedom. (Among them was a toddler called Frans Hals.) Many migrants ended up in Amsterdam, with tax registers at one point showing that no fewer than one third of the city's residents had arrived as refugees. The integration of immigrants didn't always go smoothly, and new arrivals from the south were often mocked by Amsterdammers for their simple ways. 'This is what it's like among the people of Brabant, men as well as women,' Gerbrand Bredero grumbled in 1610. 'They put on airs like cosmopolitan gentlemen and ladies, but they haven't a penny in their purse.'[30] Yet, from an economic perspective, the influx of people and money gave Amsterdam an enormous boost, opening up valuable new trading networks. If an Amsterdam merchant wanted to do a deal with Ghent or Brest or Finland or Silesia, there'd probably be someone around who had a relative or trading partner there. One study found that of the 320 biggest depositors in Amsterdam's exchange bank between 1609 and 1611, more than half had come from the southern provinces.[31] The British ambassador Dudley Carleton famously wrote in the early 1600s that while Antwerp 'was a town without people', the Dutch capital was overflowing with 'people, as it were, without a town'. Amsterdam, Carleton reported, 'goeth up apace'.[32] The stage was set for a century of extraordinary change.

With the end of today's walk almost in sight, I leave the hidden attic church and continue north along the Oudezijds Voorburgwal to the Zeedijk. This is another of the oldest streets in Amsterdam, running eastwards from Central Station roughly parallel to the River IJ. The name means 'sea dike' and that's exactly what it originally was; a defensive wall keeping water from the IJ out of the city; part of a long line of flood defences which stretched far in either direction. Pausing to look backwards I realise I've walked slightly uphill to get here — almost unheard of in this part of the world, and a reminder that this street was once raised significantly above the town it protected. Today, though, such history is hard to spot beneath all the rainbow flags. This area has long been known as a gay hangout — a bar here, called Café 't Mandje, is said to be the oldest gay and lesbian bar in the country, open since 1927. Although the Zeedijk lies a fair way off the main parade route, Pride is in full swing here. Almost every shopfront sports a rainbow flag, and the street is crowded with an eclectic mix of races, genders, and sexualities. The Pet Shop Boys are playing at high volume, and outside one bar about a dozen young men in jeans and T-shirts are carefully applying vast quantities of make-up to one another.

'Gimme gimme gimme a man after midnight ...' one sings loudly. Stopping to take a photo of some flags, I'm bumped into by a man who's so stoned and/or drunk that he can barely keep his eyes open.

'Sorry, I'm a bit … tired,' he says. My notebook fills with jotted observations:

- A Marilyn Monroe lookalike dancing in a gold dress
- A bearded man in a white wedding dress, blowing kisses
- A man aged about seventy, in an electric wheelchair, bare chested and wearing a leather harness
- Three women accompanied by a bewildered dog in a rainbow poncho
- A boy, aged about seven, happily carrying a big pink balloon shaped like a penis with a smiley face on.

It all feels, as the Dutch would say, a bit Jan Steen. Turning left along the Zeedijk, I can see in the distance the front entrance of the Prins Hendrick hotel, marked with bright neon lights and high tables on the pavement. It may look unremarkable, but it played a modest role in the history of jazz music. It was here that the legendary trumpeter and singer Chet Baker died in 1988, after falling from an upstairs window while heavily addicted to heroin. There's now a nice bronze relief of Baker on the front of the hotel, with his brow deeply furrowed and trumpet in hand.

Proceeding along the Zeedijk, I arrive almost immediately at one of my favourite pubs: In 't Aepjen, or In the Monkeys. This is, delightfully, another of the oldest wooden buildings still standing in Amsterdam, probably built around the middle of the 16th century. Back when the paint was still fresh there was an inn here that was a well-known haunt for sailors, who (the story goes) would sometimes pay their bar bills with live monkeys, meaning anyone who drank here was liable to end up with fleas. Another legend — quite possibly true — says that many customers here would drink too much and then wake up the next day realising they'd foolishly signed up to join a long expedition to Asia. There's even a well-known Dutch phrase said to originate here: if you get yourself into a tricky situation, you might say you have '*in de aap gelogeerd*', or 'stayed in the monkey'.

Today, there's no sign of any navy recruiters, but there are a few young men dressed as sailors, as well as men and women wearing colourful wigs, leather harnesses and other exotica. Despite all the glitter, inside the bar is still wonderfully gloomy and atmospheric, with dark wood floors, dark wood furniture — dark wood everything. In a nod to the place's history, there are also stuffed monkeys and model monkeys everywhere, including, on a shelf above the door, a spectacularly ugly wood carving of a monkey wearing a Santa hat. The barman slaps me on the back hard enough to knock the wind out of me, asks what I want to drink, and within moments a fresh *pilsje* (small lager) has been pulled. The ancient rafters tremble to the sound of disco music and the patrons pose, pouting for photos next to a stuffed monkey near the bar. I drink my beer, and then limp happily off back towards the Prinsengracht to rejoin the party. I end up dancing till dawn.

CHAPTER TWO

The Zuiderkerk, Entrepotdok, and the Eastern Docklands

Trade, the VOC, and the first
Golden Age

The Netherlands is not a country where vertigo is often a problem. Hills are in short supply, and the soggy ground means buildings are generally low-rise. Rock climbers in search of fame or elevator entrepreneurs in search of fortune should probably go elsewhere. Look around carefully, however, and you can still find a few high points in town, jutting proudly above the surrounding polder like upturned thumbtacks on a desk. And it is at one of these, the Zuiderkerk, or South Church, that I find myself on a bright summer morning, a few weeks after my first wander around the old city. The Zuiderkerk's tower (known as the Zuidertoren) is only about sixty-eight metres high — about a fifth as tall as the Eiffel Tower — but in a flat and mostly low-rise city, sixty-eight metres is enough to count as a skyscraper. After years living below sea level, I'm worried about altitude sickness.

My plan for today is to take a short but sight-heavy stroll through part of Amsterdam's old city centre and the adjacent docklands, focusing on the history of the city's emergence as a global trading hub and imperial power centre. In an unusual fit of foresight, I've arranged a tour of the tower today, and arrive to find my guide waiting on the front step. She's a cheerful young blonde lady who works at the church part-time while pursuing academic studies on the Dutch Golden Age. She seems disproportionately excited to have an author in temporary residence, and as we begin our tour, I do my best not to disappoint her, nodding sagely at brickwork and beams and diligently recording things in my notebook. Whenever I catch her looking at me, I try to look scholarly and thoughtful, even if I'm really just thinking about what I'll have for lunch.

We begin climbing the tower; her bounding ahead and me limping behind on my shattered ankle like Quasimodo. The steep wooden stairs have been heavily worn by centuries of preachers and bellringers, and the thick brick walls are crumbly to touch.

'The bricks they used here were taken from the old city walls,' my guide explains enthusiastically. 'We Dutch like recycling!'

At the top of the stairs, we emerge next to a massive bell, dusky green in colour and nearly the size of a small car. With the guide's encouragement, I shuffle over and stand right underneath it, nervously picturing several tons of metal slamming down over me like a clamshell clapping shut.

'Don't worry, it won't deafen you!' my guide says, before explaining that the bells are still played regularly, chiming out 'everything from Bach to Lady Gaga!'

Turning my back on the giant bell, I walk out onto the

narrow stone walkway that encircles the clocktower and am greeted by a stunning panorama of the city laid out below me. To the west lies Dam Square, and beyond it the tower of the Westerkerk. To the north is the River IJ, with clusters of new apartment blocks springing up along it. Further away, some ten miles to the southwest, I spot the control tower at Schiphol, with a blue-winged airliner taking off nearby. I remember something the poet Zbigniew Herbert wrote about how 'in Holland ... the smallest hill would be enough to take in the entire country: all its rivers, meadows, canals, its red cities, like a huge map'.[1] He also wrote that climbing even a small building or berm made one feel 'omnipotent'. I'm not sure I'd go that far — it normally takes at least two coffees before feelings of omnipotence kick in for me — but I can certainly see a long way. Slowly circling the walkway, I tick off sights like a surgeon going through a checklist: the Noorderkerk, the Royal Palace, Central Station, the Old Admiralty, the Rijksmuseum ...

The Zuiderkerk was built starting in 1603, making it probably the first Protestant church to be built in Amsterdam following the Reformation. It followed a design by Hendrick de Keyser, the prolific architect who also designed the Noord (North) and Wester (Western) churches, and who was apparently terrible at naming churches. The Zuiderkerk was the only church that de Keyser was able to see completed before he died, and he's now buried here along with three of Rembrandt's children. When it opened, the church didn't always get rave reviews. In 1663, for instance, Olfert Dapper described it bluntly as '*duister en dompig*', meaning dark and gloomy.[2] The tower was, however, immediately recognised as an impressive landmark at a time when most buildings were only a few storeys tall. It was once even painted by Monet, who came here in 1874 and produced a lovely picture of the tower standing gracefully in dappled sunlight, with its spire reflected in a canal.

At the time when this tower was built, in the early 1600s, Amsterdam was still in its teenage years. It was a successful town, but still a small one, with not much more wealth or influence than countless other fishing and trading communities in the region. Within a couple of decades, however, it would be transformed. Resting on the balustrade of the tower balcony, I unfold my copies of two of the most famous maps of Amsterdam: Joan Blaeu's map of 1649 and Cornelis Anthonisz's map of almost exactly a century earlier. I've looked at both maps many times before but opening them here now, I am immediately struck by how much of the city is still recognisable: several centuries on from the time both maps were drawn, Amsterdam still has the same tight little warrens of houses arrayed concentrically around the core; the same long stretch of riverfront along the IJ; the same little harbour of the Damrak probing inwards from the IJ towards the open expanse of Dam Square; and the same constellation of spindly church towers scattered around the centre, soaring above their low-rise surroundings like Dutchmen in a crowd of Italians.

What is more surprising, though, is how much changed between the two maps. In the Anthoniszoon map from the 1540s, Amsterdam is still small; a slender finger of developed land, encompassing just a few streets before quickly backing out onto green fields. By the 1640s, however, the city's geography had changed profoundly. The second map I hold, from 1649, shows a city which has burst outwards from its original core, roughly doubling in size as it spread from its original thumbprint into a sizeable footprint. New churches and parks and windmills have been added, and along the IJ waterfront the harbour has grown and filled with ships. Most notably, a whole new neighbourhood, the Jordaan, has been welded onto the western edge of the city. A dense mass of skinny streets is hemmed in by a jagged defensive wall that looks like a row of teeth biting into the surrounding emerald fields. Holding the two maps side by side, I am reminded of those before-and-after pictures you might see advertising diets on the metro, except in this case Amsterdam hadn't slimmed down but ballooned, like a retired marathon runner who developed an addiction to deep-fried Mars bars. As one historian put it, Amsterdam had, in the space of a century or so, become 'an urban beehive of commerce and a cultural melting pot unrivalled elsewhere in Europe'.[3]

What, then, had happened between the mid-1500s and mid-1600s to cause this epic growth spurt? While studying in the Amsterdam library over the previous weeks, I'd learned that it was partly a simple case of a small town continuing to grow, just as all towns and cities tend to do over time, attracting foreigners in search of new opportunities and people from the countryside. However, there was also a major factor that lies not in this corner of the city but further away — thousands of miles further away, in fact, on the coasts of present-day Indonesia.

At the time my first map was drawn, ties between Amsterdam and Asia were few. Since the early 15th century, Europe had been sliding headlong into what became known as the 'Age of Discovery', with great powers fanning out across the world in search of new riches, territories, curiosities, and believers.* The Spanish were occupying much of central America and the Caribbean, shipping home mountains of gold and silver, and the English were trying to find the fabled Northeast and Northwest Passages over the top of the globe. The Portuguese, meanwhile, had sponsored a generation of world-class geographers, navigators, and explorers, including Vasco de Gama and Ferdinand Magellan. In 1497 de Gama reached India, and in 1511 the Portuguese captured the great trading hub of Malacca, in the strait between present-day Malaysia and Indonesia, carting off cannons, gems, bronze statues, and jars filled with gold dust. Burma, Thailand, Sumatra, Macau, the Seychelles, and Manila all fell like dominoes to the Portuguese, and their merchants were kept busy from Bengal to Mesopotamia.

Among the most valuable goods that the Portuguese traded were spices such as cloves, nutmeg and pepper. From a modern perspective, it's perhaps hard to understand what all the fuss was about: spices are today a triviality in economic terms and something many of us could probably live without. In past centuries, however, things were very different. Ancient Egyptians liked their dead bodies well-spiced, medieval monarchs drank spiced wine, Romans added pepper to almost every meal and leaders from Charlemagne to King Henry V were also embalmed in spices.[4] Nutmeg was also thought to improve performance in the bedroom.[5] One 15th century book advised that a man "with a small member, who wants to make it grand", should rub themselves with pepper and

---

*   As we'll discuss later, the places Europeans enjoyed 'discovering' were, of course, already familiar to the people living in them.

ginger, upon which the relevant body part "will then grow large and brawny and afford to the woman a marvelous feeling of voluptuousness". [6] By the late 1500s, the appeal in Europe was partly medicinal: it was widely believed that spices like nutmeg could cure coughs, colds, flatulence, dysentery, amnesia and even the plague.[7] Mainly, though, people wanted spices for the taste. At a time food was often depressingly plain and stodgy, spices such as black pepper or cinnamon offered a welcome distraction from unpleasant tastes. [8] Spices also helped keep meat fresh for longer, and could be used to help hide the smell of slop-filled streets, or neighbours who'd never been near a bath. [9] As a result of all this, the spice trade was in the late 1500s something like the global arms or oil trade is today — a key strategic concern, and a source of great wealth and power. For individual traders, the profits could be incredible: Giles Milton reports a penny's worth of nutmeg once being sold for more than two pounds in London.[10] And it was the Portuguese who controlled the most spice ports and made the most money. Lisbon was, in the 1500s, one of the liveliest and richest cities in the world; overflowing with spices, sugar, parrots, sailors, spies, diplomats, and enslaved people. At one point, wealthy merchants in Lisbon even staged a fight between an imported white rhino and a white elephant, which upon catching sight of its opponent's horn, promptly turned round and ran away.[11]

Throughout all this, however, the Netherlands remained more nervous elephant than feisty rhino. By the second half of the 1500s, Amsterdam was already a fairly prosperous place, with a lively merchant scene, a growing population, and a decent income from Baltic, Rhine, and North Sea trade. One visitor described it as being 'in all pointes like unto Venice, and little inferior to it'.[12] However, despite this growing prosperity, Amsterdam was still not a great world city. Many visitors to the Low Countries wrote extensively about Antwerp, Brussels, Arnhem and Utrecht but found Amsterdam barely worth mentioning. Thomas Gresham, Queen Elizabeth I's agent, thought Amsterdam noteworthy only because it was a good place to buy wainscoting.

As I saw on my previous walk, the reasons for this were complex, but it was in part due to the city's limited trade links beyond Europe. Unlike some other nations, the Dutch didn't at this stage entertain many grand ideas of acquiring new territories under the Dutch flag. This began to change, however, with the publication in the late 1500s of a book known as the *Itinerario,* by an author called Jan Huyghen van Linschoten.

Van Linschoten, who was born in Haarlem in 1563, was a born adventurer who spent much of his teens and twenties roaming the Portuguese empire, including working in Lisbon and Goa. As a trusted record-keeper for an influential archbishop, van Linschoten managed to become a kind of Dutch Marco Polo, collecting reams of information about far-flung corners of the world and the Portuguese traders operating in them. After returning to the Netherlands in the 1590s, van Linschoten began writing the *Itinerario.* In Amsterdam, his efforts attracted the attention of Cornelis Claesz, who specialised in literature on seafaring and travel and soon began offering fully bound editions of the *Itinerario* in his Amsterdam store. A blend of gossipy travelogue and guidebook, the book was a revelation for Amsterdam's merchants, seamlessly mixing military reporting with cheerful observations about daily life in far-off places. From

Mozambique, for example, van Linschoten noted that 'pork is there a very costly dish, and excellent fair and sweet', but also that 'the Portuguese have therein a very fair and strong castle ... but [only a] small store of ordnance and ammunition [and] no more soldiers than the captain and his men that dwell therein'.[13] Crucially, van Linschoten's book depicted the Portuguese empire not as an unassailable titan, but as rather rickety and vulnerable; ready to be toppled by anyone who was cunning enough. It became an immediate bestseller; the *Da Vinci Code* or *Fifty Shades of Grey* of 16th-century Amsterdam.

The city's merchants, reading the guidebook, smelled an opportunity. Inspired by what they'd learned, nine of them founded a company to capitalise upon its recommendations, known as the *Compagne van Verre* (Faraway Company). The outfit may have had an Enid Blyton name, but its business was deadly serious, and investors soon pledged thousands of guilders to support an expedition seeking to get filthy rich in rising Asia. In the spring of 1595, a crew of about 250 men set sail in three ships and a pinnace from the harbour where the IJ met the Damrak, carrying an abridged edition of van Linschoten's how-to-beat-the-Portuguese guidebook.

Unfortunately, the expedition was a disaster. Its leader, Cornelis de Houtman, turned out to be the kind of guy who could start a fight in an empty cupboard. He also managed to get lost repeatedly, and began the voyage to Asia by making an enormous detour across the Atlantic to Brazil and back after being caught by unfavourable winds. Even when the flotilla was finally heading in the right direction, the crew found themselves regularly lashed by storms and ill-prepared for warm weather. The food was dreadful. (*'Our flesh and fishe stunke*, our Bisket molded, our Beere sowred, our water stunke, and our Butter became as thinne as Oyle,' one sailor of the era groused.)[14] Lacking vitamin C, many of the crew soon developed scurvy; their teeth shaking in their mouths like beads in a rattle and their sea legs growing so stiff they could hardly walk. Occasional stops at ports and islands provided some relief from the rough seas, but the goods de Houtman had brought along to trade with locals were poorly chosen — heavy cloth blankets being of little interest to people who lived in the tropics. In June 1596 the ships finally arrived at Bantam, a prized spice-trading settlement in present-day Indonesia. Well into the 20th century, Dutch school textbooks included images of de Houtman meeting natives for the first time and bowing humbly, with a friendly smile and his sword firmly sheathed. The reality was rather less romantic. When it became clear that they wouldn't be able to buy the spices they wanted at knock-down prices, de Houtman's men opened fire, blasting Bantam with cannon fire and killing any residents they could get their hands on. The Javanese were understandably riled by these tactics, and when de Houtman's ships next made landfall, a little further up the coast, some locals hacked a number of the Dutchmen to death. From there, the expedition swiftly went from bad to worse. Arriving at Madura, the Amsterdammers were given a surprisingly warm welcome, with a flotilla of local boats fronted by a smiling prince inviting them to come ashore and trade. De Houtman, however, decided that the prince was being too friendly, and was clearly plotting to turn on the Dutch later. So he responded in the usual way: he 'opened fire and killed all on the big boat', before heading ashore to hack the survivors to death.[15]

Eventually, even de Houtman's crew had had enough of

all this, and forced him to turn back to Amsterdam. It had taken Houtman well over a year to travel to Indonesia, and it was months more before his ships finally limped back into Dutch waters, in 1597. In Amsterdam, merchants and investors gathered on the quayside, eager to see their fabulous haul of spices unloaded. They must have been crushed to see instead only three of the four original ships making it back, and at least one of them carrying a crew that was too weak even to lower their own anchor. The holds of the ships were not filled with the expected mountains of spices, but rather with the same silver coins the Amsterdammers had given de Houtman many months earlier. Yet oddly, the expedition was not seen as a failure. In fact, the return of de Houtman's ships would come to be seen as a pivotal moment in the history of Amsterdam, and of the Netherlands at large. Why? Well, even the relatively tiny quantity of spices that de Houtman had procured were so valuable that their sale still yielded a decent profit. And more importantly, the voyage had proved that it was possible for a fleet from Amsterdam to beat the Portuguese at their own game; travelling halfway round the world and securing spices for themselves, rather than simply oiling the wheels of other countries' trade. If a voyage was run a little better, and secured a few shiploads of spices, it could be fantastically profitable.* For the Dutch, the door to east Asia had been unlocked.

In the months and years after that door opened, many Amsterdammers were quick to rush through it; setting up their own expeditions to Indonesia in search of what Milton called 'their spicy drugs'.[16] The undisputed winner was Jacob van

---

*   Centuries later, you may still hear Dutch people refer to something
     costly or valuable as being '*peperduur*' — as expensive as pepper.

Neck's fleet, consisting of eight Dutch ships, which arrived in the Spice Islands in the spring of 1599 and deftly repaired some of the local relationships that Houtman had previously shot to pieces. A famous painting by Hendrik Cornelisz Vroom, now in the Rijksmuseum, shows the moment that four of the ships from that expedition arrived back in Amsterdam's harbour in the summer of 1599, floating in a turquoise River IJ just outside the city centre. The ships themselves look glorious, with colourful flags flying, cannons blazing, decks crowded with merchants, and crewmen in their finest attire. On the water, dozens and dozens of small sailing and rowing boats crowd around to greet the returning heroes, like fans mobbing victorious players on a football pitch. Of the 550 men who left Amsterdam with the expedition, 'only' 85 had died.[17]

Vroom's depiction was probably a little exaggerated, but it's certainly fair to say the return of van Neck's expedition was another pivotal moment in the history of the city. Disembarking in the harbour, the four ships' crews unveiled huge cargoes of valuable spices and were greeted as heroes. (Four other ships had stayed in Asia to collect more spices.) Amsterdam's church bells rang in celebration. 'As long as Holland has been Holland there have never arrived ships as richly laden as these,' one observer famously wrote.[18] As the spices van Neck secured sold out, the expedition's investors ended up earning (by one count) around a 400 per cent profit[19] — a return on investment that the poet Vondel snappily summarised: 'He who has risked but one receives four as reward, Thus everyone is pleased and gives thanks to the Lord'.[20] Amsterdam, already mildly prosperous, had won the lottery, and would never be the same again.

As the church bells strike noon, I leave the Zuiderkerk and walk down the Zandstraat, a slender street with houses closing in on both sides like overhanging cliffs. It leads me to the Kloveniersburgwal, where a pretty canal is lined with lovely old houses. Further north, the Kloverniersburgwal becomes a riot of drug-vending coffeeshops and bars, but here the canal is still quite stately; wide and murky green, and lined with grand houses that look as if they could be banks. The canalsides are packed with parked bicycles, and the street is busy with pedestrians. I cross the water on a narrow iron bridge and, as I look left, am rewarded with a fine view of the greenish towers of the Koninklijk Theatre Tuschinski, once voted the most beautiful cinema in the world. Directly ahead of me on the west side of the canal is an even happier sight: the best second-hand English bookshop in the Netherlands, at Kloveniersburgwal 58. I'm tempted to head inside and bankrupt myself, but keep walking. A young mother cycles briskly past with no fewer than four children attached to the various appendages of her bicycle, and a dog tethered to a spring-mounted arm reaching off one side. She's also on the phone.

I'm now close to the area I passed through on my previous walk to the Oude Kerk and am again astonished by the number of tourists around. Turning left, I pass over a bridge and onto the Oude Hoogstraat, or Old High Street, which is busy with small businesses catering to customers of the brothels and surrounding coffeeshops: burger places, doughnut stalls, and stores selling smoking paraphernalia. Stopping to study my map, I find myself standing in front of a fine dining establishment called Chipsy King and another outlet selling 'Dutch hash brownies' and fridge magnets shaped like penises. As I pause to take a photo, a Spanish tourist rushes inside and enthusiastically buys a flesh-coloured cooking apron with stuffed hairy genitals attached to the groin area. '*Muy bueno*,' I say, giving him a thumbs up.

This seems an unlikely place to find one of the most important locations in the history of northern Europe, but studying my map again, I realise I'm standing practically on top of it. Just across the street from Chipsy King is a tunnel-like doorway burrowing into the side of one of the big buildings here. There are big white pillars on either side of the doorway but it's otherwise unremarkable, and a passer-by could be forgiven for rushing past and not noticing it at all. Yet, when I duck through the entrance, I find something extraordinary. Set back a few yards from the street is a courtyard, perhaps half the size of a tennis court, closed in on all four sides by the high walls of the surrounding buildings. These buildings are made of reddish-brown brick, and the many windows and archways are decorated with alternating white stones, giving the whole façade a pretty chequerboard appearance. Above many of the windows there are small stone heads, many of which look like sea captains in pointed hats and pointed beards. I'm the only one there and the space is completely silent. However, it's little exaggeration to say that in the 17th century, this pretty building — now known as the Oost-Indisch Huis — was one of the most important places in the world; the equivalent, perhaps, of the Pentagon, the White House, and the Amazon HQ all rolled into one. At the rear of the courtyard, above a small doorway, three interlocked letters give a clue as to the reason why: VOC.

The story of the VOC begins in the wake of Jacob van Neck's expedition. The news of his success in securing Asian spices triggered a frenzy of exploration. By 1601, there were no fewer than 65 Dutch vessels travelling to and from the Spice Islands, shuffling past one another on the high seas like customers in a crowded bar. The *wilde vaart*, as they called it, or 'wild voyage', was a sort of gold rush for 17th-century traders in search of spices. For Amsterdam's merchants, it must at first have seemed like unrestrained capitalism at its best, but in time it proved deeply counterproductive. Dutchmen arriving in Asia ended up competing to buy the same spices, so the costs of securing them soared; while an influx of spices arriving in Amsterdam meant retail prices cratered. Spices were stacked in Amsterdam's harbours as traders were unable to find buyers, and merchants were in danger of losing their shirts. Alarmed by the unseemly free-for-all, in 1602, the States General (that is, the government of the Netherlands) hit upon a simple solution. They would force the merger of all the competing spice-trading companies into a single mega-monopoly — the *Vereenigde Oostindische Compagnie*, or United East Indies Company, or VOC. The move amounted to what we would think of today as a big nationalisation project, with government officials effectively transforming an array of competitive private companies into a single behemoth at the stroke of a pen. (Not coincidentally, the very similar English East India Company had been founded two years earlier, in 1600.) The VOC was ostensibly a private company, but was also a tool of Dutch foreign policy, with clear instructions to 'attack the Spanish and Portuguese wherever you find them'.[21] The VOC could negotiate a treaty with a Sultan, or shell a Portuguese fortress, or sink an English ship. It could even mint its own currency. As an 18th-century poem by Jan de Marre put it: 'she [the VOC] sits enthroned; is mistress of life and death; deposes and raises up kings; makes war and peace; has her own mint; and possesses all the attributes and signs pertaining to independent sovereigns.'[22] The Company's directors had powers that would make Jeff Bezos or Elon Musk green with envy.

It's important to acknowledge here that the VOC's successes are sometimes exaggerated. As many historians have pointed out, the Company wasn't always wildly profitable, and the boring old Baltic grain trade also accounted for a large share of national income. However, there's little doubt that for the Netherlands in general, and Amsterdam in particular, the creation of the VOC, and the ensuing explosion of Asian trade, was transformative. Within just a few years of its founding, Dutch merchants had swiped the coveted Spice Islands from Portuguese control and swiftly established a near-total monopoly on the Asian spice trade. Eventually the Company would establish trading posts from Yemen to Japan, Iran, Jakarta, Sri Lanka, Mauritius, Madagascar, and Cape Verde; all of which were transformed by the arrival of hundreds of hungry Dutchmen searching for food, fresh water, and entertainment. Some of these trading posts, like Surat in India, would remain relatively obscure, but some blossomed into major settlements. (In Cape Town, Dutch sailors battling scurvy planted fruit vines, which would later form the basis for the South African wine trade.) It's said that at its peak, the VOC was worth around eight trillion dollars in today's money — more than Apple, Facebook, and Google combined.[23]

Back in Amsterdam, the rapid expansion of trade in the early 1600s changed everything. As the VOC boomed, the city began to acquire the air of a place of real importance; somewhere where big deals were done, and great fortunes could be made. As any good business studies student knows, the VOC was (along with the English East India Company) one of the world's first joint stock companies, owned by shareholders who held defined proportions of the company and could easily buy or sell those shares to other people.[24] Because shares in the VOC could easily be sold to someone else, there also arose a raft of innovative ways of gambling on future value: secondary sales, derivatives, short-selling, futures. By 1622, the company had even suffered the world's first shareholder revolt, when investors complained that VOC account books had been 'smeared with bacon' so that they might be 'eaten by dogs'. The investors demanded a *reeckeninge*, or a proper financial audit.[25]

Many shares were bought by wealthy merchants and bankers, but many others were snapped up by ordinary people: housemaids, labourers, seamstresses, and a spoon maker. If things went well, the returns could be incredible. Some individuals became spectacularly wealthy: in the 1620s, the richest man in the Netherlands was Jacob Poppen, the son of an investor in the spice trade, whose wealth was estimated at some 500,000 guilders, at a time when a whole family in Amsterdam could live fairly well on a few hundred guilders a year.[26] Within a few years of the VOC's founding, it was said that Amsterdam had more gold in it than stone.

Leaving the old VOC headquarters, I walk southeast along the Nieuwe Hoogstraat. The weather is warm, and the street is an entertaining jungle of touristic delights: steaks, pizzas postcards, vintage clothes, vegetarian shoes. One shop with a big neon mushroom sign advertises the chance to 'zoom like an asteroid through time and space to the heart of the galaxy' for only €22.50. The sign on the window says, 'Smart shop', although I imagine ingesting its products will make you anything but. At one 'headshop', displays of seeds and bongs sit incongruously alongside a poster advertising local mental health services. Glancing right down a side street, I get a nice view of the Zuiderkerk again, just past a shop selling food — churros, Twix brownies, waffles with Oreos on top — which is clearly aimed at customers with the munchies. In front of me, a young man who's taking a selfie while walking manages to blunder straight into a lamp post, sending him flying to the floor and leaving his friends in hysterics.

Crossing the Sint Anthoniebreestraat, I head down the Snoekjessteeg and into the neighbourhood known as the Lastage. Historically, this area of Amsterdam lay outside the city limits and was very boggy, populated mostly by poorer people who lived surrounded by muck. It did, however, benefit from an inlet that led more or less directly to the River IJ, and as a result, soon became one of the main shipbuilding sites in the city. Today, the Lastage is not as pretty as it once was — some of the old buildings have been replaced by ugly modern homes. But overall it's still a rather charming place for a wander, largely free of tourists and surrounded by canals so it feels like an island. Walking along the western edge I find a row of lovely old warehouses; slender, six-storey structures with big hooks protruding at the top; and across the water a pretty memorial to the Armenian genocide. The name of the street sounds like something from a children's book: Kromboomsloot, or the Crooked Tree Canal. One home, on the corner of Korte Dijkstraat, is exploding with greenery, with most of its façade covered by lush creepers that wouldn't look out of place in a sundrenched Mediterranean vineyard. On another doorstep sits an older woman in a loose jacket carefully embroidering a small patch of fabric. She looks like a character from a Johannes Vermeer painting.

After a few minutes walking in circles, I arrive at the Oudeschans canal; a wide waterway lined with nice old warehouses, shed-like houseboats, and big brown sailing barges. A mat on someone's doorstep reads: 'HOME IS WHERE THE WI-FI CONNECTS AUTOMATICALLY.' This canal connects more or less directly with the River IJ, and is busy with boats, including many greenhouse-like ones carrying dozens of tourists. On my left I see the Montelbaanstoren, a solid red-brick tower built in the early 1500s as part of the city's defensive walls following a nasty attack by gangs from Gelderland, who pelted boats with burning pitch. When the city subsequently spread eastwards, the tower lost its defensive purpose, and the octagonal brick base was supplemented by a delicate cream-coloured clock tower on top, which may have been designed by Hendrick de Keyser. Now more than 500 years old, the tower is still in wonderful condition, and looks like a cross between a church and a lighthouse. The tower is located at a sort of crossroads in the water, where two big canals meet, and I sit there for a while enjoying the view. Bikes, canals, humpbacked bridges: it's an archetypal Amsterdam scene. A boatful of young women in bikinis roars by and they all wave and smile at me. I feel childishly flattered — 'Still got it!' — until I notice that they also wave and smile at an old lady standing nearby, and at a homeless man on a bench after that.

I could happily stay here all day, soaking up the scenery in the sunshine, but press on, walking a block northwards to the Prins Hendrikkade, one of the relatively few roads in central Amsterdam that are really busy with cars. In the tattoo shop on the corner, a young man in a reclining chair is wincing as the needle buzzes. Looking north across a stretch of water, I can see the pointed green roof of the Sea Palace, a Chinese restaurant in a three-storey floating pagoda. The restaurant nearly sank when it first opened in 1983, because the owners had calculated the maximum capacity based on the average weight of Hong Kongers, not taller and heavier Dutch people.[27]

A little to the east, I also have a clear view of another significant landmark: the NEMO Science Museum, a giant structure with distinctive turquoise copper walls and a sloped roof that makes it appear to rise from the harbour like a great green whale. It was designed by Renzo Piano, an Italian best known for designing the Centre Georges Pompidou in Paris and the Shard in London. Piano, a keen sailor, complained that 'Amsterdam is a one-dimensional city'[28] and vowed to give it a new piazza with a view, perched atop what would otherwise be the ugly entrance to a road tunnel under the IJ. The view from the terrace is a treat.

I walk on to the junction with Peperstraat (Pepper Street), whose name is a nod to the goods once imported here. In the distance I can already see my next destination: a huge cuboid building of cream-coloured stone, floating atop the murky waters of the harbour. The Scheepvaartmuseum, or Maritime Museum, has long been one of my favourite places to while away an hour in the city. The attraction lies partly in the majesty of the building itself, which has huge arched doorways, whitewashed walls, and high wooden ceilings that make it look like a Portuguese castle. But the appeal also lies with what they keep inside: a rich repository of artefacts related to Amsterdam's Golden Age, beautifully presented but with a fraction of the crowds of some of the city's other museums. I enter through the front door into a beautiful interior courtyard, surrounded by high walls of whitish stone and covered by a domed glass roof, like that of the British Museum courtyard in London. The average Amsterdammer has a remarkable twenty-four museums within five kilometres of their home,[29] and the Maritime Museum isn't as popular as some of the more famous ones. But in my opinion it's easily one of the best in Amsterdam, packed with unusual artefacts and stories, and very child-friendly.

The building the Maritime Museum is housed in was built in 1656 as a supply depot for the Dutch navy. Designed by Daniël Stalpaert, it sits atop 2,300 Norwegian piles driven into the swampy floor of the harbour. I've been here many times but can't resist taking a peek at some of the treasures on display, including Cornelis Claesz van Wieringen's breathtaking painting of the *Battle of Gibraltar*, the stunning Solebay tapestries and, in a glass case downstairs, a rusty cannonball that was fired at the English when the Dutch raided Medway in 1667. I also see Cornelis Anthoniszoon's map of Amsterdam in 1544 — the same map that I took a copy of up the church tower this morning. Studying it again I can clearly see the route I just walked, along the Oudeschans and through a Lastage that was, at the time this map was drawn, still mostly green fields. It's always been something of a mystery how Anthoniszoon managed to draw the city so accurately from above when aeroplanes didn't exist. Some have boldly theorised that early mapmakers must have flown over Amsterdam in a balloon but there is of course no evidence for that; it seems more likely that the artist simply had a remarkable imagination.

The museum's most impressive exhibit is outside, moored to a jetty on the northern side of the building. As I descend a steep staircase onto the wooden walkway, it makes for an astonishing sight: a giant three-masted galleon with a rusty reddish painted hull, colourful engravings on the bow and stern, and enough rigging to net a passing whale. It looks as though it could have drifted straight from the set of *Pirates of the Caribbean*.

This isn't an original VOC ship, of course, but a replica, built in 1985. It's a copy of a ship called *Amsterdam*, which was built at the VOC shipyard in 1748 and sank in the North Sea before it got anywhere near Asia.* When this replica ship was unveiled in the 1980s, it sparked a lot of controversy, with campaigners protesting that it was a 'floating provocation' that aided the 'glorification of theft, oppression and the slave trade'.[30] They demanded the ship be sunk, but didn't get their way.

I walk across the narrow gangplank and board the vessel. In the VOC's heyday the open deck would have been filled with cages holding pigs and chickens, as well as big boxes of soil in which vegetables could be grown. Today there's just a rowdy group of schoolchildren running rings around their teacher. Inside, it's surprisingly spacious; the ceiling is low but it's very wide, with the hull on either side punctured by square portholes lined with massive cannons. In the cramped bow area, there's a remarkable cinema-like installation showing

---

*   If you go to a certain beach at Hastings in southern England at the right time, you can still see the wreck of the original *Amsterdam* protruding from the sand.

Amsterdam as it was in the 1600s, with dozens of ships in the harbour and a city skyline bristling with church towers. The camera swoops over the water and along the Oudeschans, where I just walked. What's remarkable to me is how unchanged the scenery is between the 17th century and now. The boats have engines these days, and there are cars parked along the canalsides, but architecturally the streetscape is almost exactly the same.

In the 17th century, this area, along the IJ east of Central Station, was a hive of activity: a place where giant shipyards churned out big wooden gunboats and spice trading ships like cars rolling off a production line. As the VOC grew, so did its shipyards in Amsterdam, some of the largest ever built in Europe. Inside the maritime museum there's a painting of the enormous VOC *zeemagazijn* (warehouse), which also stood near here, at Oostenburg, on an island in the IJ. It looks like Buckingham Palace, but bigger. For years, this colossal building was considered one of the Dutch Republic's greatest wonders, but in 1822 it collapsed under its heavy load, and not a trace of it now remains.

Ships like the *Amsterdam* were built at a rate of three per year,[31] and they were things of rugged beauty; great floating castles with masts as high as church towers and sails the size of buildings. Some finished ships were so big that they couldn't sail out of the shipyards and across the choppy Zuiderzee without running aground. They had to be suspended in giant floating docks known as 'camels' and hauled out into deeper water by local fishermen before being set free to fend for themselves. At the end of their life, meanwhile, many ships would be brought back home to the same Amsterdam shipyards where they'd been built, broken up, and used to construct buildings in the city. Visit a home or go for a coffee in central Amsterdam today, and the roof above your head could be held up by recycled ships' timbers that once sailed to Java and back. Building materials also travelled in the other direction. When VOC and WIC ships left Amsterdam, they were often loaded with local bricks as ballast, and once they'd filled their holds with Asian or American products, they left these bricks behind, where they were used to build forts, houses, and churches in places like Sri Lanka and Suriname.

Tiring of nautical history, I leave the maritime museum and walk south a short distance, past a nice little pizzeria called Sotto, and through a big stone archway emblazoned with gold letters reading ENTREPOT-DOK. The archway itself seems a bit out of place plonked next to a busy road, but beyond it is one of the better-known sights in this part of the city: an extremely long row of old warehouse buildings lining a tranquil canal. These days, we're conditioned to think of warehouses as having the visual appeal of a grey shoebox, but these old ones are undeniably beautiful; tall and surprisingly delicate-looking, with smooth brick façades studded with dozens of windows and colourful shutters that make them look like advent calendars with all the doors open. Faded Pride flags from the recent celebrations still flutter prettily in the breeze, and a woman kneels outside one doorway carefully upholstering an old leather chair. Nearby, three bearded guys sit on deckchairs having a meeting about a website. In one window, a sign provocatively reads: *'Verhuur hier uw woning aan Expats'* (Rent your home here to Expats) — an offer unlikely to endear the organisers to locals who are being priced out of the housing market. Just across the canal to my right is the Artis city zoo, and at one point I am astonished to catch sight of an elephant peering out at me through the foliage. It's an Amsterdam Safari.

The Entrepotdok dates from the late 1700s and early 1800s, after Amsterdam's Golden Age. However, as Amsterdam thrived in the 1600s and beyond, warehouses like these could be found all over the city, and were crucial to its economy. Described as 'Amsterdam's secret weapon', warehouses not only allowed goods to be stored safely, but enabled traders to play the market for things like grain; buying large volumes for a pittance when harvests were good and then selling them for a fortune when people were hungry. One local explained: 'When in any Foreign Country the Growth and Manufactures of that Place are very plentiful and cheap, such Commodity are presently bought up by our Merchants, paid with ready Mony, and kept in their Magazins there, till the Season of Exportation and Shipping presents for other places.'[32] 'That city,' Voltaire famously wrote, 'is the warehouse of the world.'[33]

Foreign goods and money brought a new cosmopolitanism to what had long been a slightly dour and conservative city. Harbours and warehouses that had once been filled with grain and timber were now bursting with fragrant spices, colourful silks, exotic fruits, and animals. Even the smell of the city changed. One visitor wrote that the warehouses of the VOC 'creak and groan and lean against each other for support under their fragrant burdens'. In order to maintain high prices for their spices, merchants would occasionally destroy their own goods in order to restrict supply. One year, more than a million pounds of nutmeg and cinnamon were set ablaze in

Amsterdam, sending rivers of scented oil trickling down the streets and clouds of musky smoke out across the countryside; presumably confounding people out in the surrounding areas who wondered why their cow fields suddenly smelled like a spice rack. Another new smell was coffee. In 1616, a Dutch delegation managed to secure some coffee seedlings from Aden and, after cultivating them in Amsterdam's botanical gardens, re-exported them throughout their trading empire, literally sowing the seeds for the later popularity of coffee in places like Java. Without Amsterdammers' gardening skills, Europeans and Americans might not be drinking coffee today. As the drink's popularity grew, Amsterdam's coffee houses became famous as places to gather news or swap gossip, rivalled only by the city's markets. In the 17th century dozens of markets were held around Amsterdam every week, including ones specialising in flowers, cheese, butter, spices, poultry, baskets, tobacco, chairs, cakes, ale, rags, and dogs. The dog market was held every Monday morning, and an English visitor reported seeing about twenty hounds for sale when he visited, all of them 'extremely ugly' but popular with Amsterdam women who were willing to pay a good price for a 'hairy companion'.[34]

As trade grew, Amsterdam's population exploded from roughly 40,000 in 1610 to 50,000 by the 1620s, and over 105,000 in the early 1660s.[35] Predictably, parts of the city also became crowded with bars and brothels catering to returning sailors. One can only imagine the sailors' joy at being released from their miserable floating jails, given a year's salary in cash and set loose on the town: the 17th-century equivalent of a modern stag party, with more time to fill and fewer teeth. In the streets around the Dam, raucous taverns echoed with the sounds of noisy drinking games such as 'In the cup', in which players shook dice in a beaker to decide first how many drinks they had to down and then how many ladies they had to kiss. Rowdy nights out in this city are nothing new.

The Dutch differed from other nations somewhat in that their objectives for exploring the world were almost entirely commercial. Most Amsterdammers had little interest in converting people to Christianity or claiming foreign lands for the sake of it, preferring instead to focus on getting rich. As a result, the markets for several important commodities ended up being virtually monopolised by small groups of Amsterdam merchants, who cornered the market in everything from Italian silks to sugar and saltpetre. Another big import good was porcelain, which was brought to the city from Asia by Dutch traders and became very popular in the homes of wealthy Dutch merchants – until local manufacturers figured out how to make blue-and-white china for themselves, creating a style now known as *Delfts Blauw* (Delft Blue). The Dutch allegedly bought entire forests in Germany, ready to be felled on order, and the markets for Loire wine, wood for making brandy barrels, and sugar in London were all said to have been upended by the rapacious demand of Amsterdam's merchants filling their warehouses. In 1640 one Amsterdam trader reportedly bought up such quantities of Russian furs that the famous annual market at Arkhangelsk had to be cancelled. As well as warehouses for food and spices, Amsterdam had others for storing beer — along the Brouwersgracht, or Brewers' Canal, five-storey warehouses had to be reinforced with timber to stop them collapsing under the weight of thousands of beer barrels. Another popular product was wine. Because the French wine harvest was rarely ready for export early enough in the year to make it through the Baltic to Russia before the sea froze, French wine could only be sold in Scandinavia and Russia if it could be stored conveniently somewhere along the way, and Amsterdammers were happy to help out, for a fee. There were even some warehouses dedicated to whaling, where the upper floors were stacked with massive bones and the basements held enormous brick reservoirs filled with stinking whale oil. It's hard to believe now, but whaling was once big business around here: John Richards wrote that in 1684 no fewer than 246 Dutch whaling ships were active in the seas around Spitsbergen.[36] According to Amsterdam's Maritime Museum, in the space of 200 years Dutch hunters caught a total of around 40,000 whales. The industry was considered so important to Dutch society that at one point King Willem I personally subsidised whaling and seal hunting to ensure they stayed profitable.[37]

Amsterdam's merchants went everywhere. They established trading posts not just in Asia but all over Europe, in places like Hamburg and Gothenburg. In Bristol, Dutch traders built 'small wooden houses', which observers complained 'detract much from its appearance'. In the east of England, they sold the bricks and tiles that they'd brought over from Holland as ballast in ships for use in local housebuilding – visit an old pub in somewhere like Harwich or Colchester today and you might find yourself sitting between walls made from Dutch bricks. In Newcastle, the Dutch set up shop shipping coal to London. In Sweden, they controlled mines and logging operations and traded in munitions. In Norway, they ran much of the copper industry. In Russia, Amsterdammers monopolised the export of caviar, and in Poland they operated the national Mint.

Amsterdammers even exported marble from Italy, supplying some of the stone used to build Versailles. All across northern Europe, 'Dutch capitalists were,' in Charles Wilson's words 'to be found draining swamps, clearing forests, building canals, opening mines, building shops, mills, factories for gunpowder, glass [and] textiles ... Amsterdam capital reached out into Europe's backward areas, fertilizing and fructifying as it went'.[38] The city, once a relative backwater, had become a hub of the world economy.

It's important to acknowledge here that this growth did come at a terrible human cost. Like most people of their time, early Dutch traders cared little for equality or democracy abroad, and gleefully trampled on the rights of anyone who got in their way — even as they took pride in the degree of freedom they themselves enjoyed at home. Among other crimes, the Dutch murdered and exiled thousands of residents of Banda in order to secure a monopoly on the nutmeg trade. After 1621 the Dutch West Indies Company (WIC) also played a major role in the slave trade, kidnapping people in west Africa and taking them to the Caribbean.[*] For millions of people around the world, the Dutch 'Golden Age' was anything but golden.[**]

Dutch successes were also not always appreciated by the country's rivals. The English, for example, had great respect for the trading prowess of their neighbours across the sea. 'The Dutch,' Sir William Temple famously wrote, 'are the envy of some, the fear of others and the wonder of all

---

[*]   For more about Amsterdam's role in slavery, see Chapter Five.

[**]   In 2020 the Amsterdam Museum announced that it would stop using the term 'Golden Age', but the Rijksmuseum and most historians have not followed suit.

their neighbours.'[39] However, the English were often bitterly jealous of Dutch economic success, attributing it to greed and trickery, and worried that Dutch republicanism might take root in their kingdom. Flick through 17th-century English pamphlets and you'll find endless hyperbolic criticism of the Dutch. In 1673 Henry Stubb wrote of how 'the Tongues, the outrages and the insolencies of the Dutch have done England more prejudice than Their Ships and Cannons'.[40] Around the same time, another said that the Dutch Republic was 'a State not fit to live in the World, by reason of their Treacherous dealings with all Nations ... and their Pride hath raised them to that height that their fall must be great'.[41] In 1688 another English pamphleteer wrote that 'there is a certain Bogg-land in the World, which by the Lowness of its Situation, may justly claim the honour of being the Sink of the Universe'.[42] How the Dutch responded to this, history does not record.

I continue my stroll along the Entrepotdok. I remember that atop one of the wooden mooring pillars here there's a little figurine poised for a high dive, which was installed by Streetart Frankey — a sort of Dutch Banksy who tucks little models and bits of graffiti all around the city. At the end of the warehouses, I head north, crossing a narrow bridge to the Oosterkerk, or East Church, which was built in around 1670 from mountains of brown-red brick. A plaque on one wall pays touching tribute to three local residents — Gerrit Blind, Marie Altelaar, and Corrie Scheen — who fought to preserve the historic character of this area 'during the sanitization and new-build [implemented] in the 1960s and 1970s'. Behind the church, I turn right down Parelstraat, and idly wonder which existed first: this 'Pearl Street' or the one in New York City?* A lovely old tilting iron bridge then leads into the neighbourhood known as Oostenburg, a warren of six-storey post-war apartment buildings. It's a pleasant place, but mostly unremarkable, save for one building, which I find hulking incongruously behind a children's playground. The Oost-Indisch Pakhuis, or East Indies Warehouse, is a huge cuboid building of red brick and stone, nearly encircled by water and with sheer sides studded with dozens of dark windows like holes in a cube of Swiss cheese. With walls three-quarters of a metre thick, this was once used as a storage space for millions of pounds of saltpetre, sugar, coffee, zinc, and tin imported from throughout the Dutch empire.

As well as building warehouses and shipyards, increasingly wealthy Amsterdammers also funnelled money to grand civic buildings. In 1608, the city council decided Amsterdam needed a purpose-built bourse to match those in London and Antwerp, bringing together insurance, money-changing, and commodity trading in one place. By 1611, it had been completed, following a design by Hendrick de Keyser, who used London's exchange building as an example. In the words of the historian David Rooney, the Exchange was 'hard to miss, as it was the size of a football pitch and could accommodate thousands of traders'.[43] The open courtyard design seemed optimistic given the city's climate, but the new building was a hit. Rather than huddling in a nearby church, merchants could now meet in proper exchange buildings,

---

*   Modern street maps of New York City are littered with names imported by early Dutch settlers: Bowery, Bleecker, Stuyvesant, Rikers, Bushwick. Coney Island supposedly got its name because it was once overrun with wild rabbits, and the Dutch word for rabbits is '*konijn*'.

and coordinate their trades using one of the most accurate clocks ever made — accurate to more than half an hour a day.* Upstairs there were also vendors selling books and curiosities from around the world. Filips van Zesen, a German author who lived in Amsterdam in the 17th century, wrote of 'magnificent halls and rooms' where 'it seems as if the whole world gathers to do business'.[44] Another visitor described the Exchange as 'a polylingual hubbub of bargaining',[45] while the poet Jeremias de Decker described it as:

> A strolling place where Moor with Northman bargained,
> A church where Jew and Turk and Christian gathered,
> A church of every tongue, a market field of every ware,
> An exchange which swells all exchanges in the world.[46]

At the exchange, merchants could negotiate credit, buy insurance, hire staff, and swap tips about what was happening with prices in the global market. The Dutch guilder was one of the most widely accepted currencies in the world — the euro or dollar of its day — and Amsterdam's merchants and bankers acquired a reputation for reliability. 'Every man lodges his money [in Amsterdam] because he esteems it safer,' wrote William Temple, 'and easier paid in and out than if it were in his coffers at home.'[47] One visitor reported that Amsterdam's banks were so rich in deposits that they 'resembled to a Peruvian mine'.[48] Long before Amsterdam became a place where Brits came to lose their minds, it was where they came to secure their fortunes.

In 1648 work also started on a new town hall designed by

---

*   The Exchange building itself is long gone, but the remains of the clock still sit in the Oosterkerk.

Jacob van Campen — the grand building on the Dam that is now known as the Royal Palace. The building was conceived at a time when the Treaty of Westphalia had just marked the formal end of the Eighty Years' War between the Dutch and the Spanish, and Amsterdam's rulers were in a celebratory mood. As Richter Roegholt has written, the project was not without controversy. Some religious leaders thought a new civic building was a waste of money, with one Calvinist burgomaster arguing 'God's wrath must fall on a city, when such treasure is spent on the outward appearance of a worldly building'.[49] However, the proponents of the plan eventually won out, and by 1655 the new building was complete. It had an elegant classical design including an Italian-style cupola — it was said that on a clear day, from the cupola you could see all the way from Haarlem to Utrecht. The main building material was not local red bricks, but expensive stone imported from Germany, which was initially light in colour but gradually turned darker — if you look at old paintings of the palace, its walls look much brighter than they are today. In order to hold the building up on boggy ground 13,659 Scandinavian wooden pilings were needed.[50] The building was for years said to be the largest public building in the world, and the poet Vondel called it 'the eighth wonder of the world'.[51] In a nod to old traditions, many of the decorations included Biblical symbols and acknowledged the city's humbler past. One fresco showed Icarus plunging to earth after flying too close to the sun. Yet what was most striking about the new town hall was how dominant it was. Previously, the most impressive building on the Dam had been the Nieuwe Kerk, but now that was nudged aside by the new civic building, which partly blocked the church from view from many points on the square. The symbolism of this change was powerful: while Amsterdam's centre had once been dominated by a place of worship, its landscape was now dominated by new forces: the city government and trade. God would have to take a back seat for a while.

I turn my back on the giant warehouse and walk a few hundred metres east. On my map, the names of the surrounding streets point to a nautical past: Compagniestraat, Admiraliteitstraat, VOC-kade. A woman passes me carrying a dog in a backpack, followed by a woman carrying a tote emblazoned with 'I WISH I WAS IN FINLAND'. At the end of the block, I pass the Czaar Peter supermarket on the Czaar Peterstraat in the area known as the Czaarpeterbuurt. Finding the next thing I want to see is a challenge, and I spend a good five minutes studying online maps and walking back and forth in front of a hummus bar before I eventually find it, hidden away in the garden of the first house on the Oostenburgergracht. There, mounted on a wall at head height, behind a cast-iron fence thickly coated with ivy, is a bronze plaque with a bearded man's head on it. The text on it reads: '*Hier werkte Tsaar Peter de Grote, 1697–1698*' — 'Here worked Tsar Peter the Great, 1697–1698'.

More than 300 years ago, the Russian tsar became one of the first big celebrities to come on holiday to Amsterdam. Peter had grown up admiring Moscow's German Quarter and, in 1697, when he was still in his mid-twenties, he left Russia for the first time on 'a personal voyage of discovery in a quest for practical knowledge', aiming to learn the secrets of Western Europe's economic success.[52] In August

1697 he arrived in Zaandam, a few miles along the IJ from Amsterdam, where he rented a tiny box room at the back of a blacksmith's house and attempted to go undercover as a ship's carpenter called Peter Mikhailov.* The tsar told his staff that if anyone gave the game away, he would have them executed, but one suspects that some observers might have twigged that he was a VIP, given that he left Moscow with a party of 250 people including twenty servants, several surgeons, five trumpeters and four dwarfs.[53] In Zaandam, he was annoyed to become something of a tourist attraction, hassled by curious Zaandammers at all hours, including some who climbed across his neighbours' rooftops in hopes of catching a glimpse of him. Nevertheless, staying in humble rooms and working in the shipyards was still a remarkable thing to do, for a man who ruled one sixth of the world; the 17th-century equivalent of King Charles taking a job at Burger King and making everyone call him Brian.

Peter ended up staying almost five months in the Netherlands, much of it spent visiting shipyards and windmills that he hoped to replicate back home. He also went to some gory public lectures at Amsterdam's anatomical theatre, enjoyed a trip to the ballet, and bought mountains of souvenirs to take home. According to his biographer Lindsey Hughes: 'Peter took away from this part of northern Europe the impression of a well-ordered state, well-planned towns with clean streets and ... a people in control of their environment.'[54] He also concluded that the Netherlands had been successful for two reasons: it was open to foreign trade and investment, and it had a geography which was the very

---

*   If you can beat the crowds, you can see the cottage Peter supposedly stayed in (the Czaar Peterhuisje), still standing in Zandaam.

opposite of landlocked. Returning to Moscow in 1698, Peter set out to replicate these strengths in his homeland, and sent his army to capture the patch of land where the Neva River ran into the Baltic, with the aim of turning it into a trading hub. In 1703 the first stone of Peter's new settlement was laid, and a city soon grew, centred around a port and filled with canals, red bricks, and blue-and-white tiles. Some gave it the nickname 'New Amsterdam', but the official name was 'Sankt Pieter Burkh'. It would go on to thrive and become famous around the world under another name: Saint Petersburg.

Heading south on the Czaar Peterstraat, I cross a wide bridge over a canal, passing an old lady on a motor scooter who has a big wax-covered cheese on her lap, like a shiny red bowling ball. It's dinnertime by now, and the streets are filling with bicycles as thousands of office workers head home. I pass a group of tourists immobilised with fear at the side of the road, nervous about crossing between all the speeding bikes. It's a common problem in Amsterdam — one survey found that 90 per cent of cyclists in this city jump red lights.[55] The solution, I've learned, is to treat the cyclists like a fast-moving stream: just hold your breath, jump in, and be thankful that the Dutch health system is one of the best in the world.

This part of Amsterdam is unfortunately not terribly scenic. The roads are wide and busy, and the main landmark is a petrol station. Off to my left, however, there is one attractive sight: an enormous windmill, known as de Gooyer, which has four sails and a wooden walkway strung around its waist like a tutu. There aren't many windmills left in Amsterdam these days, but there used to be dozens of them, with some used to saw wood or pump water, and others used to throw silk, make cloth, print fabric, or make gunpowder. This one was originally used to mill flour and has (remarkably) moved around the city a few times in search of stronger winds, before winding up in its current location in 1814.

Next door to the windmill, in a former bath house squatting at the foot of the tower, is another favourite haunt of mine, the Brouwerij 't IJ brewery. Compared with some other bars in the city this one is not particularly historic — it opened here in the 1980s, after being founded by a local musician, Kaspar Peterson, who went to Belgium on tour and was impressed by the range of craft beers available there. 'I thought: if you could bring that to the Netherlands, that would be a good idea,' he said. Four decades after its opening, the brewery is thriving — and is just one of about seventy small breweries currently operating in and around Amsterdam.[56] Ducking inside, I find the bar nearly empty and the atmosphere a little subdued, but the choice of drinks makes up for it: this is a good example of what the Dutch call a proeflokaal: a place selling more different beers than a supermarket has breakfast cereals. I spend a happy half hour sitting at a long wooden bench, reading the paper, sipping a delicious beer the colour of an espresso and texting a friend about our plans for dinner. The food we'll be eating will be Indonesian, of course.

CHAPTER THREE

Garden-hopping from the Grachtengordel to the Jordaan

The growth of the city and the creation of the 'Venice of the North'

When I was a child, one of my favourite books was about a secret garden. In it, Frances Hodgson Burnett tells the story of an unhappy ten-year-old girl, Mary, who finds a garden hidden behind a high wall. The garden is eerily quiet, with winding paths, moss-covered urns and 'high walls ... covered with the leafless stems of climbing roses which were so thick that they were ... like little trees'. For little Mary, it represents a hidden sanctuary where strange and magical things happen, and the chaos of everyday life is shut away. The secret garden is, she says, 'the sweetest, most mysterious-looking place anyone could imagine'.[1]

I find myself thinking of that garden one bright day in Amsterdam in June, as I walk through a narrow canal house on the Keizersgracht, on the southern side of the city centre. The house itself is fairly typical of those in this part of the city, which is to say: very nice indeed. Entering through the polished green front door, I pass through the souterrain floor, just below street level, and walk through a cool, tunnel-like space towards the rear of the house. At the end of the tunnel, I open a small door and am astonished to emerge into a beautiful garden, bursting with roses and ivy and big leafy trees; completely enclosed from the city and invisible from the street. I feel as if I have, like the girl in the children's book, stumbled into a hidden world.

The garden isn't huge by most people's standards — perhaps ten strides wide and twenty-five long — but is wonderfully leafy and green, and ringed with tall beech and elm trees. A red-brick pathway leads around the edge of a small, neatly trimmed lawn, at the centre of which stands a golden sundial, glinting in the sun. Around the lawn are flowerbeds packed with pink and white roses, hydrangeas, and ferns. A gazebo is cloaked in vines and at the rear stands a crumbling brick wall thickly embroidered with ivy. Following a narrow path, I duck through a little iron gate into the neighbouring house's garden. This garden is smaller — maybe six big paces wide and fifteen paces long — but is wilder and greener than the one next door, with shrubs reaching above my shoulders and tall overhanging trees. A narrow path is lined with steep banks of laurel bushes, and a large barbecue hides incongruously between ivy and ferns. Through another metal gate is a third garden; much bigger and much more organised than the other two, with an arrow-straight footbridge leading across a rectangular pond, and neat beds of pink and red flowers on either side. Most amazing of all is the silence. The busy Rembrandtplein is, according to my phone, only a few hundred metres away, but this spot feels completely secluded. I close my eyes and think I could almost be atop some mountain in Scotland, and not in the heart of one of the most crowded cities in the world.

My plan for today is to explore not just this garden but many others, which are open today for *Open Tuinen Dag*, or Open Gardens Day; an annual event during which roughly two dozen of the nicest houses and offices in the city centre open their gardens for visitors to see. I hope that on the way I can learn a bit more about how Amsterdam's beautiful houses and gardens were built, and how the city's famous canals came to be. Looking at the map I've been given, I see it won't be a long walk — perhaps a mile and a half in total, excluding the long stretches of time I'll spend stopping to stare at things. But the event seems to be popular. At mid-morning on a Sunday, Amsterdam's streets are quiet, but I can already see several small groups of people marching determinedly towards the next garden, with maps and guidebooks in hand. To my surprise, many of them seem to be British: women of about my mother's age who've made the trip across the North Sea especially to see some of Amsterdam's finest green spaces. Leaving the leafy garden, and walking out onto the Keizersgracht, I literally bump into a group of them, cooing happily over a canal-side box of orange tulips and horribly mispronouncing Dutch words.

'Look!' one of them says, pointing excitedly at her map. 'Next we're going near the blow-men market!'*

I walk east along the Keizersgracht and turn left onto the gorgeous Reguliersgracht. At number 92 I spy the famous *gevelsteen* (gable stone) depicting a large white stork with a carrot-like orange beak. This was supposedly put here in

---

* 'Bloemen' is Dutch for flowers, and usually pronounced 'blue-men'.

the 17th century to advertise the presence of a midwife to pregnant customers who couldn't read street names or house numbers. I continue a short distance north and then turn right onto the Herengracht, zigzagging my way towards the River Amstel. I am not exactly off the beaten path here. This area is one of the most famous urban landscapes in the world, visited by millions of people every year, and I know it well myself. Yet even for someone visiting for the thousandth time, this part of Amsterdam still has the power to astonish. Gables are shaped like staircases and front steps explode with flowers and greenery. Old buildings tilt like riverside elms, and cyclists rattle peacefully along red brick-paved streets. It's all so perfectly preserved that it looks like a film set, where I might at any moment hear a director shout 'Cut!' and see a bewigged Kenneth Branagh or Anne Hathaway collapse into a folding chair and demand a foot massage. Not for the first time, I marvel at how interesting and unusual it is that the best-known symbol of Amsterdam is not a palace, parliament building, or cathedral, but a row of ordinary canal houses like these ones. There is something quintessentially Dutch about it all, that humility. For all its ancient glories, this is still a city where if you leave a 10 per cent tip after dinner in a restaurant, your fellow diners might wonder if you've won the lottery.

The scenery around this area of Amsterdam dates to the teenage years of the 17th century. As I'd learned on my previous walk, the city was growing rapidly by then, and bursting beyond its original boundaries like a cake spilling over the sides of a cake tin. This growth was a mark of the city's dynamism and success, and a source of pride for many of its inhabitants. However, because of its speed, Amsterdam's growth in the early 1600s was erratic and unplanned. Parts of the city looked more like a farmyard than a budding world metropolis. By 1607, Amsterdam's elders agreed that it was time for their hometown to acquire an appearance that befitted its growing prosperity. Amsterdam needed beautiful houses — and beautiful gardens.

The impetus for the development that followed came largely from one man, Hendrick Jacobszoon Staets. His plan, drawn up in 1609, envisaged transforming the soggy city not just by adding roads but by controlling the water; constructing what came to be known as the *grachtengordel*, or canal ring; a stunning array of concentric canals lined with slender mansions, which radiated outwards from Dam Square like the rings on a dartboard. The canals would be mainly decorative, but would also help drain water from the surrounding boggy land, and provide an easy way of moving goods around the city, and a convenient open-air sewer system. The soil that was removed when digging the canals would be used to raise the height of the surrounding land for building. The canals would also be self-cleaning, with a sequence of sluices opened twice a day to allow water from the IJ to flow through the town at high tide, flushing the canals with fresh water. Of the four main canals, three bore aspirational names, indicative of the kind of city Amsterdam was trying to become: the Keizersgracht (Emperor's Canal), the Herengracht (Gentlemen's Canal), and the Prinsengracht (Princes Canal). (The fourth canal, which already existed before the big rebuilding project, was known simply as the Singel, or belt.)* It's often said that Staets was inspired by the Italian Renaissance, and if you walk around

---

* Locals sometimes remember the order of the canals (Prinsengracht – Keizersgracht – Herengracht – Singel) with a handy mnemonic: *Piet Koopt Hoge Schoenen* (Pete buys high shoes).

his creation today, it is indeed hard not to get a distinct whiff of Venice, both metaphorically and olfactorily.

Five minutes after leaving the first gardens I arrive at my next stop: the Willet-Holthuysen house. This palatial canal-side residence on the Herengracht was built in the late 1680s and was subsequently home to several leading members of Amsterdam society, including a couple of art collectors, Abraham Willet and Louisa Holthuysen, who gave it its current name. Louisa was the daughter of a wealthy merchant and inherited this house from her parents before marrying Abraham. According to the Museum Amsterdam, Louisa was careful to insist on a prenuptial agreement and paid her husband an annual allowance; when she died childless, she left the property to the city as a museum. I walk through another marbled entrance hall to the garden beyond. This garden is also not particularly huge — perhaps a bit bigger than a tennis court — and hemmed in on all sides by tall modern buildings. Yet it is, again, utterly tranquil. Compared with the last gardens I saw, this one is very formal, with lots of neat gravel paths and maze-like low green hedges, punctuated by large statues of women in flowing robes, dancing atop beds of pink roses. It feels a bit like a miniature version of the gardens at Versailles. The house itself is spectacular too. Peeking through the windows I see high ceilings, polished floors, priceless-looking art, and fine furniture. Much of the décor dates from long after the house was built, but it's not hard to imagine how it would have appeared at the height of Amsterdam's Golden Age, when the building was first constructed. I can imagine some titan of the Dutch trading empire standing at a window, gazing out at the manicured garden and plotting to found New York or raze Java.

Hendrick Staets's plans to transform the city weren't universally popular. Not long before construction began, some in the city council were still wondering whether it would be possible to replace one of the canals with a broad, glamorous highway that would serve as a sort of Dutch Champs-Élysées or Whitehall, which men like themselves could parade along. Others said the new canals were a health risk, and if your horse was startled, you'd be risking death in two ways: by breaking your neck from the fall, or by drowning. During the canals' construction, many workers fell ill with what they called 'polder fever' — now better known as malaria. Dishonesty was also a problem. To outsiders, Amsterdammers often seemed unusually honest — when he visited in the mid-1700s, Voltaire wrote that:

> Of the ... people who live in Amsterdam, there is not among them a single shirker, not one who is poor, arrogant or insolent. We met the governor going about on foot without lackeys in the midst of the general populace ... They don't line up to watch a prince go past; they know only work and modesty.[2]

In reality, as Amsterdam grew, it was beset by appalling corruption, with city leaders routinely arranging cushy jobs for close family and government contracts for friends, dabbling in insider trading, and arranging for council seats to pass from father to son. Those with inside knowledge of urban expansion plans stood to do particularly well. A burgomaster called Franz Oetgens, for example, reportedly earned a cool 112,000 guilders by buying up land near the Haarlemmerpoort, which he knew would be needed for the city's expansion.[3] Another businessman was reportedly able to buy a house on Dam Square for 16,400 guilders and then sell it almost immediately to the council for 25,500.[4] Locals liked to say that rich men 'ran between the drops', effortlessly dodging taxes which ordinary people were soaked by.

The first phase of construction began in 1613. Initially, the plan was that construction of the *grachtengordel* would proceed quickly, with the new canals completely encircling the old city so you'd hit one of them if you walked from Dam Square in almost any direction. However, due to a lack of funding, the project ended up being broken into phases and adapted to fit in around the curves of the old city walls. This meant that at first the main canals reached only about a third of the way around the old city, roughly from where the Haarlemmerstraat is to where the Spui lies today. Something that had been designed to be shaped like a dartboard ended up looking more like a wedge of cake. Later, in the 1660s, when new taxes were raised, the canals were extended to loop around the bottom of the city, giving the city the concentric semi-circular layout that makes it instantly recognisable on a map today. The 'magical semi-circle', Cees Nooteboom called it.[5] Albert Camus was harsher: 'Have you noticed that Amsterdam's concentric canals resemble the circles of hell? The bourgeois hell, naturally, people with bad dreams.'[6]

Looking back, it's almost impossible to imagine now just how much work it must have been to build the canals, in a time before cranes and mechanical pumps and diggers, when almost everything had to be done by hand. The Netherlands, having the overall consistency of a blancmange, doesn't have much in the way of natural rock, and so homes were built mostly from reddish bricks made from tidal river sludge or clay that could be found locally. Hundreds of men spent countless hours digging and pumping and hammering wooden poles into the ground to support the buildings. To drive the poles in, they would have to first construct a huge wooden tripod, then suspend a heavy hammering block called a *heiblok* underneath it, and then haul on a rope hundreds of times to lift the block and let it fall, over and over, bashing each long wooden pillar between seven and twenty metres into the ground. Once inserted, the poles were sawn off just below groundwater level, and brick walls were perched on top. These constructions could last for centuries, but a drop in the groundwater level could be disastrous. If exposed to air, the pilings could rot quickly, making the house tilt like a sinking ship, and landing the owner with an epic repair bill. Some houses on the end of a row would later need extra wooden joists to stop them toppling over, and many of the most famous streets in the city tilt like an oil tanker on a sandbar. Even today, many Amsterdammers' greatest fear is not a war or pandemic, but a knock on the door from the downstairs neighbour, telling them there's a financially ruinous problem with their building's foundations.

The high cost of plunging all those poles in had a profound impact on the design of the houses themselves. If you were paying a fortune to shore up every square metre you built on, it made sense to design buildings that had a horizontal footprint which was as small as possible, with the result that many houses ended up having modest frontages but being very tall, with deep, Tardis-like interiors. Houses were often six times deeper than they were wide. To maximise space further, upstairs rooms were also sometimes built jutting or leaning out over the street, so houses looked almost like inverted L-shapes, dropped there in some architectural game of Tetris. In some cases, the forward tilt also made it easier to winch deliveries up to the upstairs windows, without big crates or barrels dragging up the façade. Then, as now, a taller house could be a sign of status. VOC merchants and stern burgomasters may have frowned on frivolous consumption, but they enjoyed looking down on the rest of the city, both figuratively and literally.

Leaving the Willet-Holthuysen house, I walk down the busy Utrechtsestraat back to the Keizersgracht, or Emperor's Canal. The weather has brightened a little and the canals are growing busy with boats; a mixture of big glass-sided tourist boats and smaller motor cruisers carrying groups of people drinking beer and wine and enjoying the scenery. I get lost for a while, struggling to find the doorway leading to the next hidden garden, until I'm saved by a group of middle-aged English women laughing and gossiping their way towards a discreet doorway at Keizersgracht 689, the rear entrance of the Waldorf Astoria Hotel.

'Amsterdam is just gorgeous at this time of year,' one woman sighs happily. 'Like Harrogate.'

The Waldorf Astoria is not the kind of place I'd normally spend much time in — a weekend's stay there would, by my calculation, cost about what I earn in a month. But the Open Gardens Day offers a welcome opportunity to pry. I walk through another souterrain that opens out into a vast inner courtyard, with a big triangular lawn and a nice little white summerhouse. Compared to some of the other gardens I've already seen, this one is not hugely attractive — there's a lot of ugly modern garden furniture lying around, and half-dressed hotel guests basking on sun loungers. But the scale of it is impressive: I've walked past this spot on the Keizersgracht countless times, but never guessed that such a massive garden was hidden here.

Walking along one of the canals today, your overriding sense is of uniformity. The houses all seem to have roughly the same proportions and styles, with the same basement rooms tucked halfway below street level, the same stone steps leading up to an imposing front door, and the same big, clear windows offering views of book-lined interiors. Under the original expansion masterplan, care was taken to ensure a degree of homogeneity. A merchant building their dream home on the Prinsengracht, for example, might be told they could only use certain kinds of brick when constructing exterior walls, would have their plot carefully measured to ensure it was the correct width and depth, and might have their pilings inspected by officials before building could begin. Look closer, though, and you'll also see that the houses along the canals are more varied than they might appear at first glance. Some of the richest residents bought two plots and built double-size mansions, and the plots themselves were sometimes irregular — for example, where the canal curved sharply, homes and gardens might end up shaped more like a slice of pizza than a standard rectangle. In some places, gaps in the façade where no homes had been built were later backfilled with ultra-narrow houses that tour-boat guides enjoy pointing out today, where you'd struggle to do a pirouette in your living room without grazing your elbows. Many of the buildings also have different shaped gables on top — partly because many façades were altered in the 1700s and 1800s, and different shapes of gable went in and out of fashion as years passed. 'Ramparts against the sky,' the novelist Bernard MacLaverty called them.[7] The area's original planners might have been disappointed to see how varied the houses ended up looking, but personally I've always thought that this is a large part of Amsterdam's charm. Walk along the Herengracht or Keizersgracht and the buildings to your left and right will all be similar enough to form a pleasing repeating pattern, but also varied enough that the scenery never gets boring, and there's something new to notice every time you pass.

I leave the Waldorf Astoria and continue a few hundred metres along the Keizersgracht. The sun has broken through the hazy clouds and it's starting to feel like summer. Reaching the point where the Reguliersgracht meets Keizersgracht in large watery crossroads, I stop for a while and lean on a railing on a bridge to absorb the scene. Tour boats slide past with tannoys blaring, a parcel delivery boat executes a chugging U-turn, and there is even a pair of kayakers kitted up in helmets and waterproof vests as if they are headed for Niagara Falls. At Bridge 39, I stop for a while and watch a municipal garbage boat with a claw attached to a mechanical arm fishing for rubbish on the bottom of the canal. It quickly secures a handsome catch: a pair of very rusty bicycles, chained together and thickly coated in blackish mud, which are dumped unceremoniously on the canal bank. Such sights are common around here. Amsterdam's canals have an average depth of 2.4 metres and the Guinness World Records states that between 12,000 and 15,000 bikes are recovered from Amsterdam's canals like this every year, easily winning the city the coveted world record for 'most bicycles recovered from a waterway'.[8] I feel momentarily sorry for whoever's bike ended up in the drink this week before reflecting that it could have been worse: thirty-five cars are submerged every year too, and well over a hundred people fall in.[9]

I walk further along the Keizersgracht. On my right I spot Reguliersgracht 36, which featured in the James Bond film *Diamonds Are Forever* as the home of a nubile diamond merchant who greets Sean Connery wearing a 'nice little nothing'.[10] On the next doorstep, two young women sit sharing a big tub of yoghurt and discussing whether or not Elke really likes Daan. (She does, but he's too dumb to realise.)

A few minutes later I arrive at the van Loon house, which is another of the city's most famous old residences, now open to the public as a museum. It has an elegant sandstone façade and statues that hint at the sources of the wealth which helped pay for it: Mars and Minerva (war and wisdom), Vulcan (metallurgy), and Ceres (agriculture). Yet like many grand houses around here, its overall appearance is quite plain compared to the more ornate residences you might see in the fancier neighbourhoods of Brussels or Paris. For the Dutch, money was — and still is — best spent discreetly.

The van Loon house was built in 1672 and its first resident was Ferdinand Bol, the great painter and pupil of Rembrandt who had, by marrying a wealthy widow, miraculously managed to escape the impoverished life of an artist and live in some style. Later, the house became the home of Willem van Loon, who was born in 1537 and managed to build a sizeable fortune in the Rotterdam herring trade, before cleverly turning it into an even larger one by becoming one of the first investors in the VOC. As his bank balance improved,

Willem founded a great Amsterdam dynasty, with sons and grandsons who played prominent roles in the city's cultural and political life, intermarrying with other great families like the Geelvincks and serving as mayors and patrons of the arts.

Inside the house, things are sumptuous. Many of Amsterdam's townhouses have been extensively remodelled and redecorated over the years, making them an odd hodge-podge of architectural styles and fashions, and the van Loon residence is no exception: it looks as if it's been furnished by someone with a very large expense account and very inconsistent tastes. Walking through the front door, I'm greeted by a pleasing jumble of brass rococo banisters, polished wooden floors, French furniture, and Japanese trimmings. The entrance hall is lined with contrasting black and white tiles like a chessboard, and a series of high-ceilinged salons and dining rooms drip with fine china, tapestries, and artworks. The positioning of the windows and the layout of rooms, also means that — as in many older Dutch properties — the whole building is shaped like a corridor: closed in on both sides but with big windows at either end. This means that if you stand almost anywhere inside, you can enjoy a clear line of sight spanning perhaps thirty metres in each direction. It's a neat trick that floods even smaller rooms with an unusual amount of natural light, making them feel bigger than they really are. What strikes me most, though, is that the house is not actually that big at all. There are only six rooms on the ground floor and another six on the first floor; and I can walk across the whole width of the building in about twelve big steps. For a wealthy merchant of the Dutch Golden Age, this might have been unimaginable luxury, but a modern oligarch would probably think it too cramped as a weekend home for their pets. I stand at a window for a while, watching the boats go past and find it easy to see why a budding imperial titan might feel pretty pleased with himself, sitting here in the evening celebrating the day's profits and looking out across the water. They might even have been able to enjoy spectator sports from their windows. One popular pastime around here in the 17th and 18th centuries was a ball game known as *kolf*, in which people used a curved wooden stick to knock a leather ball stuffed with goose feathers up and down the road. The game became hugely popular and, with a few modifications, spread around the world, better known by its Anglicised name: golf.

By modern standards, grand houses in the canal ring were far from perfect places to live: freezing in the winter and sweltering in the summer. Visitors weren't always impressed: one described the canal-side houses as 'like privies, hanging still over the water'.[11] For the people who lived here, servants made life easier. The Dutch generally treated their servants equitably. One French visitor to a wealthy merchant's home reported his astonishment that a maid and a manservant were allowed to sit at the table and eat with their master and his guests. However, a servant's lot was not an easy one, due to the Dutch obsession with keeping things clean. 'Their houses they keep cleaner than their bodies,' Owen Feltham reported after a visit, and 'their bodies than their souls.'[12] Johan Huizinga once claimed the obsession with domestic hygiene arose because of the need for a germ-free environment when making cheese,[13] but in truth, it was probably more about religious conservatism and a desire to appear to be behaving responsibly, perhaps intermingled with a sense that in a country where the natural environment was always a threat, it was essential to keep everything spick and span. The English diplomat William Temple told the story of a burgomaster who visited a family in a grand house like this in the 1600s and was greeted at the front door by a maid who took one look at his dirty shoes, decided she didn't want him walking through her pristine entrance hall, and picked him up and carried him into the next room. Attending a dinner party in another home, Temple also complained that his meal had been ruined because a servant appeared with a cloth in hand every single time he spat on the floor.[14]

Reaching the rear of the house, I walk out down some steps into the garden. It's another beautiful one, with a maze-like array of low green hedges, tall trees, and colourful flowers. In the Middle Ages, gardens in the Netherlands and elsewhere were mostly functional rather than decorative; used for growing food or raising animals rather than for lazing about in. In the Golden Age, however, there was a growing realisation that a nice garden could be a good place to both enjoy your wealth and show it off to others. Gardens became increasingly decorative, with neat hedgerows and flower beds, statues on pedestals, sundials, and benches on which gentlemen could sit to discuss business or delicate personal affairs. There was some room for individuality, of course, but generally, the gardens were a way to show you fitted in with the neighbours, rather than stood apart from them. Often, the layouts subtly reflected attributes that the owners thought they possessed themselves: neat, tidy, disciplined, orderly, graceful. Because the tall houses cast such long shadows, it sometimes made it tricky to grow things, yet the plants that did thrive could be surprisingly exotic, thanks to specimens brought back from Dutch expeditions abroad. Sadly, during

Amsterdam's 20th-century post-war boom, many nice gardens were lost; filled in with home extensions or paved over for car parking. (Dutch gardens are, unfortunately, often horrible these days — many people prize convenience over beauty and are keen to turn their gardens into just extensions of the house.) Now, though, there are strict rules aiming to preserve the gardens that remain and regulating the cutting of trees. In some places, the once-orderly landscape has grown surprisingly wild — a falcon lived for years in one old beech tree off the Keizersgracht, much to the delight of local homeowners who never had to worry about pigeons or mice sullying their gardens.

Leaving the van Loon house I head along the Vijzelstraat, past the mammoth city archives building and on to the Herengracht. The weather keeps improving and Amsterdam has reverted to default sunny day mode: sunglasses, terraces, impromptu picnics by the canal. Drinking on café terraces in the summer is the closest thing the modern Dutch have to national religion and today it feels like half of Amsterdam is at prayer. Every table is filled, and every chair is carefully rotated to catch the maximum sunshine, like the solar panels on a satellite. A boat full of young men in swimming trunks passes by, broiling pinkly in the sun. They stop and moor their boat near a bar with a sign out front saying: 'Beer: Now Cheaper Than Petrol'. Nearby, a young man is cycling slowly down the centre of the road with big earphones on, drumming happily on his handlebars as a long line of traffic builds up behind him, unable to pass. Heading in the other direction is a young woman in a trench coat on the back of which reads:

'STOP LOOKING AT MY ASS'. Alain de Botton once wrote that there was 'a democratic scruffiness' about this city, and it's often easy to see what he meant.[15]

I continue walking northwest along the Herengracht. This is an area rich in memories for me, as it was here that I first worked in Amsterdam and where some of my earliest memories of the city were formed. I can't pass by here without remembering countless lunch breaks lounging in the sunshine by the canal, which, after years of dreary London office life, felt idyllic.

I'm now passing through one of the most beautiful places in the whole city, and arguably in the whole of Europe: the curve in the Herengracht known as the Golden Bend, immaculately preserved and ready for Instagram. Looking at it I think inevitably of the most famous painting of this spot: Gerrit Berckheyde's 1671 *View of the Golden Bend in the Herengracht*. It depicts the view along the water from the bridge on the Vijzelstraat, with monumental buildings lined up like massive tombstones and cast in strong sunlight and shadow. It's a beautiful image, but if you look closely what strikes you most is that Berckheyde caught the neighbourhood at a moment when it was still under construction. The houses in his picture are beautiful but still unfinished, and there's no colour or chaos in the streets, and no trees or greenery. Building materials lie scattered on the canalside, fences shield the undeveloped lots from the public road and the last building on the south side of the canal is even clad in scaffolding. Today everything looks a good deal tidier, although I do pass a group of yellow-jacketed workmen who are lifting the brick road surface to access a water main. That's one advantage of brick streets like this: if you need to get under the surface, you can open the ground up like a zip, and then close it smoothly again when you're done.

For the next hour or so I happily zigzag my way up and down the canals, visiting more gardens and filling my notebook with short summaries:

Herengracht 460: another cool dark tunnel-like entrance leading through the house to a lovely little garden, compact and green, with pink hydrangeas, cherubic fountains, and winding paths made of seashells.

Herengracht 450: a modern office interior leading to a huge garden that stretches behind half a dozen houses. Roses the size of teapots. Gravel paths and low beech hedges. People sitting in the sun drinking Prosecco.

Herengracht 386: a *stiltetuin*, or quiet garden, with signs asking guests to speak softly and avoid using mobile phones. Garden with French elements, including marble statues and a fountain twice as tall as I am, ringed with winged horses and cherubs.

Huis de Vicq: neat low hedges in fractal patterns. In the centre a golden sundial. Rhododendrons. Bushes trimmed in helter-skelter shapes. High walls covered in creepers. Hydrangeas like colourful fireworks.

Keizersgracht 369: small, leafy, tranquil. A young woman entering ahead of me leaves her sleeping baby alone in his stroller out on the pavement while she goes in the house to look around, confident that in this city he'll come to no harm. She wouldn't do that in London or Paris.

One thing that surprises me about the gardens I've seen is the lack of tulips, which once would have been the centrepiece of any self-respecting garden in this neighbourhood. Tulips first arrived in the Netherlands from the Middle East and thrived in the sandy soil south-west of Amsterdam, where the famous Keukenhof Gardens are now. Today, tulips are seen as appealing partly because they're graceful but simple, but they once were anything but — as Anne Goldgar has written, in the 17th century the flowers represented 'novelty, unpredictability, excitement – a splash of the exotic east, a collector's item for the curious and wealthy'.[16] 'The tulip was the ultimate status symbol', the historian Anna Pavord explained, 'the definitive emblem of what you were worth'. [17] As incomes rose, it all sparked what is often said to be the world's first speculative bubble — the famous 'Tulipmania' of the mid-1630s. Common tulip bulbs were traded feverishly in Amsterdam and elsewhere, and prices soared overnight. A single Admiraal van Enkhuijsen bulb reportedly sold for 5,400 guilders — the equivalent of fifteen years' salary for an Amsterdam bricklayer.[18] At another auction, 99 bulbs were sold for a total of 90,000 guilders – or roughly €6 million in today's money. The extent of the mania is often exaggerated — it wasn't as if the whole country lost its mind over bulbs, and the number of individuals involved was actually quite small. But there were fantastical tales of fortunes gained and lost. One anecdote told of a city brewer offering his whole brewery in exchange for a single bulb; another of a lady who commissioned an artist to paint her a bouquet of flowers because she could not afford a real one. In Haarlem, people told the story of a merchant who supposedly paid the enormous sum of 3,000 florins for a bulb and then carelessly left it on his desk while he went to finish some paperwork. Returning a short while later, the poor merchant found a passing sailor had assumed the bulb was an onion and chopped it up to eat with his herring. Needless to say, the boom couldn't last. In February 1637 the market slipped, losing traction like a drunk cyclist spinning into a canal. Some people lost everything, and others were left holding large stocks of bulbs or contracts that were now essentially worthless. One Amsterdam gardener supposedly bought a single bulb for 1250 florins in early 1637, then found he could not sell it on for even a tenth of that amount a few weeks later.[19] Those who lost out received little sympathy. The poet Roemer Visscher wrote that for people who invested too much 'lust is surely costly',[20] while Jan Brueghel the younger produced a painting of tulips being praised by a group of monkeys.[21] 'Our descendants,' one Haarlem historian wrote a few years after the boom, 'doubtless will laugh at the human insanity of our Age.'[22] He clearly couldn't have predicted bitcoin.

Proceeding along the Herengracht, I reach the area known as the *Negen Straatjes*, or Nine Small Streets. This is one of the most popular parts of Amsterdam for tourists and it's not hard to see why; it's a delightful warren of brick-paved streets that are packed with boutiques, bars, and cafés. If you want a summer dress in a Frida Kahlo print, or some vintage Levi's, or some expensive candied almonds, or a pair of designer wooden sunglasses, or a smoothie that costs more than you'd usually spend on a pizza, then this is the place to go. Ten or fifteen years ago, this part of Amsterdam was still fairly quaint, but sadly, it's now a little overexposed and many of the older, quirkier shops have been driven out by rent rises. Today the streets are crammed with dawdling tourists, and outside one ordinary chip shop there's an enormous line, separated from the street behind by thick ropes like a film premiere, with two security guards shepherding people into place. Googling the name of the place, I remember why it's famous: some videos of people eating chips here for some reason went mega-viral on TikTok a while ago, and the place is now more popular than ice cream in a heatwave. Clearly, strange fads didn't end with Tulipmania.

I can feel my energy flagging, so make a brief stop for coffee. Amsterdam seems to have a coffee roastery or café for every resident these days, but I opt to go to a café that I used to visit daily, which is so dedicated to good coffee (or so pretentious?) that when I once ordered a coffee with milk there, the barista steadfastly refused to provide it on the grounds that 'milk ruins the taste'.* Today I do get my milk, and the coffee is excellent, but the waitress reacts grumpily when I speak Dutch to her. In this part of Amsterdam, the local tongue is practically a second language.

I walk north, passing the famous Pulitzer Hotel on the Prinsengracht, where George Clooney's gang of thieves stays while plotting a heist in *Ocean's Twelve*. Just north of the hotel stands the towering Westerkerk. The church is

---

*   Tellingly, if you want a coffee with milk in this country, you'll usually order a *koffie verkeerd* or 'coffee gone wrong'.

another Amsterdam landmark; a gracious monolith of red-brick and buttery stone, with a tall clocktower (known as the Westertoren) which was built in the 1620s and 30s under the oversight of the prolific Hendrick de Keyser. Rembrandt is buried somewhere here, although no one remembers exactly where. Approaching the base of the tower, I scan a QR code displayed there and am directed to the church's website, which tells me in slightly Borat English that 'Westerkerk was not the first Protestant church in Amsterdam, but it was the first biggest in the world.' Indeed. I remember there's also a beloved song about the church tower, by the singer Willy Alberti, which you might still hear being sung in some of the area's scruffier bars late on a Friday night:

Oh, beautiful old tower
You've been standing there for years now
Wherever I walk in the Jordaan
You follow me everywhere
If you were to tell me
What you have seen all these years
You could tell us so much
But old man, you just don't do it.[23]

It sounds better in Dutch.

Rounding a corner, I turn away from the canal and find myself on the Westermarkt, a short row of gorgeous 17th-century townhouses, each with white-framed windows, sheer brick façades and gabled rooftops. One house in particular — number 6 — stands out from the rest because of a plaque mounted high on the façade explaining that in 1634 *'le celebre philosophe Francais'* lived here. It's referring to a famous resident who lived here at the time when the city was being transformed: the philosopher René Descartes, best known for his dictum that 'I think, therefore I am.'

Descartes moved here in his thirties, after many years soldiering and travelling, yearning for somewhere he could work in peace. When he arrived, Descartes was still in the early days of his philosophical career, sporting a pencil moustache and a flowing bouffant of dark hair, which made him look like a glam rock guitarist. The political climate in Europe at that time was not exactly conducive to open debate, but Amsterdam offered a rare sanctuary, with an intellectual climate that was expansive, energetic, and unusually tolerant of divergent views. Descartes loved the city, devouring piles of books and walking the canals and building sites. Above all, Descartes — like many others before and since — relished the bustle and colour of the growing city, enjoying the noise of people in the streets 'as if it were the murmur of a country stream'. 'I invite you to Amsterdam for your retirement,' he wrote to a friend.[24] 'A country house may be very well run, but there are always all sorts of things missing which can only be obtained in a town ... In this great city everyone except me is in business and so absorbed by profit-making that I could spend my entire life here without being noticed by a soul.' When a friend dared to say they preferred Italy to the dreary Dutch Republic, Descartes famously wrote back with a five-star review of the city. 'What other place in the world could one choose, where all the commodities of life and all the curiosities to be desired, are so easy to come by as here? In what other land could one enjoy such a complete freedom?'[25]

I leave Descartes' place and walk west over the Leliesluis into the Jordaan. The Jordaan is another neighbourhood that is popular with tourists, and it's easy to see why. Like the nicer areas of many cities, it feels almost like a small town in its own right, with a distinct flavour and feel; a sort of Notting Hill on the Herengracht. The origins of the neighbourhood's name are disputed — 'Jordaan' is sometimes said to be a biblical reference to the River Jordan, but the most common explanation is that it comes from the French *jardin*, or garden. Today, it's not much like a garden at all, but study a map and you'll soon notice that many canals and streets are still named after plants and flowers, including the Palmgracht (Palm Canal), Lauriergracht (Laurel Canal), Rozengracht (Roses Canal) and Bloemgracht (Flower Canal), where Rembrandt had a studio. On a sunny day — or, in fact, on a rainy one — the streets here are packed with visitors, including many coming to see the bustling Noordermarkt (North Market) and many more joining the endless queues to get into the Anne Frank house, which lies on the edge of the Jordaan. Yet despite the crowds, this area still often feels like the distilled essence of all that's good about Amsterdam; the perfect place to sit on a friend's front step with a glass of cheap wine before going for dinner. I don't have any particular destination in mind today, but while away a happy half hour wandering up and down busy little streets, visiting the famous statue of the singer Johnny Jordaan, and fantasising about one day living here in a sundrenched flat with a view of a tree-lined canal.

The Jordaan wasn't always so refined. When, in the early 1600s, the fancy new canal houses were being built along the Grachtengordel, an obvious problem arose: where to put the poorer locals who were being displaced? The Jordaan offered an easy solution, and a densely packed neighbourhood of smaller homes was soon being built just past the Prinsengracht.

The layout was unusual: if you look at a map of the Jordaan today, you'll see slanting, dog-legged streets that reflect the orientation of the drainage ditches which once lay here; a glitch in the matrix of the neat cobweb covering the rest of the city. By the 18th century the area was horribly overcrowded, with many families crammed into tiny apartments with terrible hygiene, beset by minor floods and disease outbreaks. In the 19th century, as Amsterdam industrialised, things got worse, and the Jordaan came to resemble something close to a slum. In 1866, a cholera epidemic in part of the Jordaan killed about a tenth of the residents in the space of a few months.[26] In the 20th century, things improved, but the neighbourhood retained a feisty working-class reputation. The novelist Cees Nooteboom, who lived for years on the edge of the Jordaan, once wrote that:

> The neighbourhood retained an at times almost
> provocative sense of identity, completely different
> from other parts of the city; it was a family of sorts,
> a tribe with its own customs, sayings and above
> all laws. Marrying outside the neighbourhood was
> frowned upon, solidarity was strong and people lived
> literally on top of one another and knew everything
> about each other.[27]

Another minor celebrity who grew up here (in a flat on the Eerste Egelantiersdwarsstraat) was the criminal Willem Holleeder, who became a bizarre Amsterdam anti-hero after being involved in various murders and kidnappings, including the abduction of the brewery heir Freddy Heineken. In court, Holleeder once tried to explain that tapes recording him losing his temper simply reflected the place where he'd grown up. 'We come from the Jordaan,' he said. 'We argue, we shout and we swear. That's all allowed. The next day we talk about it and it's all over.'[28]

Well within living memory, old canal houses in and around the Jordaan were not that desirable or expensive, and many were still inhabited by squatters, students and ageing hippies on a budget. In the 1970s, the city authorities seemed determined to demolish big parts of the Jordaan and replace it with modern roads and blocks of flats. However, after a lot of resistance, they wisely changed their plans and focused on small projects to fix up the neighbourhood instead. Whatever they did clearly worked, for the Jordaan gradually went from undesirable to unaffordable. Old timers grumble that the locals have all been forced out now, replaced by overpaid expats and yuppies. They're probably right, but traces of the old, scruffier Jordaan still remain, and there are some lovely little businesses tucked away on the quieter back streets — it was near here that I found an old German silversmith to make my wedding ring. Such businesses may not be here for much longer, though. Between 2014 and 2022, the average house price in the Jordaan nearly doubled. Fiddling with my phone, I check the property prices: not far off €2 million for a smallish apartment above a shop. That sundrenched view of the tree-lined canal will have to wait.

The day is slipping away, and I've only time to see one more garden before everything closes. Leaving the Jordaan, I walk back towards the city centre, stopping briefly for a drink at a busy bar on the Prinsengracht. Bars like this — known as *bruine kroegen*, or brown bars — are a Dutch institution; a sort of lowlands variant of a traditional English pub, with a gloomy but irresistibly welcoming vibe that seems immune to changes of fashion or season. The playwright Gerrit Komrij described one such *kroeg* as being like 'an oven glowing darkly', while the Dutch–Moroccan novelist Hafid Bouazza wrote that they were like 'wooden wombs'.[29] Sadly, *bruine kroegen* have been in steep decline in recent years, as property values soar and a younger generation decides they like their bars with shinier fittings, exotic drinks, and fast wi-fi. According to the national broadcaster NOS, in the last ten years the number of bars of this type has fallen by about a third.[30] Today the atmosphere in this one is unusually rowdy, thanks to a local student fraternity playing drinking games in the small bar. They are, I notice, adhering to the bizarre, inverted dress code of young Dutch men, who will happily turn up for a job interview or even a funeral in jeans, but consider it amusing to wear a jacket and tie when out boozing with their mates.

My last stop for the day is a somewhat unlikely one: the Amnesty International headquarters at Keizersgracht 177. I arrive to find that from the outside it's another grand old building like many others in the area, impressive but forgettable. Behind the historic façade, it's all been heavily modernised and looks roughly how you'd expect a charity HQ to look: linoleum floors, bright yellow placards and posters, a faint smell of bleach, and no traces of the 17th century. The garden at the rear of the property is, however, astonishing; perhaps the best I've seen all day. I walk out of the rear doors into a small grove of slender trees, which remind me of the olive groves van Gogh painted in France. Thick bushes burst with white and pink flowers, shaded under chestnut and purple beech trees which look far too big to be anywhere near a city centre. A man sits quietly on a bench with a cup of coffee, and I spy a teenaged couple exchanging giggly kisses behind a tree. I wander in circles gaping at the garden for a solid five minutes, giving serious thought to quitting the writing game altogether and taking a job with Amnesty just so I could spend my lunch breaks here. It's sunny and I feel drowsy; the kind of drowsy happiness that you only feel on a sunny day when you've walked a long way and done everything you need to do that day. I lie down on a bench and fall blissfully, deeply asleep.

CHAPTER FOUR

Along the Amstel from Ouderkerk to Rembrandt's House

How Amsterdam became a haven for artists and inventors

Amsterdam is not a city of early risers. Walk through the centre of, say, London, New York, or Nairobi at breakfast time and you're likely to see hordes of people bustling about; on their way to work or study, heading home after a night shift, or running an early-morning errand. Here in Amsterdam, though, much of the old city centre remains deserted even at about eight thirty. As I walk sleepily from the Dam to the metro station at Waterlooplein, I pass only a handful of locals cycling to work and the odd half-drunk reveller stumbling home in last night's clothes. Dutch working hours are by far the shortest in Europe, and it shows.[*]

---

[*] According to the OECD, the average Dutch person works thirty hours per week in their main job, compared to thirty-seven hours in the UK and thirty-five hours in Belgium and Germany. The difference is partly due to the fact that nearly half of Dutch people work part time. (OECD, Average Weekly Hours Worked, 2023)

From Waterlooplein I catch a half-empty metro and then a bus south to Ouderkerk aan de Amstel; an attractive little place that lies about seven miles upstream from Amsterdam along the River Amstel. Ouderkerk is in many ways a typical Dutch small town, much like hundreds of others scattered through the surrounding countryside: a warren of busy little streets filled with cafés, bakeries, and bike shops, centred around a stout little church tower that looks like a lost piece from a board game. Ouderkerk is, however, different from some towns in that it's buoyed and gentrified by its proximity to Amsterdam. On weekends, hundreds of cyclists, runners, and hikers head here from the city in search of fresh air, open space, or somewhere to drink coffee while looking at the river.

Today I am planning to walk along the river all the way from Ouderkerk to Amsterdam's city centre. By the standards of someone with a recently broken leg, it's quite a long way to hobble — seven or eight miles — but I have plenty of time, and am looking forward to seeing the city from a slightly different perspective, approaching from the outside and exploring its rural hinterland. My itinerary is not an entirely original one: I'll be following in the footsteps of a certain Rembrandt van Rijn, who also liked to walk this way nearly 400 years ago. I hope that along the way I can learn more about how he came to love Amsterdam, and how the city became a magnet for all kinds of artists and innovators in the 17th century.

Ouderkerk doesn't boast much in the way of major attractions, but I start by making a quick detour to see the Catholic Urbanuskerk: a sturdy brick church designed by Pierre Cuypers, the architect who produced the Rijksmuseum and Amsterdam's central train station. Along the road, I'm also moved to happen upon the old Beth Haim Jewish cemetery, which I haven't visited for years. It's a charmingly picturesque place, with big gravestones sinking into the soft peaty soil, fences woven from local willow branches, and a nice miniature museum giving a brief overview of the area's Jewish history. Sephardic Jews started arriving in and around Amsterdam in large numbers in the 16th century. By the end of the 1600s there were about 7,500 of them in the city, of whom perhaps two-thirds were immigrants from Eastern Europe.[1] In keeping with the prejudices of the time, Jews were initially refused permission to establish a Jewish cemetery in Amsterdam, but in 1614 were finally allowed to establish a burial place here, at a safe distance to the south of the city, which eventually grew to hold nearly 30,000 graves. Today, I find the cemetery deserted, but it was once a popular tourist attraction. Jacob van Ruisdael produced a moody painting of the cemetery bathed in moonlight, and visitors used to come from all over the place to see the unusual horizontal tombstones, with John Evelyn writing of a 'spacious field ... which was full of Sepulchers and Hebrew Inscriptions, some of them very stately, of cost'.[2] By the 1920s, the cemetery was so popular for funerals that the ground was getting full, and a new layer of earth was added on top of some existing graves so new bodies could be added; a move that the authorities expected would enable them to keep accepting new customers until the 1960s. Sadly, though, so many of Amsterdam's Jews were subsequently murdered in concentration camps elsewhere in Europe that, more than half a century after the original deadline passed, the authorities say they've still got enough space here to keep running for decades.[3]

I leave Ouderkerk and walk north along the Amsteldijk, on the west bank of the river. Glancing over my shoulder, I catch a view similar to the one Rembrandt must have enjoyed when he walked here in 1641 and produced a nice etching of the winding river with a sailing barge moving along it and a tall church steeple on the horizon.

In my experience, Dutch people often have a slightly distorted view of nature — given the lack of real wilderness in the Netherlands, they end up revering scruffy little patches of green as if they were Yosemite, and going for walks along flat tarmac paths dressed as if they're climbing Everest. There is, however, no denying that this stretch of the Amstel is beautiful. For the first ten minutes or so, the riversides are crowded with terraced houses and parked cars, but after a while the landscape opens out into empty countryside and the footpath becomes a narrow ribbon of gravel, tracking the waterway like a handrail. Chalk boards outside farm cottages advertise local apples and honey for sale, and riverside bulrushes reach higher than my head. It's idyllic. Because the Netherlands is so flat, many rivers have barely any detectable current, and the Amstel is no exception: the water looks as tranquil as a village pond. On both sides of the river, lush grassy fields stretch into the distance, with black-and-white dairy cows moving slowly across the landscape like chess pieces on a giant green board. The landscape here is unremittingly flat and dizzyingly green, to the extent that it's difficult to judge distance or scale. A 'civilized steppe,' a poet once called it.[4] I'm now at the edge of what's known as the Groene Hart, or Green Heart; the large diamond of predominantly rural land wedged between Amsterdam, Rotterdam, Utrecht, and the Hague, where it always feels a bit like it's 1925. Amsterdam's city centre, with its cheerful bustle of bicyclists and tourists, tram bells, and dance music, is only about six miles from where I stand, but feels a hundred miles (or perhaps a hundred years) away. My ankle starts to hurt a little and I pause for a minute or two in front of one amazing old house; a beautiful cuboid palace with little turrets on the roof, which looks like an oversized townhouse somehow shipped upriver from the Herengracht. I fantasise about one day buying it, should my rambling book about Dutch history somehow get made into a Hollywood movie and leave me richer than John Grisham.

I'm not the first person to be enraptured by this liminal zone between city and country. From the Golden Age onwards, many of Amsterdam's wealthiest residents had country retreats here along the Amstel or along the River Vecht, roughly eight miles east of here, where they could escape the noise and grime of the city while not straying too far from it. The Amstel was also a source of inspiration for many artists, including Adam van Breen, Jacob Maris, Gerrit Toorenburgh, Johan Conrad Greive, and Aert van der Neer, who all painted or sketched it — along with Rembrandt. These days, Rembrandt is remembered mostly as a painter of people, but after the death of his wife Saskia in the early 1640s he spent many hours wandering along the Amstel and sketching here. In the words of the scholar Deric Regin, Rembrandt's city home 'had become oppressive to him, and the flight into landscape ... meant a temporary relief'.[5]

Right on cue, I round a bend in the river and am interrupted from my thoughts about Rembrandt by the sight of a life-sized statue of Rembrandt, kneeling on the riverbank in front of a pretty windmill, with a sketchbook in hand. There's something a little odd about the statue — to me, it looks like a mechanic kneeling down with a clipboard to inspect a faulty brake pad — but the setting is lovely; a wide curve in the river, flanked by emerald-coloured countryside and tall bulrushes. A pair of hikers who are absurdly over-dressed for the pancake-flat landscape — Gore-Tex, walking poles, and trousers covered in zips — speedily overtake me and then stop to take a selfie with Rembrandt. '*Prachtig*,' one of them announces to no one in particular. 'Beautiful.'

By the time Rembrandt was born in 1606, the Amsterdam art scene was already undergoing a profound change. Painting was, like empire-building, another area in which the Netherlands had somewhat of a slow start. This was partly because the austere Protestant Dutch church had little interest in buying art to adorn churches and residences in the way that the authorities in Catholic countries like Italy did. Lacking wealthy patrons, Dutch painters in the 15th and 16th centuries were often very good, but rarely managed to achieve true fame or greatness. All this began to change, however, around the time of the wars with Spain and the dawn of the Golden Age. Refugees fleeing Flanders carried artistic influences northwards, and the rapid emergence of Amsterdam as a wealthy trading hub put rocket boosters under the burgeoning Dutch art scene. As merchants, burgomasters, and diplomats began buying art to fill their grand homes, a distinctive style of Dutch landscape painting emerged, focused on exactly the kind of scenery a traveller might see on a journey from Ouderkerk to Amsterdam: serene rivers, church steeples, boats, cows, trees, and vast skies forever studded with clouds and pierced with shards of golden sunlight, illuminating distant towns as if they were spotlit set-pieces on a gloomy stage. Dutch artists, as Zbigniew Herbert noted, often 'never traveled to the other side of the Alps, or even neighboring countries. They remained faithful to the trees, walls, clouds of their homeland'.[6] Yet despite these limitations, their output was prodigious: one scholar estimated that up to 1.4 million paintings were produced by around 700 Dutch artists in just two decades in the mid-1600s.[7] Their work quickly became wildly popular, purchased in huge quantities not only by wealthy VOC empire-builders but also by ordinary clerks, teachers, priests, maids, and farmers. One study found that in Amsterdam in 1610, households owned an average of twenty-five paintings each, and by the 1670s this had risen to forty per household.[8] The Englishman John Evelyn visited an art market and wrote of his astonishment that 'it is an ordinary thing to find a common farmer lay out two or three thousand pounds in this commodity, their houses are full of them'.[9] In the space of a generation, fine paintings had become like Netflix subscriptions: something almost everyone felt they had to have. Not everyone was impressed though: Sir Joshua Reynolds, President of the (British) Royal Academy, did a tour of Holland and complained that 'we did not see less than twenty pictures of dead swans'.[10]

The hike from Ouderkerk is already by far the longest I've done since smashing my leg, and at the four-mile mark I can feel my ankle swelling like an apple pie in a hot oven. But I don't actually mind that much: it's a beautiful day, the scenery is glorious, and I'm secretly happy to have an excuse to take things slowly, gawping at beautiful houses and watching crews of rowers whizz past like shuttles on a loom. A 'NIET MAAIEN' sign begs workmen not to mow the riverside foliage, and another explains that although the riverbanks are home to grass snakes, people shouldn't be too alarmed if one slithers over their foot: they're harmless. At one point I see a trio of young boys floating past on a raft made of wooden pallets, on the verge of capsizing but utterly gleeful, enjoying the delights of growing up in a land where health and safety rules are largely unheard of. Childhoods in this area were not always so cheerful. The Protestant faith put great emphasis on people being able to read the Biblc, so schools were often quite good, but in the 17th century thousands of children were put to work in shops, on farms, or in factories. In Amsterdam, many orphaned boys were signed up for a life at sea with the VOC, while others were put to work winding silk from the age of seven, often working thirteen hours a day.[11] Flipping through my notebook, I find a letter I've copied from a British female traveller in 1834 who was amazed to see one boat carrying a huge load of hay crewed by only 'two little children'; and another being towed along the river by 'a girl with a strap around her neck, and another round her breast ... tugging a boat in which sat two men and a great lubberly boy ... all of whom the poor girl had to tow along, and apparently with much effort, for her head was bowed down to her knees, besides which, a great child of two years old whom she carried in her arms, and who clung to her neck, added to her fatigue'.[12]

The idyllic landscape can't last forever, of course, and as Amsterdam draws nearer, the scenery becomes less pastoral and more urban. The river passes under a big concrete bridge — the A10 ring road, Amsterdam's *périphérique* — and after this I begin to see large houseboats moored along the riverbanks, faded rainbow flags flying, and dozens of bicycles parked along the riverbanks. A little further on comes a cluster of ugly modern tower blocks stretching away from the water; all grey concrete and reflective glass. One bears the logo of the struggling Dutch conglomerate Philips; another is emblazoned with the name of a prominent bank. Across the river to the east, the sky is a forest of cranes, and I can see new apartments sprouting up like seedlings.

This area, known as the Omval, was once a green and leafy place lying well outside the city. Browsing through Amsterdam newspaper archives, I found countless references to the area's popularity with walkers and boaters. One journalist who walked here in 1938 complained that his walk was ruined because 'it turned out, once at Omval, that a thousand Amsterdammers had the same idea, and it was teeming with people'.[13] In 1947, Het Parool reported that:

> Walkers and cyclists along the Amstel near Omval
> saw a remarkable natural phenomenon in the
> afternoon: two tornadoes. Real windstorms with
> houses and cows into the air you will only see in
> Texas or Zanzibar. But gusts here were still a cause
> for panic. Hats and hair in the air. A torn mainsail
> of a sailboat. An ice cream man who has to hold his
> waffles tight, because the waffles would otherwise be
> dumped into the Amstel.[14]

Studying my map, I suddenly realise that I know the Omval for another reason. Rembrandt produced a famous etching of it in 1645. It shows a man with a cape and big flat hat

(Rembrandt himself, maybe?) watching a crowded passenger boat passing by on the tranquil river while two lovers frolic under a willow tree. The scenery looks quite different now.

Records show that Rembrandt's first meaningful encounter with Amsterdam came in 1624 or 1625. He was born in Leiden, the son of a miller, and in his late teens came to the city to complete an artistic apprenticeship with Pieter Lastman, a well-known painter. Such apprenticeships were, back then, the standard way for a young middle-class man (and they were almost always men) to become a real artist. In exchange for payment, someone like Rembrandt could live with and learn from a master artist while carrying out chores such as cleaning, washing brushes, and stretching canvases.*
Pieter Lastman, lived near one end of Sint Antoniesbreestraat, almost in the shadow of the Zuiderkerk tower, which I climbed a few weeks ago. The area was at that time packed with the homes of painters, art dealers, antique merchants, writers, and printers, as well as junk shops stocking a delightful jumble of things that an artist might need as props for a still life: swords, shields, chandeliers, skulls, fruit, maps, globes. Rembrandt's stay there probably wasn't entirely pleasurable — an apprentice like him would have been worked hard, and it seems he left his apprenticeship after only about six months. However, his early days in Amsterdam clearly had a lasting influence. Lastman had spent years training in Italy (in an

---

*   If students produced work that the master liked, the master would probably retouch it slightly and then sign it as his own — one reason why scholars often disagree over whether a particular painting is genuinely *by* a certain great artist rather than just produced by his entourage.

effort to give his works an air of international glamour, he sometimes signed his paintings 'Pietro') and had been heavily influenced by the way artists including Caravaggio portrayed light and shade. That influence seems to have trickled down to Rembrandt himself, who began experimenting with contrasts between light and shade, developing the subtle, smoky, moody style he's best known for.

After the apprenticeship, Rembrandt moved back to Leiden, but within a few years found himself back in Amsterdam again. This time he moved in with an art dealer called Hendrick van Uylenburgh, who lived close to Pieter Lastman, near where the Rembrandt House Museum is today. Van Uylenburgh's place was a sort of cross between an art factory, an art school, and an auction house, and it's not hard to imagine it might have had a cosmopolitan, relatively swinging vibe, with dozens of artists coming and going. Staying with van Uylenburgh also brought other benefits — it was through him that Rembrandt met Saskia van Uylenburgh, the daughter of a mayor of Leeuwarden. She became one of Rembrandt's favourite models, and soon his wife.

At the time Rembrandt moved back to Amsterdam, in 1631, the city's great 17th-century boom was already underway. The VOC was thriving, the harbour was always filled with ships and the city's population had exploded to well over 100,000 — nearly four times what it had been forty years before.[15] The historian Charles Mee memorably described the cityscape that would have greeted Rembrandt when he arrived:

> The odors of Amsterdam were those of fish and salt water, of roses and tulips in the fields at the edge of

town, of garbage and raw sewage coming through
the canals in the middle of the town, of wet while in
the market squares and pipe tobacco in the taverns,
of beer and wet dogs, of pancakes and turnips and
roast pork ... The colors were dark: clothes of black
and grey and brownish yellow; a touch of orange-
brown; the brown of coffee, cocoa and chocolate ...
The IJ was filled with ships. [16]

For an aspirational young artist, it all must have made
quite an impression.

Walking north from the Omval there's an even stronger sense
that the countryside has ended and the city begun. The Amstel
becomes wider and more canal-like, lined with busy roads and
houseboats, reminding me of the Thames in the busier parts
of Richmond or Putney. The footpath I'm walking on has also
narrowed to a sliver, squeezed out by a cycle lane that hosts a
constant stream of bikes. Next to one houseboat, a wooden
sign reads: 'WARNING! Joy, our cat, ATTACKS DOGS! She
has no fear or shame. We are sorry!'

As I enter Amsterdam proper, the riverbanks fill with
slender homes. Central Amsterdam often feels cosy to the
point of being cramped, with its myriad narrow streets and
small buildings meaning you usually can't spill a beer without
getting six people wet. But here on the Amstel there's a great
sense of space, with several hundred metres of clear air
between houses on one side of the river and those on the other.
Many of the houseboats are flying XXX Amsterdam city flags
and on more than one occasion there's an unmistakable whiff

of weed smoke in the air. I see the Amstelkade on my left, and remember that further up this waterway there's a pizzeria, the San Marco, with a special window at canal height from where you can collect a takeaway by boat. (Local sometimes call it getting a *drijf-by* – a float-by.)

I cross the Nieuwe Amstelbrug to the east bank, which has several delightful little bistros and bars with people sitting outside. I quickly spot an old haunt of mine; a bar with the pleasingly nautical name of *Ysbreeker*, or Icebreaker. It has a wide terrace filled with fashionable youngish people eating burrata and drinking Aperol. In sweaty walking clothes, I don't feel particularly young or fashionable, but pull up a chair nevertheless, eat a burrata, drink an Aperol, and enjoy it very much. A youngish couple at the next table are discussing which is the best way to invest their spare money: buying a boat or buying a holiday cottage in the forest. Proof, I suppose, that rich people have problems too.

After half an hour or so, I tear myself away from the café and keep walking north along a pleasant bike-filled street — the Weesperzijde — which is slotted between the river and a bank of tall houses. The Amstel is at this point wide and murky. I pass the Amstelsluizen, a wide set of locks spanning the river that were built in the 1670s to improve the flow of water between the Amstel and the canals, alleviating the terrible stench which pervaded the Golden Bend on hot summer days. I also see several big old metal sailing barges that have been converted into handsome houseboats. A generation or so ago, houseboats like these offered a relatively affordable place for people on low incomes to live, but now they're some of the most desirable locations in town. I remember almost moving into one about a decade ago. Fearful of cold winters on the river, I ended up baulking at the price, and have regretted it ever since. What a place to wake up every day!

I cross the river again via the Magere Brug, whose delicate metalwork the novelist Dubravka Ugrešić once compared to a dragonfly's wings. I walk up the steep slope of the bridge to its peak and pause to admire the view, only to be interrupted by a pair of middle-aged cyclists wheezing and cursing as they haul themselves over the summit. 'Typhus!' one exclaims as he grinds to a halt and is forced to put both feet down. Dutch inventiveness in swearing knows no bounds.

Continuing northwards, I walk a short way to the point where the Keizersgracht meets the Amstel; one of the key nodes of the web of canals and rivers that entangles the old city centre. After walking up and down a few times, I find what I'm looking for: a solid brown brick building that is significantly larger than most of the other old canal houses in the city. A wide staircase leads up from street level to a big front door with lanterns on either side, and the rooftop is adorned with what looks like a pair of big golden globes. The building looks more like a bank than a residential home, yet it is one of the most famous residences in the city: the so-called Six Huis, or Six House; the home of a famous family who amassed huge wealth in the textile trade and played a major role in city life from the 1600s on. One of the family patriarchs, Jan Six (1618–1700), famously sponsored Rembrandt, commissioning major works that helped keep the artist afloat financially. Today the front door is tightly locked, but I went on an invitation-only tour just a few weeks ago and marvelled at the lush interior, as well as the art collection. In one of the front rooms there's a stunning portrait Rembrandt did of Jan Six in 1654, depicting his patron in a big black hat and red cape, looking so lifelike that he could almost step out of the frame and walk across the room in front of you.

Rembrandt was lucky to have friends like Jan Six. In 17th-century Netherlands, as today, being an artist was not an easy way to get wealthy. Frans Hals had his home raided by bailiffs after he failed to pay his bakery bill, and many other artists were forced to take on a side hustle or two, painting by night and working by day in bars, restaurants, or shipping offices, decorating carriages or painting shop fronts. Jan Steen and Vermeer both helped run taverns while Cornelis Brisé, a noted still-life artist, ran the bar in an Amsterdam theatre. When money was tight, some painters even used their art as currency. An artist might, for example, pay off their bar bill in the Jordaan with a nice portrait, with the result that many tavern owners (including Vermeer's father) found themselves running a profitable sideline as art dealers. The painter Joos de Momper reportedly liked a drink, but struggled to pay his booze bills, which led to one lucky wine merchant ending up with twenty-three landscapes by de Momper displayed in a special room in his house; a collection to rival the greatest museums today.

Leaving Jan Six's house, I walk a short distance northwards and cross back over the Amstel on the Blauwbrug, a wide stone structure that looks like somewhere spies might swap secrets in a misty Cold War thriller. This was another favourite spot of Rembrandt's, where in the late 1640s he produced a well-known drawing of the view of the Amstel from the Blauwbrug, imaginatively known as *View of the Amstel from the Blauwbrug*. Looking down into the murky water, I'm hit by a sudden memory of once having swum across the river somewhere near here in the middle of the night. On a warm summer's evening it was great fun and very refreshing, although I had a sore throat for a week afterwards.

Next comes the hulking H'ART museum, previously known as the Hermitage. It's a massive red-brick building which was once one of the largest care homes in the city, the Amstelhof, and reportedly had the longest façade in the country. I still have a way to walk, so am reluctant to linger too long, but can't resist popping into the museum briefly. Inside, it's beautifully cool and open, with windows everywhere and picture-postcard views out across the barges on the Amstel. The museum has had a tough few years, with its main exhibitions decimated after it abruptly (and rightly) cut ties with its St Petersburg partners following Russia's brutal assault on Ukraine. However, other museums have rallied round and arranged to loan various exhibits to fill the gaps. In one room, I find a small but glorious collection of relics and paintings, including Gerrit Berckheyde's famous view of the Golden Bend, on loan from the Rijksmuseum. There's also a lovely view of Amsterdam from the Amsteldijk painted by Jacob van Ruisdael in 1680, showing the area I'd just walked through when it contained nothing but windmills and trees. Tucked away towards the back of the museum there's even a Rembrandt, which I study keenly; the *Anatomy Lesson of Dr. Deijman*, from 1656, depicting the gruesome dissection of an executed criminal's brain. It's not the most famous anatomy lesson painted by Rembrandt, partly because it was badly damaged in a fire in the 1720s and only a fragment remains. But even a fragment of Rembrandt is still worth seeing in all its gory glory, with a doctor's hands dissecting the brain of a man whose skull is peeled open like a banana.

I walk north and then west, heading away from the river

towards the Rembrandtplein, or Rembrandt Square. This is a place that, amid strong competition, could lay claim to being one of the most touristy places in Amsterdam. It was originally a parking place for horse-drawn wagons that couldn't enter the city centre, and this is reflected in the names of some surrounding streets: Wagenstraat (Wagon Street), Paardenstraat (Horses Street). In the 1720s, there was a plan to fill one end of the square with a spectacular domed church with an enormous steeple. It was never built, though, and as a result, the square has developed a rather less pious character than it might have. The streets around the main square are filled with bars with backpacker-friendly, un-Dutch names like Woody's and Coco's Outback. Most implausible of all is the K2 ski bar, situated hundreds of miles from any hill big enough for a dog to hide behind, let alone need oxygen to climb. Although best known for its nightlife, early in the afternoon the square is already busy with Brits, Italians, Spaniards, and Americans, many of whom are queuing patiently to take photos in front of the famous statue of Rembrandt. The square itself barely existed in Rembrandt's time but in the 1850s, Amsterdam's leaders decided they needed a grand statue to match Antwerp's one of Rubens, and so they came up with the rather flattering depiction that delights visitors today. Rembrandt here looks nonplussed and youthful, burnished to a pleasing Ferrero Rocher gold and gazing serenely towards Coffeeshop Smokey and Café Club Smokey. A seagull lands atop his head as two Newcastle lads perch nearby to eat Subway sandwiches and talk loudly about all 'the birds' they saw last night. Ornithologists in Amsterdam, I think, how lovely.

From Rembrandtplein I walk west along a street lined

with souvenir shops and snack bars, narrowly avoiding getting squashed by a tram when I stop to tie my laces. At the end of the street a beautiful tower looms: the Munttoren (Mint Tower), which originally formed part of one of the main gateways in Amsterdam's city walls, before partly burning down and then being rebuilt and eventually used as the city mint. A few years ago, there were fears the tower might topple over when a new North-South metro line was built underneath it, but the city stumped up a few million euros to bolster the foundations and it now looks pretty solid; looming over the surrounding streets like somewhere Rapunzel would be held captive in a fairy tale.

I leave the tower and head off along the Nieuwe Doelenstraat, a quieter side street lined with a scattering of overpriced hotels and cafés. They all look similar, but one leaps out at me when I see its name: de Jaren café. I remember reading that this stands near the site of a house which Rembrandt lived in for a couple of years in the 1630s, soon after marrying Saskia. A few doors further along stands a hotel with a pair of red flags above the door called de Doelen. It doesn't look like much, but this too is one of the most important locations in the history of art, as it was here that Rembrandt delivered, in 1642, his most famous work: *The Night Watch*.

I popped in to see *The Night Watch* in the Rijksmuseum yesterday and was, as always, blown away by the scale and majesty of it: the unusual composition, the brilliant juxtaposition of gloom and light, the endless little details that I still keep spotting anew on my fiftieth visit to the museum. Rembrandt was commissioned by the Night Watch themselves — a sort of citizen militia who ran a neighbourhood watch patrol in their spare time — to produce a grand portrait for their headquarters at the Doelen. The commission was a good one – each man included in the picture paid a fixed fee to the artist – but it ended up taking Rembrandt at least a year (and probably much longer) to complete. What makes the painting special, though, is that Rembrandt resisted the temptation to produce something like a modern school photograph, with neat rows of people staring glumly straight ahead, and has instead managed to give a real sense of drama and motion to what might otherwise have been a static frame, with almost every character in it seemingly caught mid-motion. Most striking of all is the inclusion of someone who you would never normally expect to see in a formal portrait of men with guns: an angelic young girl in a bright butter-coloured dress, standing in a beam of sunlight like an angel who's been dropped into a war zone. (Some scholars have claimed she bears a resemblance to Rembrandt's wife, Saskia.) Oddly, the girl has a dead bird hanging from her belt; probably because its claws resembled a traditional emblem of the company. Another interesting feature is the gold jacket worn by the man in the centre holding a sword: look very closely at the embroidery and you can see a vertical XXX — the symbol of Amsterdam. The Xs are neatly placed between the thumb and fingers of the shadow of a hand — a clever trick by Rembrandt, indicating that the city is safe in the hands of the militia. Yet there is one undoubted star: the militia leader Frans Banning Cocq, who stands proud as a cockerel at the centre of the painting, sporting a hipster's pointy beard and a ruffle like a shuttlecock. Banning Cocq was in some ways lucky to find himself in such a painting: the son of a German pauper, he'd tried to give himself an aristocratic air by inserting his mother's surname in front of his father's and battled to become a well-connected young man with a nice house on the Singel. A social climber to his fingertips, he looks understandably pleased with himself for being at the centre of Rembrandt's masterpiece. Some also say that Rembrandt included a self-portrait in the picture — just to the left of the man in the centre wearing a helmet like a Roman soldier's, you can see a little slice of another man's face peeking over his shoulder. The partly obscured man looks a lot like the artist himself.

Sadly, the painting is not what it once was. In the 17th century the civic guards' headquarters would have been filled with peat fires and smoking candles, with the result that the painting got darker over time. This perhaps explains why the painting acquired the name *The Night Watch* in the 1790s: it was initially created without a title, but after years of smoke exposure looked a lot like a night-time scene. When the painting was moved to a new location in the mid-1700s it was also, incredibly, trimmed to fit between a couple of pillars, losing sizeable strips of canvas around the edges – meaning the original *Night Watch* is now significantly smaller than the copy of it which Gerrit Lundens produced in the 1640s. (Despite repeated searches, the pieces which were cut off have never been found.) Clumsy attempts at restoration also left cuts and scratches on the canvas. In the 1970s a vandal attacked the painting with a knife, and in 1990 someone sprayed it with acid. All the damage doesn't seem to have done too much harm though: Rembrandt's 'greatest failure' is now said to be worth in excess of €500 million.[17]

Looping back on myself again, I walk north along the Kloveniersburgwal. At number 29, I see one of the most famous houses in Amsterdam: the Trippenhuis, or Trips' House, which was built in the 1660s for the brothers Louis and Hendrick Trip. They were among the wealthiest men in Amsterdam in the 17th century, having become hugely rich supplying the VOC with cannons and muskets. Over the years, the Trip family firm grew into a vast conglomerate, with interests in everything from Dutch cannon-making to Swedish iron mines. The family home is predictably massive: a dark sandstone mansion with two symmetrical front doors and big stone columns reaching up the façade. As I look closely at it, I can see the house is also adorned with military symbols, including a frieze decorated with weapons and two chimneys shaped like mortars. The Trippenhuis is supposedly Amsterdam's widest home, with a frontage spanning more than twenty metres (seventy feet). Right across the road is its counterpart: the Kleine Trippenhuis, or Little Trippenhuis, which is less than two and a half metres (eight feet) wide — that is, not much wider than a man lying down. Local legend says that one of the Trip brothers' staff was once overheard saying he'd be happy to have a house as wide as his bosses' front door, and they then built him just such a house as a surprise.

I reach the Nieuwmarkt: a wide plaza ringed by bars and cafés. The space is dominated by the Waag, a big turreted building at the centre of the square, which looks like a miniature Disney castle. The Waag originally formed part of the city's outermost defences; a large gateway through which Rembrandt and many others would have passed on their way from the city to the surrounding countryside. (You can see the resemblance to the central train station, which was designed to look like an old city gate.) Just outside the gate was a hospital for lepers called the Sint-Antonies. Later, as the city expanded around it, the gate ceased to serve any defensive purpose and its moat was filled in to create the surrounding square, which in turn became one of the main markets in the city. The Waag itself served at various times as a weighing house, a meeting place for guilds, a fire station, and a museum. Today it's a restaurant. I walk inside and find a high wooden ceiling, an uneven brick floor, and a candlelit chandelier the size of a dining table overhead. I think about staying for lunch, until I see the prices: a 'double Waagburger' will set me back twenty-five euros. Perhaps I could pay with a painting?

Back outside, I circle the building, and find a gateway under one of the turrets that has a small engraving reading 'Theatrum Anatomicum' above it. In Rembrandt's time, this served as the entrance for the surgeon's guild, and it was upstairs in the large central turret that they had their anatomy theatre, where the curious could come to see bodies dissected.* In the 17th century, public dissections of cadavers were a fairly common source of entertainment around Christmastime, with dissections usually done in the winter because the cold weather meant corpses lasted longer before they started rotting. Admission fees from anatomy lectures sometimes helped pay the wages of the hangman, and tickets to the dissection of a female corpse were a guaranteed bestseller.

It was on this spot that Rembrandt created one of his most famous works, *The Anatomy Lesson of Dr. Nicolaes Tulp*. Nicolaes Tulp was born plain old Claes Pieterszoon but

---

*   The fact that audiences enjoyed watching dissections and operations explains why in English we speak of 'operating theatres'.

after changing his name rose to become one of the city's most distinguished citizens, taking a seat in council many times and serving as burgomaster. He was also by all accounts a pretty good doctor — records show him claiming to have sewed up a man who had been stabbed until his lungs were visible. In 1632, Tulp gave an anatomy lesson at the Waag and commissioned Rembrandt to produce a flattering picture of the event. Like Frans Banning Cocq, Tulp probably assumed Rembrandt would produce something in keeping with the custom of the time: a group of prominent Amsterdammers posing rather stiffly and formally, as if in a group mugshot. However, Rembrandt, left to his own devices, ended up producing something far more daring: an action shot of a surgeon halfway through dissecting a dead patient's arm while colleagues crowd around, eagerly inspecting his progress. The 'patient' in question was a recently executed criminal, and Rembrandt made little effort to depict him sympathetically; his broken neck flops like that of a dead chicken. The fact that it looks like the anatomy lesson has begun with the arm suggests Rembrandt may have taken some liberties: dissections usually started with the stomach because it's the guts that rot first. Yet, according to scholars, Rembrandt's depiction of the arm's interior muscles is so medically accurate that it's quite plausible that he took a severed arm home with him to study. Looking at the painting now, it's hard not to marvel at its technical virtuosity — and the fact that Rembrandt painted it when he was only twenty-five.

I leave the Waag and turn south along the Sint Anthoniesbreestraat, into the area where Rembrandt once lived. Compared to the other parts of the city that I've just walked through, this is a remarkably unattractive street; lined with plasticky low-rise apartment blocks which look like a historian's bad dream. If you squint a bit, though, it does still have a chaotic charm. Shops selling tourist tat are squeezed between independent bookshops, international eateries, and odd little shops hawking tie-dye clothing, joss sticks, and drug paraphernalia. 'Breathcatchers' is the name of one such store selling leather bondage gear. If I look closer, I can also still see traces of the city of old, including the Sluyswacht café — perhaps the prettiest café in all of Amsterdam. Built in the 1690s to house the guy in charge of opening the adjacent lock gates, it looks like a children's toy cottage, with black painted walls and crisp white window frames; perched on a narrow stub of land jutting into the water.

Just after the Sluyswacht the Sint Anthoniesbreestraat curves left and I head off to the right, towards the Stopera. This oddly named building was designed in the 1980s as a combined town hall (*Stadhuis*) and opera theatre (*Opera*), and was once crushingly described by the critic Gerrit Komrij as epitomising 'that cut-price philosophy of two for the price of one that is so dear to the Dutch commercial soul'.[18] During the first Gulf War, the composer Peter Schat publicly hoped a stray Scud missile would hit it.[19] It's a big, ugly, white building, which looks like a spaceship that landed on the riverbank. Along the water next to the Stopera a few market stalls are selling everything from antique coffee grinders to old shoes. There are only a few stalls here today but the markets around this area are another landmark, held regularly for hundreds of years. In the 19th century, the great novelist Multatuli described the goods being sold here in his novel *Max Havelaar*:

There lay lonely legs of tongs, and blades of scissors,
cruelly separated from their twins. There lay
decapitated nails, toothless saws, chisels without a
blade, locks without a spring, keys without a lock …
There were hinges, hoops, pins, clamps, rings, door
handles, bolts, sabres, bayonets, axes, hammers,
fire pokers, coal shovels, pots, pans, cauldrons, lids.
There lay everything that could once have been made
of iron, but now unusable, twisted, cracked, split,
twisted, incomplete, and above all: rusted! This is the
essence of trading.[20]

Multatuli and Rembrandt weren't the only famous figures
to hang out here. Consulting my map, I realise I'm standing
right next to the next thing I wanted to see: a big statue of
the philosopher Spinoza, wearing a great bronze cape studded
with parakeets. Spinoza was born on the Houtgracht in 1632
to a wealthy Portuguese Jewish trading family and grew up as
a fully fledged Amsterdammer.* When he was about eighteen,
he went into business selling fruit from a nearby street stall
much like the ones that stand here today. From these humble
beginnings he rose to become one of the seminal figures of
the Enlightenment; espousing the quintessentially Dutch
view that everything could be logically explained and every
religious and moral issue should be extensively debated.
Spinoza paid a price for his beliefs, though — in 1656, he
was ordered by the leaders of the synagogue to retract some

---

* Intriguingly, it seems quite possible Spinoza and Rembrandt might
  have crossed paths, given that the future philosopher was a regular
  attendee at the synagogue just down the street from Rembrandt's
  house, and one of Rembrandt's pupils lived with Spinoza's teacher
  Frans van den Enden.

of his more controversial views, and even offered a large payout if he shut up. Spinoza declined and members of the synagogue were forbidden to have any relationship with him. 'The Lord will destroy his name under the heavens,' an official condemnation read. 'Nobody shall ... read anything which he has composed.'[21] To this day, there's still much debate about why Spinoza was excommunicated, but his biggest offence may have been being what *Encyclopedia Britannica* describes as 'aggressively obnoxious in his criticism of established religion', making him just one in a long line of Dutchmen who think they are being charmingly 'direct' while everyone else thinks they're just rude.

Today's Spinoza statue isn't really to my taste — dressed in his funnel-shaped cape, he looks a bit like one of the women from *The Handmaid's Tale*. He does, however, provide a helpful reminder that Rembrandt was far from the only talent who was attracted to Amsterdam during the Golden Age. As the city's wealth and status grew, its unique climate of liberalism and tolerance attracted thinkers, poets, and dissidents from across Europe. The Athenaeum Illustre, which would become the city's first university, opened the year Spinoza was born, and slowly but surely, Amsterdam emerged as a kind of 17th-century Silicon Valley, packed with bold entrepreneurs and inventors. Jacob de Graeff, for example, not only served as a burgomaster of Amsterdam but was a proficient lute player who had a laboratory at his home where he conducted chemistry experiments and claimed to have invented a perpetual motion machine. (Spoiler: he had not invented a perpetual motion machine.) Appalled by the regular fires that swept through parts of the city, Jan van der Heyden invented the fire engine and the flexible firefighting hose. Another inventor, Cornelis Drebbel, has been largely forgotten today but was the archetypal Renaissance man: a trained engraver who dabbled in writing, research, lens-making, explosive-making, and alchemy, and impressed the English royal court by demonstrating a submarine 'which traveled from Westminster to Greenwich without emerging from the waters of the Thames'.[22] Less usefully, he also invented a ladder to help people with obesity mount a horse and a special miniature hammer to hit parasites on the head.

Alongside these crankier types there were also serious giants of experimental science. Jan Swammerdam, whose father owned a pharmacy near Dam Square, trained in medicine but opted to focus his career not on human bodies but on something smaller: insects, which he studied 'wing by wing, and leg by leg' for years 'until his mind broke, and he renounced the whole fruit of his learning'.[23] More famous still was Anthonie van Leeuwenhoek, who was born in Delft in 1632 and apprenticed as a draper in Amsterdam before taking up the grinding of magnifying lenses. Lens-making might seem an odd hobby today, but it led van Leeuwenhoek to many remarkable discoveries, including what he himself called 'animalcules': 'living creatures in rain ... more than ten thousand times smaller than the animalcule which Swammerdam has portrayed ... which you can see alive and moving in the water'.[24] Van Leeuwenhoek went on to be called by more than one scholar the 'Dutch Benjamin Franklin' and (in the words of Deric Regin) 'the "father" of almost everything that could bear a pompous name in biology', from protozoology to micrography, cystology, and haematology. Van Leeuwenhoek's scientific notes also remain a treasure trove of discoveries, including the bold announcement that 'the testicles have been made for no purpose other than to produce the little animals in them, and to preserve them until they are ejected'.[25]

Other beneficiaries of the city's rich intellectual climate included Gerbrand Adriaenszoon Bredero, a sort of Dutch Shakespeare who was brought up in an butcher's shop on the Nes[26] and wrote pieces lauding his hometown in strident terms:

> 'Amsterdam shall rise to such a height of grandeur
> That she shall outshine Rome in her majestic
> splendor.'[27]

Joost van den Vondel, meanwhile, was born in Cologne but grew up to become the unofficial poet laureate of Amsterdam, producing texts which extolled the virtues of the city, its riches, its cultural life and even its orphanages. Vondel's writing could be pretentious — there was an old saying that he couldn't mention a waterfall without first consulting Virgil to check what one should look like[28] — but it was also rich with local references, and spiky on the fluctuating fortunes of Amsterdam's traders:

> 'A merchant's guesthouse [is] full of sorrows
> The Exchange also has its Martyrs
> The profit changes with the win
> One misses what another finds
> It is an art to win and keep.'

Shortly before the poet died, he supposedly suggested his own unimprovable epitaph: 'Here in peace lies Vondel old / he died because he was so cold'.[29]

As Amsterdam became (in the words of one historian) 'crowded with major and minor scholars', bookshops and printers also proliferated. By the middle of the 17th century there were at least forty different book printing businesses in Amsterdam, and Blaeu's printing house on the Bloemgracht was the largest printing shop in Europe, with about eighty staff. A particular speciality was books that were considered unpublishable elsewhere. Religious texts that were forbidden in England or Scotland were often printed in Amsterdam and then smuggled overseas, and it was in Amsterdam that John Locke's *Letter Concerning Toleration* was first printed in 1689. Galileo, Descartes, and Voltaire all had their books printed in Amsterdam at times when it was impossible elsewhere, while Thomas Hobbes enjoyed reading 'bookes of an Amsterdam print'.[30] Interestingly, Adrien Delmas argues that the VOC helped boost the city's verbosity, because the company's original charter declared that 'generals and commanders' completing a voyage must always provide a written summary of 'the journey and its achievements'.[31] As Matthew Stewart has written, Amsterdam became known as a city of 'freethinking bibliophiles', where visitors could 'while the afternoon away discussing novel theories, plotting revolutions, and bantering about the latest developments in the republic of letters'.[32]

Amazingly, many of the first English newspapers that circulated in England were actually printed in Amsterdam and delivered with labels saying they were 'truthfully translated out of the low Dutch copies printed at Amsterdam'.[33] As early as 1618, the city even had what was probably the world's first broadsheet newspaper, the snappily titled *Courante uyt Italien, Duytslandt &c.* The strength of Dutch free speech was sometimes exaggerated: Willem van Focquenbroch* attracted censure when he wrote spiky satirical verses about the city ('Avaricious Amsterdam with all her sweet children / Brags all too imprudently about her fat moneybag ...').[34] However, compared with most other European countries, the press in Amsterdam was extremely free. As John Ray wrote, 'the people say and print what they please, and call it liberty'.[35] There was clearly something in the water.

Bidding Spinoza farewell, I walk back along the water to the Jodenbreestraat. As the name suggests, the 'Jewish Broad Street' was once the heart of Amsterdam's Jewish Quarter, home to hundreds of Jewish families and two big synagogues. Today much of that is sadly gone, destroyed by the Holocaust and by rash post-war redevelopment. In Rembrandt's time, though, this area would have been a proverbial melting pot of religions, races, and backgrounds, and was a well-known hangout for artists. Paulus Potter and Hendrick Avercamp both lived here, albeit at different times.

I turn right and almost immediately arrive at my final destination for the day: the house where Rembrandt spent many years living and working, which is now a museum. Rembrandt's former home has long been a popular tourist attraction — Vincent van Gogh visited in the 1870s — but I'm pleasantly surprised to find it empty today. There's just me, some bored-looking staff, and a young Japanese man in

---

*   Focquenbroch isn't well known today, but it's hard not to admire his lifestyle. One encyclopaedia said his hobbies were 'smoking, drinking, sleeping around, playing the flute and the violin, conversing at great length and writing poetry'. (André Lefevere, *Translation, Rewriting and the Manipulation of Literary Fame*, 2017)

a Ramones T-shirt who's carefully photographing everything. I haven't been inside the house since I was here with my parents more than two decades ago, and I'm curious to see how it appears to me now. The answer is, sadly, a little underwhelming. The Rembrandt house is a beautiful building, to be sure, with some fine old features. But it has also clearly been heavily renovated, and most of the interior consists of modern wooden floors, smoothly painted walls, shiny staircases, and scattered furniture that has obviously been implanted for display purposes. It feels a bit like one of those little showrooms at IKEA where gleaming furniture has been neatly packed in to demonstrate how happy your life would be if only you'd invest in an Ogglo or a Burklapp. At some spots it's hard not to be moved, though. Ascending to the top floor I find myself in the studio where Rembrandt would have spent much of his day working. It's a long, wide room with big windows looking out onto the Jodenbreestraat. There's something genuinely jaw-dropping about being here and imagining one of the greatest artists who ever lived, standing in this exact same spot and producing pictures that are now among the most famous images in the world.**

In Rembrandt's day, the big windows in his studio would have offered ample opportunities for people-spotting. Browse his works and you'll soon notice that alongside Rembrandt's depictions of wealthy men like Nicolaes Tulp and Jan Six, there are also portraits of beggars, paupers, old men, mothers with children, market women and stray dogs, turbaned soldiers, a man peeing in the street, a dog trying to steal a pancake from a baby. Somewhat unusually for the time, he

---

** *The Night Watch* probably wasn't created in the house, but in a shed outside.

was also fond of painting Jewish people: one scholar later estimated that about a fifth of all Rembrandts portraits of men featured Jewish people. Not everyone was impressed with his eclectic tastes: Rembrandt's own assistants reportedly would grumble that while other apprentices got to help their bosses paint beautiful women, they were stuck with 'figures before which one feels repugnance', such as toothless beggars.[36] Yet the artist himself seemed unashamed, and happily spent hours painting people who many others would have unthinkingly passed by. Were Rembrandt alive today, you could almost imagine him running some sort of *Humans of Amsterdam* viral webpage, with a portrait of a different colourful city-dweller published every week.

Sadly, Rembrandt's time in this house did not end happily. Ironically, soon after finishing his greatest masterpiece, *The Night Watch*, in the early 1640s, his career seemed to stall, grinding painfully to a stop like a barge scraping along a canal bank. The warehouse he used to house his pupils on the Bloemgracht stood largely empty and the big house in which I now stand became a financial millstone. (With a typical lack of good sense, he had effectively agreed a mortgage with a term of only six years, and struggled to make the repayments on time.) In 1654 Rembrandt was forced to sell the house, move to a rented property in the Jordaan, and declare a kind of bankruptcy that gave his family control of his money. Rembrandt occasionally tried to restore his finances, including by bidding on his own works in order to boost the price. However, the problem remained the same: Rembrandt spent like a lottery winner with a coke habit. To give just one example: records show that not long after being pursued by his landlord for unpaid rent, he was trying to buy a wildly expensive painting by Holbein. Rembrandt was, unfortunately, not much of an investor — in the words of one observer, he 'bought high, and sold for what he could get'.[37]

It didn't help that by the 1650s, Rembrandt's style was going out of fashion. As Europeans began to enjoy finer, more detailed, Italian-style paintings, Rembrandt's smoky, smudgy, thickly painted works no longer held quite the same appeal. The quality of his work also became inconsistent: Rembrandt biographer Charles Mee controversially claimed that his later pictures were 'so bad that his admirers still hope the scholars will come along and decide that a lot of these paintings were not done by Rembrandt at all'.[38] However, Rembrandt's late-career decline wasn't that steep. Even during his period of bankruptcy, English royals were proud to own his work, and when Cosimo de' Medici visited Holland in 1667, he made a point of calling on the painter. As he aged, Rembrandt was still capable of remarkable pieces, most notably the *Jewish Bride*, painted after 1665, which van Gogh described as 'an intimate ... infinitely sympathetic painting, painted with a glowing hand'.[39]

Rembrandt died in October 1669, aged sixty-three, of unknown causes — perhaps the plague, perhaps something else. Many in Amsterdam must have been saddened by his departure, but he left little money behind, and no one was willing to step up and organise a decent funeral, so he was consigned to a pauper's unmarked grave somewhere in the Westerkerk. The most famous Amsterdammer of all time — and perhaps the most famous Dutchman in history — disappeared into the boggy ground.

Centuries after his death, the debate over Rembrandt's true nature continues. As revisionist historians like Gary Schwartz have noted, there's something uncomfortable about the way he is venerated despite having been — to put it diplomatically — a bit of a shit. As far as we can tell, Rembrandt had few friends. He also juggled lovers in an unkind way, including having a long marriage-like relationship with his housekeeper, Geertje Dircx and then dumping her for a twenty-year-old. Incredibly, once Rembrandt had ditched Geertje he then claimed she was insane and had her locked up in an asylum. She ended up staying there for five years.* Other modern historians including Svetlana Alpers have also sought to revise the view of him as wistful, noble artist, portraying him as ruthlessly commercial; a sort of 17th-century Andy Warhol. That seems a little harsh, but there is, I suppose, something quite fitting about an artist associated with light and shade having lived a life that was not entirely sunny, but peppered with brilliance and breakdowns, kindnesses and evil deeds, incredible achievements and tragic losses.

I leave Rembrandt's house and step back out onto the Jodenbreestraat. It's early evening now. The light is failing, the streetlights are flickering on, and the red tail lights of hundreds of cyclists zip past me like fleeting fireflies. My ankle hurts from the long walk, and I rest for a minute near the museum doorway, gathering my senses and enjoying that strange kind of peace you get in a big city when everyone's rushing around except for you. Across the road the Sluyswacht Bar is lit up like a Christmas decoration and looks about as welcoming as a bar can be. I cross the road towards it and on the way

---

*   There's now a plaque marking the site of the asylum at Gouda's Casimirschool.

am nearly swept away by a large group of teenage tourists, bristling with backpacks and smart phones, apparently just completing their own speedy tour of the city's Rembrandt remembrance sites.

'Do they actually have *The Night Watch* here?' one asks loudly, 'Or just the *Mona Lisa*?'

CHAPTER FIVE

The Oosterpark to Multatuli's House and the Royal Palace

Keti Koti, the dark side of empire, and French Amsterdam

I can hear the party long before I arrive. As I walk towards the Oosterpark (East Park) from Muiderpoort train station, the sound of distant drumming fills the air like thunder, growing louder and louder as I get closer to the edge of the park. Crossing the busy Linnaeusstraat, the crowd becomes visible: a giant conga line of dancing men and women, mostly dressed in colourful African wax prints, sashaying down the middle of the street with a tram crawling along patiently behind them. Dozens of drums are being slapped with an open palm, and somewhere in the distance a brass band is belting out a jazzy tune. Surinamese and Brazilian flags are flying everywhere, and people have come out of shops and cafés to stand and stare. There aren't quite as many revellers as at Pride, but I feel as if I've somehow stumbled through a wormhole and been transported to Rio de Janeiro during Carnival.

Feeling a little self-conscious about my lack of colourful costume, I join the flow of the crowd and walk towards the Oosterpark. I overtake three women in electric wheelchairs heavily garlanded with plastic flowers, and a woman riding a cargo bike filled to bursting with plastic tulips. Many others are carrying white placards on sticks with upbeat political slogans: '*Jouw bijdrage vandaag bepaalt de koers van morgen*' (Your behaviour today decides the course of tomorrow); '*We delen niet alleen het verleden, maar ook de toekomst*' (We share not only the past, but also the future). It is, unfortunately, not great weather for partying, or for walking around the city — there's a mist-like drizzle in the air and heavy rain is forecast later. But that clearly hasn't dampened the mood. As I wait to squeeze through the park gates, a man with a fat joint hanging from the corner of his mouth nods a friendly greeting at me then bends down to tend to his baby daughter, who's sitting between us in a pushchair festooned with flags and flowers. 'Papa's just having a little smoke and then we'll go and play together, okay?' he tells her gently.

Inside the park gates, the music reaches a deafening crescendo. Dozens of drums are being banged, and the crowd surges back and forth in time to the beat. Off to one side, a big circle of people has formed on the grass, and I join it to find, at the circle's centre, a choir consisting of about a dozen Black men and women in dark suits. The crowd falls relatively quiet for a moment and the choir begins to sing softly; a beautiful prayer-like gospel song that immediately makes everyone in earshot fall silent. I can't make out all the words, but it's about freedom.

It's my first time attending this Keti Koti event, which is held in Amsterdam every summer, and commemorates the day when slavery was abolished throughout the Dutch empire. Keti Koti means 'broken chains' in the language of Suriname: the former Dutch colony that was one of the epicentres of the transatlantic slave trade. The event occupies an unusual place in Dutch civic life, in that it both commemorates past suffering and celebrates freedom and diversity, as if Notting Hill Carnival and Remembrance Sunday have been combined into a single event.* In keeping with that, I've come here today with mixed motives. I've heard from friends that the celebrations are not to be missed if you're a party-lover, but I'm also hoping to use the event as an excuse to learn more about the negative side of Amsterdam's history. These days many people are vaguely aware that empires are bad, that a lot of nice things in European museums were pilfered from elsewhere, and that a lot of early explorers and traders did not behave like nuns. However, much of the Netherlands' colonial history still feels downplayed or ignored. Some prominent books about the Netherlands and Amsterdam rhapsodise for dozens of pages about the glories of the Golden Age while barely mentioning slavery or colonialism. Yet there's little doubt that slavery and subjugation played a central role in the history of this corner of the world. In many accounts — including, perhaps, the first few chapters of this book — it's easy to get the impression that Amsterdam's ascent in the 17th and early 18th centuries was an unalloyed success story. But Amsterdam's prosperity came at a terrible cost for people

---

*   In Suriname, and some places in the Netherlands, the two sides of the event are kept separate: commemoration on 30 June, and celebration on 1 July.

living in Africa, Asia, and South America. This is, in many ways a city built on blood and bones.

My plan today is to walk through central Amsterdam again, revisiting some of the same places I've already seen, as well as some new ones. Along the way, I hope to learn more about the less sunny elements of the city's history, as well as what happened to Amsterdam in the 18th century, when it rapidly fell from grace and became a rather shabby place once more.

Back in the Oosterpark, there's a lull in activities. The drumming has stopped, and the choir is taking a break. The crowd starts moving towards the south-west corner of the park, where an official remembrance ceremony will start soon. I've a little time to spare before the ceremony begins and so nip out of the park for a quick lunch — a roti curry wrap from the takeaway counter at Roopram, generally agreed to be one of the best Surinamese takeaways in Amsterdam. Colonial history left many marks on this city, but one of the most obvious is in the food: in a land of pork and potatoes, Surinamese roti and Indonesian nasi goreng offer rare culinary bright spots. As Anthony Bourdain once said: 'If you can't go to Indonesia for its food, go to Amsterdam.'[1]

The roti is delicious, and after inhaling it I walk back west, recrossing the bustling Linnaeusstraat. By the time I get back to the Oosterpark, people are converging on one corner, where rows of chairs for VIPs and a big TV screen have been set up. The backdrop for the ceremony will be the impressive national monument commemorating slavery; an array of Giacometti-like skeletal figures marching forward in chains and then ascending to the sky like angels. A large crowd is gathering behind the VIP seats, and I join the back of it, in a spot where I can just about see the podium. In other countries, I'm usually tall enough to see over the tops of most people's heads in a crowd, but in the Netherlands my six-foot-something height is merely average, and I find myself straining on tiptoes to get a good view.

Keti Koti is celebrated in this park every summer, but this year's event will be a particularly notable one, as a special guest is expected soon: King Willem-Alexander. Peeking over the top of the crowd, I see him walk through the park's tall gates with his wife Maxima, on foot and umbrella-less despite the steady drizzle, grinning and waving like a film star on a red carpet. He takes his seat, and right on cue, the heavens open and it begins to rain heavily. The crowd erupts in a flurry of dark-coloured umbrellas opening, like a flock of crows suddenly taking flight. I shuffle sideways, trying to maintain my line of sight on the podium through dozens of raised umbrellas. After a minute or two the crowd falls silent, and the ceremony starts. A Black woman steps up to the podium, accompanied by an older man with a guitar, and begins singing a slow, mournful song. At the front of the crowd, three little blonde girls clamber over the steel fence separating them from the VIPs and start dancing on the grass, oblivious to the rain.

The music ends, and after a brief introduction from another speaker, the King steps up to the podium. He has the ruddy and unshaven look of someone who just got back from a long skiing holiday, which he probably has. He's heckled almost immediately, with a long-haired man standing near me bellowing in Dutch: 'Give the slavery profits back!' The

King ignores — or doesn't hear — him and begins by paying forceful tribute to Amsterdam:

> Ladies and gentlemen, here in the Oosterpark, on the Museumplein, in Suriname, in the Caribbean part of our Kingdom and wherever in the world you are watching …
>
> Together with you I stand here in a city which has loved freedom above all for centuries. The capital of a country that, in the march of history, acts again and again against tyranny and oppression. But what was self-evident within this city and within this country was not true beyond our borders. Slavery was forbidden here. But not overseas.

In the early years of their rise to global prominence, the Dutch didn't have much interest in the slave trade. The Portuguese and others began trading African enslaved people in the mid 1400s, but by the early 1600s most Dutch merchants were still unenthusiastic. The Pope had said Catholics had the right to enslave 'Saracens, pagans and any other unbelievers'[2] but the Protestant Dutch still mostly thought the trade in people was a little distasteful. That dynamic began to change, however, with the development of a Dutch trading empire in the Americas to match the one in Asia. By the early 1620s, the VOC had become a great success and had taken over much of the Asian spice trade from Portugal, but the Dutch were still envious of the trading empires that the Spanish and Portuguese had constructed in the Americas. And so it was that, in 1621, the *Geoctroyeerde West-Indische Compagnie*, or Chartered

West India Company (WIC) was founded. The WIC remains far less well known than the VOC, but it essentially followed the same playbook: a group of merchants clubbed together to form a joint company to trade in the Americas, backed by private capital but also strongly supported by the Dutch state, with the power to conquer territory, build fortresses, sign peace treaties, and attack European rivals. Like the VOC, the WIC was ostensibly a national enterprise, carefully structured so power was split between different areas of the Netherlands, but Amsterdam was the dominant player, holding eight out of nineteen votes on the company's governing board. Amsterdam also hosted the WIC's primary headquarters; a mansion-like edifice that you can still see at Haarlemmerstraat 75 today. (It's now a nice bar and wedding venue, and as I pass by I often wonder how many of the well-dressed people going there for birthday parties or wedding receptions know anything of its controversial history.)

There were some important differences between the VOC and the WIC. Unlike the VOC, the WIC never had anything resembling a private army, and never achieved a full monopoly on trade in the Atlantic. However, the WIC did succeed in expanding the Dutch sphere of influence in the western hemisphere, establishing Dutch trading posts in Curaçao, Aruba, Sint Maarten, Suriname, Brazil, and Guyana. Crucially, the WIC also opened up new markets for Amsterdammers in many goods, including tobacco and furs from the area around what would become New York City. Amsterdam quickly assumed a central role in the sugar trade, with refineries along the River IJ processing sugar imported from Brazil, Java, and Suriname, and then re-exporting it to the Rhineland and Flanders. By 1662, there were around fifty sugar refineries in Amsterdam — about half of all the refineries in Europe at the time.[3] Amsterdam also became a centre of fine chocolate making, using cocoa beans from Suriname, which were crushed by wind-powered chocolate mills. By 1670, there were also about thirty Caribbean tobacco importers based in Amsterdam, and the city had become (in the words of Jonathan Israel) 'the central reservoir' for all tobacco trade in Europe.[4]

The rapid growth of trade in Caribbean goods created a problem for the people running the WIC, in that it required huge amounts of labour. As the historian Johannes Postma explained: 'forced labour became a necessity because the intense regimen required for harvesting sugarcane and toiling at the sugar mills had no appeal to workers who had a choice.'[5] In 1637, a Dutch fleet sailed to Ghana and snatched the castle of Elmina from the Portuguese, swiftly converting it from a trading post used mainly for exporting gold into one used for human trafficking on an industrial scale. Within a few years, the Dutch had built or captured a string of fortified slave stations in places like Angola and Sao Tome, 'virtually eliminating the Portuguese from western Africa'.[6] For a nation of traders, Black Africans had become simply another commodity to be bought and sold.

Once they reached the Americas, enslaved people were forced to work nearly naked in sweltering conditions, harvesting sugar cane or stirring vats of scalding syrup, chained and beaten. Terrible injuries were routine, and insubordination was punished brutally. WIC records tell of one female enslaved person called Lohkay in the colony of Sint Maarten being punished for running away by having her breast cut off.[7] Enlaved people were also routinely branded with the letters 'WIC', or with other letters. The Rijksmuseum collection includes a hefty, poker-like metal stamp bearing the letters GWC, which one enslaver in Suriname used to burn his initials into the skin of people he had bought. The enslaver Willem Bosman once defended the branding of enslaved people by saying, 'I doubt not but this Trade seems very barbarous to you, but since it is followed by mere necessity it must go on; but we yet take all possible care that they are not burned too hard, especially the Women, who are more tender than the Men'.[8]

The exact number of people who the Dutch enslaved is often disputed, but the Rijksmuseum has calculated that during the colonial era, 'the Netherlands enslaved more than a million men, women and children from Asia and Africa and shipped them to faraway places unknown to them'.[9] It's also generally agreed that between 1600 and 1650 the Netherlands was the world's second biggest trafficker of people, trading fewer enslaved people than Portugal but nearly twice as many as Britain.[10] It's also clear that Amsterdam was one of the primary beneficiaries of the growing trade in people — one official report estimated that Amsterdam's share of the Dutch slave trade amounted to at least 135,000 enslaved people, of whom 20,000 did not survive the journey from Africa to the Americas.[11] That's a hundred and thirty-five thousand people — men, women, and children, kidnapped from their daily lives, chained and beaten and tortured; to help pay for the beautiful canal houses and artworks that Amsterdam's Instagrammers and TikTokers coo over today.

Back at the Oosterpark, the King's speech continues. This year marks 160 years since the abolition of Dutch slavery, and the media has for months speculated that the King might use his speech today to make an official apology for the Netherlands' role in the slave trade — something campaigners have been demanding for years. Debates about how to handle this part of Dutch history are nothing new: in 1984, a child was wounded by a bomb placed by anti-imperialist activists at a monument in Amsterdam-Zuid dedicated to Johannes Van Heutsz, a former governor of Dutch Indonesia.* But inevitably, the idea of a Royal apology for slavery has proved very controversial. Years ago, the populist politician Pim Fortuyn wrote that 'those who say [they] suffer even now from the past of their distant ancestors' enslavement should go to a psychiatrist'. More recently, Geert Wilders, one of the most popular politicians in the country, said the government was *helemaal gek* (completely crazy) to apologise for slavery and should instead focus on apologising for 'breaking the Netherlands'.[12] However, left-wing campaigners have long argued that the government needs to not only apologise, but pay financial compensation. 'A true reckoning of colonial crimes, including slavery and other forms of exploitation, requires reparations,' said Almaz Teffera of Human Rights Watch.[13] For her part, Amsterdam's left-wing mayor Femke Halsema also said that it is now 'time to engrave the great injustice of colonial slavery into our city's identity'.[14]

Whatever one thinks of such apologies, Dutch attitudes to the country's history are often surprising. For many years, slavery and the victims of empire were barely mentioned in the press or in Parliament, and children were taught little

---

*   In 2004 the memorial was belatedly renamed, and a plaque was added referring to the mixed human rights record of the man known as 'the Slaughterer of Aceh'.

about them at school. Polling by YouGov has found that about 50 per cent of Dutch people think their country's former empire is something to be proud of, compared with only a third of Brits, and a quarter of French and Belgians.[15] In media-political circles, it's also still surprisingly common to hear the VOC and WIC mentioned as examples of Dutch business prowess — in 2006, then-Prime Minister Jan Peter Balkenende famously referred to the country's 'VOC mentaliteit' (VOC mentality) in glowing terms.[16] In 2023, Geert Wilders won Dutch national elections after pledging to withdraw all previous apologies for the slave trade.

Today's mooted Royal apology is also complicated by the waning popularity of the King himself. Willem-Alexander's mother, Beatrix, was a beloved national grandma but since taking over the throne, her son has struggled to generate similar affection. Many Amsterdammers love celebrating King's Day but are rather less enthusiastic about the monarch himself. A nationwide survey in 2024 found that only 52 per cent of people support keeping the monarchy, down from 58 per cent two years previously.[17] Today, however, the King is clearly planning to please the crowd. As his speech continues, it becomes clear that he is indeed going to apologise, and a ripple of excitement spreads through the crowd. 'Eindelijk, eindelijk!' an older Black woman standing next to me murmurs, choking back tears. 'Finally, finally! He's actually going to do it! He's going to say sorry!' The King continues:

> On 19 December last year, the Prime Minister
> apologised on behalf of the Dutch government for
> the fact that people have been made commodities,
> exploited and mistreated for centuries in the name of

the Dutch state.

Today I stand here before you. As your King and
as part of the government, I make these apologies
myself today. They are intensely experienced by me
with heart and soul.

He tries to continue speaking, but is swiftly drowned out
by thunderous, jubilant applause. 'He did it, he did it!' the
woman next to me shouts. 'He really said he's sorry!'

The ceremony is set to continue following the King's
speech, but the weather is still what the Dutch would call
snert weer (pea soup weather), which makes you want to stay
indoors and eat something hearty. I'm cold and wet and tired
of standing still, so weave my way back through the crowd
and leave the park. I haven't been in this part of the city
for a while and decide to have a quick wander through the
neighbourhoods known as the Dapperbuurt and the Indische
Buurt. Walking east along the Insulindeweg the scenery isn't
immediately appealing. Most of the buildings are low-rise
modern apartment blocks, similar to those found in the
colourless suburbs of any European city. When I stop to look
at my phone, I'm almost run over by an old lady on a mobility
scooter who's careering down the pavement as if she's training
to replace F1 driver Max Verstappen. As I approach Javastraat,
things get more interesting. This neighbourhood has what must
be one of the greatest concentrations of bars and restaurants in
the city, and the businesses I pass are a pleasing mish-mash of
cultures, with the chic-looking 'Le French' café next door to
a travel agency offering pilgrimages to Mecca, a Turkish café
with pillowy flatbreads in the window, a sushi place, a Yemeni
restaurant, Saeed's Curry House, and Haq's international

phone centre. A text on the wall at Bar Basquiat reads:

DEAR GUEST
WE WOULD LIKE TO REMIND YOU OF THE
FACT THAT WE HAVE NEIGHBOURS
EVERYBODY WHO DOESN'T
BEHAVE GETS KILLED.

I don't linger long, but can't resist popping into the lovely Java bookshop and then making a detour into the Dappermarkt, which was judged one of *National Geographic Traveler*'s 'Top 10 Shopping Streets'.[18] I'm not sure that accolade is deserved, but the market is certainly eclectic, with colourful stalls selling everything from fake watches to fried fish and sacks of garlic. One popular product is colourful African wax fabrics of the kind that the women at Keti Koti were wearing earlier. I don't check the labels but there's a good chance these exotic textiles were made in the Netherlands. Interestingly, it was the Dutch who pioneered the production of wax-printed fabrics based on batik designs from their Indonesian colonies, before exporting 'Wax Hollandais' to Africa, where it became wildly popular. Today, many of the colourful fabrics worn in places like Ghana and Kenya are still made by a company called Vlisco in the quiet town of Helmond, near Eindhoven.

It stops raining. Resisting the temptation to buy myself a Nelson Mandela-style shirt, I head back past the Oosterpark and then walk southwest, along the Sarphatistraat. After I cross the River Amstel the streets start getting busier, and by the time I've reached the area around the Rijksmuseum, they're almost too packed to walk along. There are thousands and thousands of people here, all celebrating Keti Koti but in a very different way from those at the Oosterpark. Turning left, I plunge into a sea of pedestrians walking through the famous tunnel that cuts through the heart of the Rijksmuseum. There is, as there often is, a cellist playing classical music inside the tunnel, but today I can hardly hear him, due to the pounding music pouring into the tunnel from the other end. Emerging from it, I find that the whole of the grassy Museumplein has been converted into festival terrain, with big music stages in the distance, huge banners saying KETI KOTI, and dozens of pop-up bars and food stands. The whole span of the Museumplein, from the Rijksmuseum to the Concertgebouw, is packed with people. Compared to the crowd at the memorial ceremony earlier, most people seem much younger and much whiter. In the distance, a gospel choir is singing exuberantly on the main stage, nearly drowned out by an even noisier reggaeton group on a smaller stage next to the Van Gogh Museum. A dozen barbecues send thick plumes of smoke over the Leidseplein. A woman passes me carrying a tiny baby wearing ear defenders, followed by a man carrying a sign which reads: 'Our World Is For Everyone, Undocumented Migrants Welcome'.

This side of Keti Koti is great fun, but I feel a little tragic hanging around by myself, and so after about half an hour I walk back under the Rijksmuseum, towards the city centre. The streets are seething with people, and a man furiously rings his bike bell as he cycles through the crowd at speed, parting waves of pedestrians like Moses splitting the sea. Having celebrated the end of slavery earlier in the morning, I'm now curious to see some more evidence of its impact on the city. In my hand I have a list (which I've cobbled together from

various books) of places in Amsterdam which were linked to
the slave trade. Once you know to look for them, such sights
turn out to be everywhere. Albert Camus even mentioned
them in his novel *The Fall*, in which the protagonist looks at
one house and says:

> Charming house, isn't it? The two heads you see up
> there are heads of Negro slaves. A shop-sign. The
> house belonged to a slave-dealer. Oh, they weren't
> squeamish in those days! They were self-assured;
> they announced: 'You see, I'm a man of substance;
> I'm in the slave-trade; I deal in black flesh.' Can you
> imagine anyone today making it known publicly that
> such is his business? What a scandal![19]

My first stop is hard to miss: an enormous box-like
building of zebra-striped light and dark brick, squatting on
the Vijzelstraat, just before the Golden Bend. It looks like a
fortress, or perhaps a mansion where Bruce Wayne might live
in a Batman film. This is the *Stadsarchief Amsterdam*, or the
Amsterdam City Archive, a place I visit often. The building
(known as the Bazel) was for many years the headquarters of
the *Nederlandsche Handel-Maatschappij*, or Dutch Trading
Company. This was a sort of successor to the VOC, founded
in the 1820s with the aim of promoting Dutch trade with
Asia.* Although much less famous than the VOC, the NHM
dominated Dutch trade in the East Indies for decades. Slavery
and exploitation helped pay the bills, and the entrance to

---

* The bank headquarters at the Bazel and the nearby Vijzelbank are
still linked by a secret tunnel that passes under the Keizersgracht,
which was once used to transport sacks of money.

the building is still adorned with a statue of Jan Pieterszoon Coen, who oversaw the massacre of thousands of Indonesians in 1621.** I take a photo and then turn back east, heading a short distance along the Herengracht to number 502, a massive canal-side house with a façade of brownish brick and grey stone, and big marble columns on either side of the front door. This is the official residence of the Mayor of Amsterdam, and although there are none of the bodyguards or barriers you might find at such an esteemed address in other cities, the building is bristling with discreet security cameras. The first resident of this house was, I remember reading, a man called Paulus Godin; a successful merchant, director of the WIC, and director of the Society of Suriname. He paid for the construction of this building using money he earned selling enslaved people to plantation owners in the Caribbean. A few steps further along the canal comes Herengracht 520, a handsome double-width canal house, with a flagpole jutting above the front door like a unicorn's horn. In the 18th century, this building was home to the richest woman in the city, Anna de Haze de Georgio. She gained most of her wealth (including this property) as an inheritance from her wonderfully named uncle Jeronimo, who served as a director of both the VOC and WIC and grew rich from the slave trade.

Slavery within the Dutch Republic itself was not allowed, and so it was not common for enslaved people to be in Amsterdam. However, it was not unusual to see Black servants working in homes around the city, and Black people passing through the city. Around the Kloveniersdoelen, where Rembrandt delivered *The Night Watch*, there was a small

---

** Following various mergers and restructurings, a direct descendant of the NHM still exists today: ABN Amro.

Black community that included servants, but also sailors and diplomatic envoys from Africa. Black people also often featured in art. If you look at Golden Age paintings, you can often see a Black face peering out from the background somewhere — usually a servant included in the picture to add a little exoticism. In 1661, for instance, Rembrandt produced a picture known as *Two African Men*, which depicted exactly that. The artist Samuel van Hoogstraten once recommended that the best way to enhance a painting was 'to add a Moor to a Maiden'.[20]

I continue zigzagging along the canals, consulting my scrawled list and jotting observations in my notebook, in a grim repetition of my previous walk between the Golden Bend's gardens:

Herengracht 436: a wide, imposing brick building with an immense blue front door. Once home to the Insinger family, who made money in the slave trade in Suriname. When slavery was abolished, the family forced their enslaved people to work for them for another decade to pay for their freedom.

Herengracht 456: a big house with a plain brick façade and small plaques listing the villainous-sounding companies currently operating inside: Brack Capital Properties, Pallas Athena Group, Stark Narrative. In the 1670s, this was home to Joan Corver, a renowned VOC administrator and mayor whose family grew fabulously wealthy from trade in both Asia and the Caribbean.

Herengracht 500: a stunner, with black-painted brick walls and sharp white window frames. Once the home of Gerrit Hooft (1684–1767): mayor of the city, WIC director, director of the Society of Suriname, and member of a family that owned several sugar plantations.

Herengracht 514: the home of Henrik van Hoorn, who grew rich through the sugar trade and was director of the Dutch colony in Guyana, which relied on the labour of enslaved people. The wide stone doorway is capped with two slightly cartoonish busts of Black African figures, including a woman with her breasts exposed.

Keizersgracht 672: the famous Van Loon house, which I visited during the open gardens event. Jan van Loon was a director of the Society of Suriname and actively involved in running the WIC; the coat of arms of the Van Loon family includes the heads of three Black men.

At Singel 460 I find a home with a somewhat happier history: the former headquarters of the 'Women's Committee for Promoting the Proclamation of the Gospel and the Abolition of Slavery in Suriname', founded by an Amsterdammer called Anna Amalia Bergendahl in 1856. Unlike Britain, the Netherlands had few movements pushing for the abolition of slavery. However, Anna Bergendahl's Committee was an honourable exception; holding lotteries to raise funds to free enslaved people at a time when most Dutch people thought emancipation was a joke. The British fully abolished slavery in 1833 and France gradually did so a few years after that. The Netherlands, however, didn't ban slaving in the Caribbean until 1863, and even then, the ban was not fully implemented for another decade.

The Bergendahl home isn't the only one around here to have an abolitionist history. Walking north to the unpronounceable Korsjespoortsteeg, I find at number twenty an attractive little house, only a few paces wide, with a bell-shaped gable and a steep flight of stone steps leading to a black front door. I came here a couple of times many years ago and recognise it immediately: the former home of Eduard Douwes Dekker, perhaps the most famous Dutchman who most non-Dutch people have never heard of. Born in Amsterdam in 1820, the son of a sea captain, Dekker went to the Dutch East Indies at the age of eighteen and spent about a decade and a half in colonial government jobs. Eventually tiring of life in the tropics, Dekker returned to the Netherlands and began working as a writer, specialising in articles and pamphlets that cast the Dutch empire in Asia in an unusually critical light. Few paid much notice until, in 1860, he published a novel with the unwieldy title *Max Havelaar: or, the coffee auctions of the Dutch Trading Company*. The novel's first sentence would become famous in the Netherlands: '*Ik ben makelaar in koffie, en woon op de Lauriergracht No. 37*' — 'I am a coffee trader, and I live at number 37 Lauriergracht.'[21] Also famous was the pen name Dekker adopted: Multatuli, derived from the Latin *multa tuli*, meaning 'I have suffered much.' The Max Havelaar novel was partly autobiographical and reads something like a feisty version of George Orwell's *Burmese Days*, describing the vain efforts of an enlightened official to expose Dutch exploitation of Indonesians. The book's conversational style has aged surprisingly well, yet for its time, it was quite radical: unsparing in its criticism of colonialism, razor-sharp in its satire of middle-class mores, and passionate in its pleas for justice in Java. 'Famine? In the rich, fertile, blessed land of lava — famine?' Multatuli wrote. 'Indeed, reader. Only a few years ago entire districts died of starvation. Mothers offered their children for sale to obtain food. Mothers even ate their own children.'[22] Some reviews of *Max Havelaar* were scathing: D. H. Lawrence wrote that 'as far as composition goes, it is the greatest mess possible'.[23] Yet Multatuli's impact on Dutch history was significant. The Indonesian writer Pramoedya Ananta Toer once wrote that 'just as *Uncle Tom's Cabin* gave ammunition to the American abolitionist movement, *Max Havelaar* became the weapon for a growing liberal movement in the Netherlands'.[24] The Society of Dutch Literature once proclaimed Multatuli the most important Dutch writer of all time, and he's now celebrated with a striking car-sized bust on the Torensluis, next to where I had coffee in the very first pages of this book. He looks like a windswept Albert Einstein.

Looking back, it's tempting to view the abolition of slavery as a watershed in the history of Amsterdam; a tipping point at which the city's trade networks suddenly became less exploitative and less profitable. In truth, however, Amsterdam was already showing signs of wear long before that. The big trading companies were among the first to stumble. For all their successes, the VOC and the WIC often operated on tight profit margins, and the expense of maintaining bases around the world meant fixed costs were huge. Competition from the

(British) East India Company, founded just before the VOC, was fierce, and the VOC was hollowed out by corruption and mismanagement. Visiting Ceylon in the mid-eighteenth century, Captain Robert Percival observed that 'the Hollander began his day with gin and tobacco, and he ended it with tobacco and gin. In the interval, he fed grossly, lounged about, indulged in the essential siesta, and transacted a little business'.[25] Other travellers gleefully noted that in Asia it was almost impossible to find a sober Dutchman.

Like many struggling businesses before and since, the VOC tried to stay afloat by taking out loans, but then found itself in worse trouble when it couldn't afford to pay back those loans. Struggling to improve its margins, the company cut spending on things like mapmaking and shipbuilding, further locking in its own decline. The fourth Anglo–Dutch war in the 1780s also seriously undercut profitability. By the late 1700s, both the VOC and the WIC were essentially bankrupt; propped up only by cash infusions from the state. In 1791, the WIC was taken over by the Dutch state and in 1799, the VOC was dissolved. It was an ignoble, undignified end for two institutions that had changed the world. They ended like a firework on a misty polder night: not with a spectacular bang, but with a slow fizzle.

Other problems lay closer to home. Amsterdam is not much further from Norfolk than it is from Brussels, and the city's merchants had long viewed the English as something akin to cousins. As Anthony Bailey wrote, England and the Netherlands 'were both beer-drinking, trading, expanding nations, proud of their ability to handle ships and make money, having Protestant sympathies and joint inclinations to distrust the king of France'.[26] Wealthy young Englishmen were frequently sent to study in Amsterdam, while many Dutch engineers built fine careers advising the English on how to drain boggy landscapes or pump water. The first successful project for supplying London with drinking water was completed by a Dutchman, 'Peter Morice' (Pieter Maurits), who installed a waterwheel under the arch of London Bridge, which generated enough pressure to spray water over the top of a nearby church steeple, 'greatly to the astonishment of the Mayor'.[27]

However, these similarities and connections also meant that England and the Netherlands frequently found themselves bumping up against one another, like siblings who can't help fighting over toys. English texts from the mid-1600s are riven with anti-Dutch sentiments and rhymes:

> The Dutchman hath a thirsty soul
> our cellars are subject to his call ...
> to the new world in the moon away let us go
> for if the Dutch colony get thither first
> 'tis a thousand to one but they'll drain that too.[28]

The history of Anglo–Dutch rivalry is complex, and the Netherlands ended up fighting no fewer than four naval wars against the English in the 17th and 18th centuries; including three between the early 1650s and early 1670s alone. For a merchant city like Amsterdam, these conflicts were a disaster. When fighting broke out, Amsterdam's trade slumped, its stock market fell, and unemployment spiked. Tempers frayed: when the minister at the city's English church offered prayers for survivors of the Great Fire of London in 1666, he was scolded for it.

The summer of 1667 brought a happy moment for the Dutch when a fleet led by the naval hero Michiel de Ruyter managed to race up the River Medway and destroy much of the English fleet at Chatham before stealing the flagship *Royal Charles*. The gunfire could be heard in London. Samuel Pepys, who was working for the admiralty, thought the monarchy would fall. That didn't happen, and a few weeks later, the two countries signed the Treaty of Breda, under which the Dutch gave up control of Manhattan in exchange for the tiny island of Run, in present-day Indonesia — perhaps the worse real estate deal ever completed. However, within a few years, fierce conflict had broken out again, this time as part of a broader European war. In 1672, the French invaded and occupied southern Dutch provinces. There was fierce fighting as far north as Muiden, only ten miles from Amsterdam, where the castle very nearly fell to the French, and prices on the Amsterdam exchange went into freefall. Thankfully, Amsterdam itself was spared. Eventually, the Dutch army, under William III of Orange, managed to drive the invaders out, but 1672 would forever be remembered as the *rampjaar* — the 'disaster year'.

The city faced other crosswinds, too. One problem was that thanks to the cost of all the wars and empire-building, Amsterdam's taxes were very high. The statistician Gregory King once calculated that in the late 17th century the average Dutchman was paying nearly three times as much in taxes as his equivalent in England or France.[29] The English diplomat Sir George Downing wrote home in 1659: 'it is strange to see with what readyness this people doe consent to ... an infinity of other taxes, so that I have reckoned a man cannot eate a dishe of meate in an ordinary (inn) but that one way or another he shall pay 19 excises out of it.'[30] Adam Smith said Dutch bureaucracy was so intense that a man had to buy a licence to drink a cup of tea.[31] In 1696, there were even angry demonstrations in Amsterdam by undertakers, who were furious that the state was trying to set up a public burial service. Protestors held a mock burial on Dam Square before ransacking the homes of the officials held responsible for introducing the tax and filling the canals with fancy furniture. The damage from such riots was thankfully not widespread — one visitor observed that 'the conduct of a Dutch mob is strongly marked with the characteristic frugality of their nation ... as they carefully avoid the destruction of property'.[32] However, the unrest was, as the saying goes, a sign of the times. Amsterdam, once bland in its uniform prosperity, was increasingly febrile.

I leave Multatuli's house and walk half a mile southeast to the Royal Palace, which stands on the western side of Dam Square. I must have walked past this building thousands of times, watched the King wave from its balcony on King's Day, and seen foreign presidents come and go here, but until today have never been inside. Passing under the famous royal balcony, I enter the building through a small doorway that leads into a cool marble hallway, and then ascend a red-carpeted staircase to the first floor. Here I emerge into the spectacular *Burgerzaal,* or Citizens' Hall; a vast, cathedral-like space where almost every surface is made from silvery marble. Six chandeliers the size of dining tables drip with cut glass, and at one end of the hall an enormous marble statue of Atlas holds a blue globe aloft. I've read that the engravings in this hall include clear references to colonialism and the slave trade, and after craning my neck for a few minutes I begin to spot some. High above one huge archway, leading from the Citizens' Hall to an adjacent hall, is a white marble sculpture of an African woman raising a dish with a phoenix standing on it. Round the corner, there's a painting by Jan Lievens depicting a Black man holding up a shield on which stands one of the leaders of the Batavian revolt against the Romans — commissioned by city leaders who liked to compare themselves to previous generations of Dutch freedom fighters, and to promote the idea that leaders should have the support of the people rather than just inheriting their power by birthright. (Outside, the roof of the palace also features a tympanum showing some grandly dressed Europeans alongside Africans, who are nearly naked and surrounded by exotic animals.)

At the centre of the Citizens' Hall there's a big display board, which I study keenly. It tells the story of a splendid piss-up that took place in this hall in 1768. Willem V, the Prince of Orange, and his wife Wilhelmina were paying a rare visit to Amsterdam, and the city spared no expense in entertaining them, hosting a ball here that was described as 'the gala of the century'. The Citizens' Hall was given a wooden dance floor, and the walls were festooned with colourful candles and lanterns. Beneath the statue of Atlas, an orchestra played in an impromptu orchestra pit while over a thousand guests danced the night away in their finest gowns and costumes. The last guests didn't leave until five o'clock in the morning.

The cost of the ball was astronomical: 102,874 guilders,[33] equivalent to the salary of an average shipbuilder for 340 years. For those who attended the ball, it must have felt like money well spent, but looking back on the event it's tempting to see it as another symptom of Amsterdam's decline. During its boom years, Amsterdam had been run by what Montesquieu called 'an aristocracy, but a most sensible aristocracy' — an elite of benevolent oligarchs, who attained huge wealth but also channelled funds to public works projects and were careful not to live too lavishly. Sir William Temple wrote of the great admiral Michiel de Ruyter that 'I never saw him in Cloaths better than the commonest Sea-Captain ... and in his own house, neither was the size, building, furniture or entertainment at all exceeding the use of every common merchant and tradesman in his town.'[34] After about 1680, however, the merchant-politician class was replaced by a rentier class more interested in enjoying the finer things in life. As the historian J.H. Plumb put it: 'Dutch society lapsed contentedly into inert, bourgeois self-enjoyment.'[35] Like well-fed tigers in a cage, Amsterdam's merchants had lost the old hunger to succeed.

Seeing what was happening, the city authorities made some efforts to promote humility. In 1655, for instance, new city-wide rules tried to restrict the size of wedding parties and celebrations, after a few notable residents had been seen indulging in Beckham-style extravaganzas that would have made their Calvinist forefathers turn in their graves. Some parents also made efforts to ensure their children knew how fortunate they were. Legend tells of one Amsterdam man who rose from humble beginnings to great wealth and had a palatial home built on the Herengracht, but then worried that his children were growing up spoiled. To fix the problem, he ordered a wedge of small homes to be built on the canal bank opposite his family's grand home, so his children were 'able to grow up with the poor constantly in view'. Unfortunately, however, those trying to reintroduce a dash of humility and frugality into Amsterdam life were rowing against a racing tide. Even people lower down the food chain weren't immune: pamphleteers reported that ordinary shopkeepers were now dressing in such fine silk and velvet that you couldn't tell them apart from their richest customers.

War, slavery, debauchery, corruption — there's a lot to unpack here. But the essence is that, after a wildly successful early 17th century, Amsterdam had a tougher time later in the 1600s and beyond. By the 1700s, it was common to see empty and abandoned houses throughout Amsterdam, and the city's workhouses and orphanages were struggling to meet demand for their services. Foreign visitors who'd once marvelled at the city's prosperity were now often dismayed. When the Scottish diarist James Boswell visited the Netherlands in 1764, he wrote to a friend: 'Most of their principal towns are sadly decayed, and ... there are whole lanes of wretches who have no other subsistence than potatoes, gin, and stuff which they call tea and coffee.' Also unimpressed was the future American President John Adams, who served as ambassador to the Dutch Republic and lived at Keizersgracht 529 in the 1780s.[36] Rushing around Amsterdam trying to obtain loans from bankers sympathetic to the American revolutionary cause, he at first wrote to his wife Abigail in glowing terms: 'The Country where I am is the greatest Curiosity in the World ... Their Industry and Economy ought to be Examples to the World.'[37] A few months later, however, Adams reported to the Congress that Dutch prosperity was an illusion. 'This Country,' he wrote, 'is indeed in a melancholy situation; sunk in ease, devoted to the pursuits of gain, overshadowed on all sides by more powerful neighbours, unanimated by a love of military glory, or any aspiring spirit ... divided among themselves in interest and sentiment, they seem afraid of everything.'[38] Adams was right. Amsterdam's glory days were over.*

Continuing through the Royal Palace, I leave the Citizens' Hall and walk along a wide marble corridor to what a small sign announces is the 'Bedroom of the English Quarter', adjacent to the 'Salon of the English Quarter'. Both rooms are, even by the standards of a royal palace, luxurious. Enormous paintings hang above enormous fireplaces, facing enormous mirrors and enormous beds. In the throne room, a table as long as a swimming pool is set with dozens of places for dinner and adorned with large white sculptures made out of sugar — a perfect way for hosts to show off their wealth, at a time when sugar was wildly expensive.

Reading the small displays that have been placed throughout the palace, I notice that most of them refer to Willem V, Prince of Orange, (1748–1806) as the most notable resident of the building. However, the person who arguably had the greatest influence on this building's function and décor was not Dutch but French. Early in the 1790s, in the wake of the French Revolution, France attacked the Netherlands again. A famous picture by Jacob Cats shows the moment Napoleon's armies arrived in the north during the icy winter

---

*   John Adams' tenure isn't the only link between Amsterdam and American history. When the US completed the Louisiana Purchase in 1803, the Amsterdam bank Hope & Co provided much of the finance.

of 1794–5, with dozens of horses and men in thick long coats
trudging through a snowy landscape. French sympathisers
displayed a 'Tree of Liberty' on Dam Square, and a helpless
Willem V abandoned the throne and fled to England.* The
French seized the city.

At first, the French occupation of the Netherlands was
relatively laid back, with the occupiers claiming to adhere to
the principles of the Revolution: equality, liberty, fraternity;
power to the people. Over time, though, their grip tightened
considerably. By 1803, Napoleon was bluntly telling a visiting
Dutchman: 'You have no political independence … you can
claim civil, municipal and commercial independence, but the
rest is a chimera.'[39] In 1806, Napoleon installed as leader
of the Netherlands his brother Louis Napoleon Bonaparte
(known to the Dutch as Lodewijk Napoleon), a kindly but
somewhat bumbling soul who was then still in his twenties.
The Dutch government was at that time based in the Hague,
but Louis swiftly decided that only one building was grand
enough to be his home: the Town Hall on Dam Square. At a
stroke, the Town Hall was converted into the Royal Palace,
and modifications began. Thick carpets were laid over the
cold stone floors, a public balcony was built facing the Dam,
and hundreds of chairs, tables, beds, and lamps were brought
up from Paris. Louis even had the prison cells downstairs
converted into wine cellars, as any good Frenchman would.**

For Amsterdammers, life under Louis seemed all right at

*   In the Royal Palace, a small glass case near the *Burgerzaal* now
     displays a trunk that Willem used on his journey.
**   The Netherlands remains somewhat unusual in that some of its
     major functions are split: Amsterdam is the capital and the largest
     city, but the Hague is still the seat of government and home to the
     Dutch parliament.

first. The new king displayed an interest in helping his subjects, and even did his best to learn the Dutch language. Legend has it that Louis sparked hilarity when trying to say '*ik ben uw koning*', he actually said '*ik ben uw konijn*' — not 'I am your king', but 'I am your rabbit'. He also donated a lion, a tiger, a panther, and some monkeys to the Hortus Botanical Gardens. However, as time passed, Louis's enthusiasm for Amsterdam waned, and he began escaping the stench of the canals by spending more time in breezy Haarlem. He sparked uproar with efforts to forcibly recruit Dutch orphans and beggars into the French military and even ordered the Waag (Weighing House) on Dam Square — one of the prettiest buildings in Amsterdam — be pulled down, as it was blocking his view. More seriously, hostility between the English and the French meant that French-run Amsterdam soon found itself banned from doing trade with England. The effect on Amsterdam was severe. The number of ships visiting the city plummeted, and many jobs were lost. Foreseeing Amsterdam's possible collapse as a financial centre, some wealthy residents transferred assets elsewhere — the economist David Ricardo, for example, arranged to send much of his wealth from Amsterdam to Sweden and Russia, while the financier Alexander Baring took his business to London.

As living standards flatlined, there soon came rumblings of serious dissent. Rebellious Amsterdammers produced pamphlets protesting French rule, including one that called on people to steal guns from the arsenal and rise up against French 'tyranny and slavery'.[40] In the spring of 1809, another widely read pamphlet criticised Louis's regime as a 'cursable tyranny' and said Napoleon was 'the destroyer of Europe'. [41] This pamphlet caused a sensation and spread quickly, with copies moved around by barge and pushed under front doors in the dead of night. The document was cryptically signed 'P. Monitor', and the French authorities embarked on a hunt to find the author's true identity. Eventually, they found her: Maria Aletta Hulshoff, an Amsterdammer in her twenties. After the personal intervention of Louis, Hulshoff was handed what most Amsterdammers would surely think of as a punishment worse than death: confinement for life in Woerden, a small town south of the city. However, Hulshoff was clearly a wily character, for during her transfer from Amsterdam to Woerden, she managed to switch places with a maid before fleeing to England in a fishing boat, and then onwards to New York. Other forms of resistance were gentler, and funnier: when ordered to register their full names with the authorities, some Dutch famously responded by registering with made-up comedy surnames such as *Slaaf* (slave), *Halvebil* (half-bottom) or *Naaktgeboren* (born naked).

I leave the Royal Palace and walk briskly south along the Kalverstraat, across the Muntplein, and then further south along the Reguliersgracht: a pretty little canal lined with large trees and red-brick townhouses. The weather improved while I was in the palace, and the sky is now brightening nicely. (As a friend once said, misquoting Mark Twain: if you don't like the weather in this country, just wait ten minutes and it'll be completely different.) After a few minutes I come to a gorgeous spot where the canalside street widens out into a leafy square: the Amstelveld. Children squeal happily in a playground and a pair of elderly men play *jeu de boules* on a gritty oblong of pavement by a greenish canal. One side of the square is dominated by an unusual-looking but handsome building, which is made partly from dark brick and partly from slats of cream-coloured wood. It looks like a large church, and that's exactly what it used to be: the Amstelkerk, commissioned by the city planner Daniël Stalpaert in the 1660s as a temporary wooden structure designed to last until a proper stone church was made. However, the stone replacement never got built, and the church ended up being preserved in wooden form for centuries.

After circling the church a few times, I belatedly find the main entrance and press the buzzer next to it. I expect a receptionist to ask why I'm visiting but to my surprise the door immediately clicks open, and I walk through into a remarkable space: a large inner courtyard with a high white wooden roof and a big silvery organ reaching up one wall. The walls around me on the ground floor are decorated with Basquiat-style modern artworks, while on the first floor, looking down on the courtyard through thick glass walls, are modern offices. The glass windows of one room are engraved, for some reason, with an oversized quote from the Welsh poet William Henry Davies: 'A poor life this if, full of care/We have no time to stand and stare.'

Under French rule, this church played an important role in the system of conscription. Thousands of young Dutch men were selected for compulsory service in the French military via a lottery, and the Amstelkerk was one of the main venues where such lotteries were held. One engraving from 1811 depicts a young man in a long coat nervously picking a ticket from a basket surrounded by French soldiers, presumably wondering whether he's about to be shipped off to fight for Napoleon or allowed to go home for tea. At other times, the church was filled with horses. In 1811, roughly a decade and a half after the French army marched into the Netherlands, Napoleon and his wife Marie-Louise came to visit Amsterdam. A famous painting by Mattheus van Bree shows the moment of their arrival, with the little Corsican riding a gleaming white horse and reaching out to pluck the keys to the city from a red cushion held aloft by the mayor. Napoleon attended a ceremonial reception on the Dam, then visited the great shipyards and the theatre on the Leidseplein, took a trip to the Tsar Peter house in Zaandam, and went by boat to Pampus Island. He naturally chose to sleep in the palace his brother had fancified on the Dam, but also wanted to ensure his prized horses were kept as close to him as possible. And so, the story goes, the Emperor's horses slept here, in a wing of the Amstelkerk that is now probably the kitchen of the café Nel. For a Frenchman, Dutch food was only good for horses.

By the time Napoleon visited Amsterdam, his little brother Louis had already been shown the door. Tensions between the brothers had been running high for years, with Napoleon furious at the way Louis seemed to put Dutch interests ahead of French ones, including by turning a blind eye to Anglo–Dutch smuggling. 'Are you an ally of France or of England?' Napoleon is supposed to have asked Louis. 'I am sorry I ever put you on the throne.'[42] In 1810, Napoleon rudely turfed Louis out of office and made the Netherlands a department of France. Amsterdam became the third-largest city under French control, after Paris and Rome, and (in the words of the city council) '*het trotse Amsterdam was een gewone gemeente geworden*' — 'proud Amsterdam became just an ordinary municipality'.[43] Louis himself was reportedly crushed by his dethroning, saying: 'Dutchmen! Never will I forget a good and virtuous people like you. My last thought and my last sigh will be for your happiness.'[44] Napoleon, though, was less warm-hearted, declaring, 'I did not take over the government of Holland to consult the common people of Amsterdam, or to do what other people want.'[45] Tensions rose, and there was a series of revolts against conscription. In 1814, Napoleon was overthrown and exiled to Elba. The embattled French withdrew from the Netherlands, and within months Dutch statesmen had manoeuvred to re-establish the country as a constitutional monarchy. The Prince of Orange arrived back at Scheveningen, close to the spot from where he'd left the country years earlier, and was later crowned Willem I.* For the second time in its history, Amsterdam had seen off a foreign oppressor.

Some 200 years after the French departure, the French legacy in the Netherlands remains clear to see. As the historian Lotte Jensen has written,[46] during his reign, Louis not only made Amsterdam the capital of the Netherlands but also laid the foundations for the Rijksmuseum, introduced the *Burgerlijk Wetboek* (Civil Code) and a legal system based on French civil law, and founded institutions including the National Archives and the National Library. The French were also responsible for introducing the metre and kilo, along with a practice of military conscription that (remarkably) remained in place until 1997.

At the time when the French first left, however, Amsterdam was in a sorry state. The blockade against the English meant

---

* There's now a square in the Hague named in honour of Willem's return — Plein 1813.

trade was at a standstill, and many Amsterdammers were out of work. Parts of the city began to look quite shabby. When Sir John Carr toured Holland in 1807, he reported that 'Amsterdam has no noble squares ... nor is there any bridge worthy of being noticed.' 'The canals of this city are very convenient,' he wrote, 'but many of them most offensively impure, the uniform greenness of which is chequered only by dead cats, dogs, offal and vegetable substances of every kind, which are left to putrefy at the top, until the canal scavengers, who are employed to clean the canals, remove them.' Another French traveller's verdict was more succinct, but crushing. 'There is nothing here ... to remind one, even remotely, of Venice,' he said.[47]

Such one-star reviews were not entirely accurate, of course. Well into the 1800s, Amsterdam remained a global financial centre, with extensive colonial possessions and one of the most beautiful urban centres in the world. However, it's also clear that by the teenage years of the 1800s, Amsterdam was not what it had been. The city's artists, writers, and officials were no longer 'the shapers and shakers of European thought',[48] public finances were stretched, and the population was restless. Tellingly, after decades of rapid growth, the city's population had gone into decline again: the headcount would eventually shrink by more than a tenth between 1795 and 1815 alone. As one historian put it, the French had 'mangled Amsterdam into poverty and disrepair'.[49]

I leave the Amstelkerk and walk a few blocks west along the Prinsengracht, then turn left along the Spiegelgracht, which is flooded with wandering tourists, but very beautiful. The weather has continued to brighten, and the canalside café terraces are filling with people enjoying the patchy sunshine.

I make a quick detour to pay tribute at Tesselschadestraat 15, once the home of the feminist icon Alette Jacobs. She was the first woman in the Netherlands to become a doctor and a passionate campaigner for women's rights, birth control, and legal sex work. A plaque above the door says: 'women of future generations owe her a great deal of gratitude'.

Approaching the Rijksmuseum, I can hear the Keti Koti celebration long before I can see it. People are still pouring through the tunnel under the Rijksmuseum, and I join them, emerging at the far end to find the grassy Museumplein even busier than it was a couple of hours ago. A Sean Paul song plays at ear-splitting volume; hundreds of people stand around talking and dancing and drinking in groups. I wander up and down for a while, listening to bands play and marvelling at the range of cuisines on offer: Surinamese, Jamaican, Brazilian, Portuguese … I buy a cocktail that costs almost as much as a small car and slurp it happily while watching a reggae group cheerfully mangle the songs of Bob Marley. Thoughts of slavery and economic decline seem very far away. I sit on the grass and let the music wash over me like water.

CHAPTER SIX

De Pijp, Museumplein, and
the Amsterdamse Bos

*How Heineken and van Gogh helped
create a second Golden Age*

If you don't like crowds and noise, I would not recommend going to the Heineken Experience on a Friday afternoon in the summertime. The museum celebrating what most locals would consider Amsterdam's worst beer is one of the most popular tourist destinations in the city, and by the time I arrive, at about one o'clock, it's filled to bursting with noisy tourists. Almost all of them are under the age of thirty, and almost all of them seem to have had a few beers already. Pausing to check my phone on the way in, I am elbowed aside by a twenty-something American enthusiastically bellowing 'Let's do this shit!' while sporting backpacks on both his back and his stomach, like an angry turtle. Nearby, a group of men in T-shirts emblazoned with 'LIAM'S STAG' are passing round a big bottle of whisky and drinking it neat, like babies glugging from a bottle. I've been in the place less than a minute and it already feels less like a museum and more like the world's biggest bachelor party.

I walk to the counter and buy a ticket, then join a group of other visitors waiting to be allowed inside. Faux-cheerful staff in Heineken-green bow ties issue me with a green plastic armband and encourage me to post on social media about my #heinekenexperience. I join a group of about a dozen visitors, who seem to be roughly 50 per cent American and 50 per cent British. 'Are you ready to get excited?!' shouts one of the bow-tied young tour guides. 'YES!' the group cheers in response. 'Well, I'm about to get you even more excited!' bow tie replies. The crowd cheers again and loud dance music starts playing, and I start to wish I'd brought something stronger than Heineken to drink.

Until now, I have avoided spending too much time in museums during my walks through Amsterdam, preferring to spend my time outside. Today however, I plan to break my own rules and spend much of the morning dawdling through some of the museums, parks, and neighbourhoods that stretch along the southern edge of Amsterdam's historic core. My planned route for the day is firmly on the well-trodden tourist trail — I'll pass through two of the top twenty most-visited museums in Europe, and one of the most popular parks. Yet I am looking forward to revisiting an area that I haven't been to for a while, and to learning more about another era in the city's development — the period of time, about 150 years ago now, when Amsterdam went from being a bit downtrodden to again becoming one of the most prosperous cities in Europe — and the stomping ground of a certain Gerard Heineken and Vincent van Gogh.

The tour begins and my group shuffles through some

electronic barriers and into a cellar-like space piled with wooden Heineken crates, barrels, and bottles. This is, a cheery guide explains, one of the original silos for the brewery, where barley was stored after being brought in by boat. We all gaze dutifully skywards at a fairly crappy video installation fixed to the ceiling, depicting some imaginary barley falling into an imaginary silo above us. The guide then provides a quick canter through the history of the site. 'Do you like history?' he asks at one point, after spotting someone yawning.

'No', a tourist with a red hoody and Unabomber beard says loudly.

'Well, I can see a lot of smiling faces!' says bow tie. 'It's fantastic to be here!'

I feel as if I've inadvertently joined a terrible team-building exercise.

Our group proceeds up a spiral staircase to a small room containing holy Heineken relics, including a big photo of the company's founder sporting an epic handlebar moustache. I stop to take a photo and am heavily bumped into by another tourist who is, bafflingly, busy looking at other people's Instagram photos of the Heineken Experience while he himself ignores the Heineken Experience unfolding around him. Round the corner, yet another cheery young man in a green bow tie is briskly explaining the beer brewing process. There are, he discloses in a stage whisper, only seven people alive who know the exact specifications of the yeast used in the Heineken recipe, which is 'kept under lock and key in Zoeterwoude'.

To any true beer lover, describing Heineken as a 'premium-quality beer' would probably be a bit like telling a die-hard Beatles fan that the best ever Beatles album is *Best of The Beatles.* However, there's little doubt that the beer has emerged as an icon of Amsterdam, providing countless people around the world with yet another reason to visit the city.

The Heineken company as we know it dates back to the 1860s, when a young man called Gerard Adriaan Heineken bought a brewery called the *Hooiberg*, or Haystack. The company, which was based just off the Nieuwezijds Voorburgwal, had once been the largest brewery in Amsterdam but had fallen on hard times. And so, apparently on a whim, young Gerard Heineken bought it in the winter of 1864 for 48,000 guilders,[1] and immodestly rebranded it as 'Heineken and Co.' As Marielle Hageman wrote in a neat little history of the brewery, Gerard was only twenty-two at the time and knew almost nothing about making beer, but had the confidence and zeal of a young start-up founder, and thought with a bit of focus and innovation he could quickly turn things around. One of the brewery's problems was that its inner-city location meant there were constant squabbles with the neighbours about the pollution discharged into canals and the heavy stench of beer. And so, in 1867, Heineken moved his brewery here, to what was then the southern edge of the city. At the time when the brewery was built, the road that is now the Stadhouderskade didn't exist, and the factory site was surrounded by green fields. However, Heineken pressed ahead, and quickly opened a wooden café temporarily 'furnished for the sale of beer', which the council said would have to be pulled down once the Stadhouderskade was built. The little café was known as *De Vijfhoek*, or The Five Points, and its entrance was decorated with a five-pointed star, which soon became the logo of the whole Heineken company. In May 1867, there was a ceremony at which a small crowd watched

Heineken's sister Anna lay the first stone of the brewery itself. Someone read out a poem that Heineken had commissioned which poked fun at the rival brewing town of Schiedam: 'May this stone you have laid, serve to become a blessing, to precious Amsterdam. By brewing good beer, may the People's wish be fulfilled: farewell for good to Schiedam.'[2] Everyone clapped and cheered, and then went for a celebratory meal of turtle soup.

Heineken wanted his brewery to be an advertisement for its own success and ordered his architects to design something that would 'appear attractive' and not be 'a factory in the usual sense i.e. a box with a few openings'.[3] The lead architect, Isaac Gosschalk, responded by producing a design that consciously echoed the old warehouses of seventeenth-century Amsterdam, with their tall brick façades, white stone trim, and steeply gabled roofs. (Gosschalk also designed the city's Westergasfabriek gas factory, and if you visit it, you'll soon see the similarities). By 1871, the brewery's workforce had doubled to forty. According to Marielle Hageman, about half the staff were Germans, who mostly lived at the brewery and were paid not only with money but with free beer. The beer they produced, to a German recipe, was wildly popular. A reporter from one local newspaper said that Heineken's Bavarian beer was well on its way to becoming as popular in the Netherlands as Guinness was in Ireland. Between 1873 and 1884 production nearly doubled,[4] and what had been modest premises had expanded to cover a whole city block. An Amsterdam icon had been born.

Continuing our #heinekenexperience, our group walks on into the brew house. In contrast with some of the previous exhibits, this is genuinely impressive: a large, tiled hall with colourful stained-glass windows and eight huge gleaming copper vats, polished to a high sheen. It looks like somewhere Willy Wonka might cook up some magical candy, except that it smells overpoweringly of beer. These days no beer is actually brewed at this site, and the vats are just for show, but the effect is still powerful. 'Don't sniff too deeply or you might get drunk!' a female member of staff chuckles, prompting prolonged bouts of sniffing all round. Against one wall stands a smaller open-topped tank filled with what looks like runny porridge. The rest of the tour group queues up to take photos wearing leather aprons and stirring it with a massive spatula, like witches around a cauldron. Eager to up the ante, one young Brit gets a friend to take a photo of him pretending to climb into the vat and is quickly told off by a member of Heineken staff, who is not amused.

'I can't help myself, I just bloody love beer!' he declares, to laughter. The sweet, yeasty, slightly vinegary smell is almost overpowering.

'It stinks like our hotel room this morning,' another of the British lads says.

'No weed smoke, though,' his friend replies.

Finally, after altogether too much walking and talking, comes the bit we've all been waiting for, and have paid twenty-one euros for the privilege of: the free beer. After queuing in a gloomy cellar bar, I receive my two small glasses, served the usual Dutch way, with a head of foam so thick you could take a bubble bath in it.

'The glass should always be full exactly up to the horizontal lines of the red star on the logo,' the bow-tied barman explains.

A few metres away, another staff member is giving an impromptu pep talk to a group of fellow drinkers who haven't been showing the necessary enthusiasm. 'Just take a few minutes to appreciate the perfection,' he says, gazing into a glass and speaking in the blissed-out tones of a cult leader telling us to enjoy the Kool-Aid. Across the room, another tour group is getting a tasting lesson from their guide; swirling their glasses and lifting them to their noses as if they are sampling a fine wine.

'What does it smell like?' the guide asks.

'Last night's mistakes,' one of the English lads responds.

'That's deep, Dave ... Fucking deep,' one of his friends replies, before downing his drink in one. I down mine too and leave, my ears ringing with the sound of another cheery young staff member telling me to 'Have a brewtiful day!'

At the time Gerard Heineken began dreaming big, Amsterdam was only just emerging from what you could call its difficult teenage years. As I'd learned on my previous walk, by the time the French packed up and left the city in 1813, its shipyards were in decline and its overseas trade had collapsed. It still wasn't a poor place: in 1820, the Netherlands had a GDP of about $1,800 per person, compared to $1,700 in Britain and less than $1,200 in the USA.[5] But many houses in Amsterdam stood empty, the harbours on the IJ were silted up, and the canals in the city centre were literally crumbling, with bricks regularly breaking free from the walls and splashing into the water. As the historian Geoffrey Cotterell once wrote, by the early 1800s, Amsterdam was 'still a great city, [but] it seemed to have become a dinosaur ... [where] the middle and upper classes lived dull and stuffy lives in pale imitation of the past'. The city was, he said, 'a cozy backwater [stuck] in a long drawn-out post-eighteenth century hangover'.[6]

At this point, your average Amsterdammer could probably have been forgiven for sobbing into their Pilsner. However, the story doesn't end there, of course. Just as it had miraculously been transformed from a muddy little trading town into a bustling city in the 1600s, in the 1800s Amsterdam repeated the trick and boomed again; going from fading metropolis to one that was pulsing with life again. In 1800, the city's population was about 200,000, but by 1900 it had soared to more than 500,000,[7] and many local businesses — Heineken's brewery among them — were thriving. Less than two centuries after the first Golden Age ended, Amsterdam enjoyed a second Golden Age.

How did it happen? It's hard to pick a moment when things changed decisively, but if forced to do so, a British-born writer might be tempted to go with the day in 1816 when a ship called the *Defiance* appeared in the IJ, flying the Union Jack. In a nautical metropolis like Amsterdam, there was nothing unusual about a foreign vessel arriving, but what made this one special was its method of propulsion: a steam engine. As the vessel puffed and clanked its way along the river at speed, with no oars or sails in sight, it caused a sensation, with spectators gathering on the banks and people stopping work to stand and stare. The *Defiance* was small, with only a single tall chimney and a paddlewheel on each side, yet it made a big impression: one Dutch newspaper described it as 'ingenious and beautiful', reaping the 'great pleasure of a multitude of spectators' while moving at 'great speed against the wind'.[8] Where the *Defiance* went, many others followed.

In the 1820s, Amsterdammers founded the *Amsterdamsche Stoomboot Maatschappij* (Amsterdam Steamboat Company, or ASM), and by the mid-1820s there was a regular steam ferry service between Amsterdam and London. A city built on sails had entered the steam age.

As ships grew bigger and faster, Amsterdam's leaders dusted off plans to build the North Sea Canal, a sixteen-mile channel that would connect western Amsterdam with the North Sea at IJmuiden. This Pharaonic project had been a long time coming. In 1853, the Dutch Royal Society of Engineers offered New York newspaper readers a reward of 'two thousand florins Dutch currency' for proposals for a waterway 'uniting the harbor of Amsterdam with the North Sea, through the isthmus west of that city'.[9] After many years of discussion and delay, construction of the canal finally began in the mid-1860s. For Amsterdam, the new canal represented another transformation: just a few years earlier, the journey from the city to the coast typically consisted (one traveller reported) of 'a barge dragged by a donkey [and] a market-boat scudding under full sail, laden with milk-cans, and steered by an old woman'.[10] Within a few years, though, large steamships were busily puffing their way along the new channel and new harbours and quays in the west of the city were alive with activity. In 1892, another new canal, later known as the Amsterdam-Rhine Canal, also connected the city more smoothly with the southeast. The shipping industry boomed as a result: between 1890 and 1910, the Dutch merchant fleet doubled in size. Justus van Maurik wrote memorably of how the city was changing in *Toen ik nog jong was* (When I was still young):

As far as the eye can see, a sea of houses, towers and
buildings, an infinity of roofs, chimneys and gables.
No more trees, no more meadows in the distance,
but roofs, houses and more roofs ... a new city
everywhere! ... Like a devouring monster, the city has
... thrown itself on all the pasture and garden around
it, and greedily swallowed up what it could achieve
... Amsterdam has become a world city. [11]

The advent of steam power also meant it became much
easier to reclaim land. The Dutch had for centuries used
windmills to drain water away, but the advent of steam-
powered pumps made the process much easier and faster.
Early pumping projects were modest in size, but in the 1840s,
came the big one: the Haarlemmermeer, a huge lake just
outside Amsterdam which had long been viewed as a threat
to the city. The authorities spent years debating the best
way to drain the lake, until a commission appointed by the
King paid a visit to Cornwall and was impressed with steam
pumps used to keep mines dry. In the late 1840s pumping
finally began, using imported Cornish machines; it would
take an astonishing four years before all the water was gone.
Amsterdam was protected from a major source of flooding
and acquired hundreds of square kilometres of new land for
building and farming to boot. (In fact, if you land at Schiphol
Airport today, your plane will touch down at what was once
the bottom of the lake.) Other reclamation projects soon
followed: in 1908, for example, the Nieuwe Bullewijk was
reclaimed; the Amsterdam Arena stadium now sits where it
was, more than three metres below sea level. Later still, in
the early 1930s, came an ever bigger engineering project: the

closing of the mouth of the Zuiderzee with the twenty-mile *Afsluitdijk* (Closing-off Dike), converting the vast tidal bay to Amsterdam's east into a placid lake — or, as one reporter described it, 'a young and spirited Mediterranean right in the place where every other self-respecting country has its centre!'[12] One of the areas behind the dike which was later drained — the Flevopolder — is now said to be the largest man-made island in the world. One journalist compared the reclamation projects to adding new rooms to the country's 'ground floor'. [13]

Steam power also changed the city in other ways. In 1839, the first steam train began running on a new 'iron road' between Amsterdam and Haarlem. By the early 1840s, there was a line to Utrecht too, with steam trains travelling the 24 miles between the cities in a stunning one hour and eight minutes. Some of the first passengers worried that the train moved so fast that they wouldn't be able to breathe. By the 1860s, there were lines all over the place: from Amsterdam to Rotterdam, Antwerp, Maastricht, Harlingen, and beyond. Faster travel even enabled Amsterdammers to turn back time. For years, the Netherlands had no single unified time zone, and midday in (say) Maastricht wasn't necessarily the same as midday in Amsterdam. As rapid travel between cities became possible, however, people needed to synchronise clocks and so, in 1909, a single time zone was introduced to cover the whole country. *Amsterdamse Tijd* (Amsterdam Time), was roughly equal to GMT plus nineteen minutes, based on the time when the sun was highest in the sky over the Westerkerk. (Later, when the Nazis invaded in 1940, Dutch time was moved to align with Berlin time, and has remained this way ever since.) In 1900, the steam trains were complemented by the city's first electric tram service, running from Leidseplein to the Zoutkeetsgracht. Trams reached the blistering speed of about twenty miles an hour, astonishing onlookers, with the only drawback being that passengers grasping the railings inside sometimes got electric shocks.*

In the early years, trains to and from Amsterdam travelled via a temporary wooden train station, but in 1889 the city acquired another new landmark: the neo-Gothic Central Station, designed by Pierre Cuypers, who also designed the Rijksmuseum in a similar style. The opening of the station followed years of debate about the best location — the city's Chamber of Commerce said the idea of putting it near the IJ was 'a great folly',[14] and serious thought was given to putting it in de Pijp or on the Leidseplein. In the end, though, Cuypers and his backers decided to use steam pumps to build the station on new land reclaimed from the IJ. The building was, by the standards of the time, vast, with enough space to handle forty trains a day (it now gets about that many every hour). Inside, the station was lavishly decorated, with a dedicated spot for the Queen's carriage — go to platform 2 today, walk past the Starbucks, and you can still spot the magnificent gilded gate that once marked the entrance to the Royal Waiting Room. The building's distinctive arched roof, spanning about forty metres, also became a source of local pride, even though it was (whisper it) partly manufactured for Amsterdammers by the English, at the Handyside ironworks in Derby. Even for non-Royals, the experience of arriving in Amsterdam was transformed. There would be no more bumpy

---

*   One technology which didn't arrive until more recently: the metro. London opened its first underground line in 1863 and Paris got one in 1900 – but Amsterdam didn't get its first metro station until 1977.

wagon rides or long hours on a sailing barge creeping along the canals, but instead a smooth, sooty arrival at a grand station that looked like a low-slung cathedral. A city that had grown rich from the river now turned its back on it.

Back outside the Heineken brewery, I stand on the pavement feeling slightly dazed, having drunk two beers in the previous four minutes. Stumbling slightly, I walk south along the Ferdinand Bolstraat into the area known as De Pijp. I know this area well and it is one of my favourite parts of Amsterdam — many happy days off begin with a brunch at the Bakers and Roasters café followed by a walk to one of the nearby museums. As neighbourhoods go, De Pijp is in many ways unremarkable: densely packed five-storey houses, leafy streets, bicycles, bistros. Yet it's lovely to wander through, and has a lot of nice cafés where bums like me can while away the day eating avocado toast and drinking flat whites while feeling vaguely superior about themselves. I stop at one such café now — the inaccurately named Locals, where the English-speaking waitress stares at me blankly when I try to order in Dutch. At the table to my left, a grey-haired lady is reading the *New Yorker* and giggling at the cartoons, while to my right a young man who looks like a model is telling his dog how much he loves her. '*Mijn schatje*,' he keeps calling her: 'My little treasure.' His girlfriend comes outside after using the toilet and half-jokingly tells him: 'You love that dog more than me.' He doesn't disagree.

One of the many delights of the Netherlands is that café owners are usually happy to let you linger for a long time after buying a single drink, with no expectation that you should rush off to make room for another paying customer. Today, though, I do not linger, and as soon as my coffee is finished I resume walking southeast. After a few minutes, I come to the Albert Cuypmarkt. The street the market is held on is unusually wide compared to others in the area, because it was once filled with wood-cutting windmills, which were demolished in the late 1800s. These days, the market is supposedly the largest outdoor market in the Netherlands and has many fans. The novelist Dubravka Ugrešić once described the market in particularly potent terms:

> The market [was] engulfed ... in a mist of pollen and the strong scents of spices from beyond the seas – cinnamon, cloves, nutmeg – shot through with wind and salt. The air fairly sparkled with the bolts of rich silk and thick plush, of exotic jewels, of gold and beads, of the mother-of-pearl of immodestly open shells, of the glittering silver of fresh fish ... Each grape glowed like a tiny lantern; the milk was as rich and white as a Vermeer woman's skin.[15]

I browse the eclectic array of goods from locales near and far: feathery dream catchers, chunky bike locks, batik shirts, big round cheeses like bright yellow wagon wheels. The surrounding side streets also offer the usual pleasing jumble of cultures and cuisines. Within the space of a hundred metres or so I see for sale raw herring, Flemish fries, 'American-style cocktails', Turkish flatbreads, Lebanese platters, sushi, Italian deli supplies, French croissants, and vegan pizzas. A woman with Cruella de Vil-style black-and-white hair walks past eating a massive portion of fries, and a man who looks like

Mick Jagger is taking close-up photos of a pigeon.

This neighbourhood was also, somewhat indirectly, the work of Gerard Heineken. In the autumn of 1867, while his new brewery was still being built, Heineken began a separate project to build affordable housing for his workers, with running water and proper kitchens 'where the woman could carry out the rougher kitchen work'. The houses were small — typically six by twelve metres — and were rented out to workers at low rates. That was the beginning of the neighbourhood that would come to be known as De Pijp. (The origin of the area's odd name is unclear, but it's sometimes said to be a reference to the stream of commuters who would flow through its streets on their way to work, like water rushing through a pipe). Initially, city planners foresaw De Pijp modernising in a way that would rival Paris, with its own train station, wide boulevards, and handsome villas. In reality, budget issues meant that what was delivered was more modest, but by 1930 De Pijp was already home to some 75,000 residents,[16] including many Heineken workers. Among those who lived here was the artist Piet Mondrian,* who was born in Amersfoort but lived at ten different addresses in Amsterdam between 1892 and 1911, including one near the Sarphatipark, one on Albert Cuypstraat and another on the Stadhouderskade.[17] By all accounts, the young Mondrian relished living in the area, making sketches of the city, plunging himself into its nocturnal activities, and (according to one biographer) acquiring a reputation among local women

---

* Oddly, Mondrian's name is spelled differently at home and abroad. Within the Netherlands he's still known by the correct Dutch spelling, Mondriaan, but in other countries he chose to be known as Mondrian, which non-Dutch speakers found easier to pronounce.

'for interesting, prolonged kisses, sometimes lasting for more than half an hour'.[18]

For a long time, De Pijp was considered an undesirable part of town. As recently as the 1960s, one eminent historian described it as 'full of long, narrow, lightless and depressing streets'.[19] Cheap houses attracted a motley crew of local characters in search of affordable housing — sex workers, students, starving artists, and others — who didn't quite fit with the authorities' original Paris-on-the-Amstel vision. However, the influx of immigrants and rebellious types ultimately proved to be De Pijp's making, with what one journalist called 'bohemian spirits, thinkers and creative pioneers' gravitating there from across the city, 'earning De Pijp the reputation of Amsterdam's lively Latin Quarter'.[20] In recent decades the area has gentrified to the point where it's now considered a very desirable (and expensive) place to live — a neighbourhood where, in the words of the local tourism authority, a visitor can 'just as easily pick up a poke bowl as you could a fresh herring'.[21]

I rest for a moment in the Sarphatipark, which was originally planned to be the site of the city's main train station and is now an oasis of dense green foliage squeezed between the busy streets. On the bench next to me a British mother — an expat, I think — is sternly instructing her children about the day's plans to have fun. 'We are going to STROLL without any urgency, LOOK at interesting things, and just ENJOY ourselves, okay Rupert?' Poor Rupert does not look happy. A few yards away, meanwhile, a Dutch mother of about the same age is reading a thick novel while her two children happily wade into a nearby lake, soaking their shoes and jeans. After well over a decade in the Netherlands, I've still never been quite able to shake my surprise at the way British parents helicopter over their children and treat them as if they were naughty dogs to be controlled, while the Dutch treat theirs like little adults and largely let them run free.

I wander over to examine a temple-like memorial to Samuel Sarphati, the man who gave his name to this park. Sarphati's name is rather less well known today than Heineken's, but he was another Amsterdammer who did much to change the way this city looked in the late 1800s. A Portuguese-Jewish trader's son, Sarphati was born in Amsterdam in 1813 and completed a PhD on tuberculosis before working as a doctor in a hospital catering to poorer people who lived in terrible conditions. The young Sarphati was alarmed by what he saw, and realised that, if he wanted to really change people's lives, he would need to improve public health. By 1847, Sarphati had created his own waste collection company, based on Roeterseiland. In 1851 he visited London and was reportedly aghast to see how far behind other countries Amsterdam was when it came to sanitation. On his return, he established an organisation called the *Vereeniging voor Volksvlijt* (Association for People's Industry), which aimed to help Dutch industry share expertise with others abroad, based in a spectacular glass-walled headquarters on the Friedriksplein inspired by London's Crystal Palace and illuminated by thousands of gas lamps. (Sadly, it burned down in 1929.) Less glamorously, Sarphati also established a bread factory, based on the very Dutch belief that there's nothing healthier for a person than a diet of brown bread. His bakery on the Vijzelgracht was soon distributing thousands of cheap loaves every week, transforming the diets of many of the city's poorest residents. As the city grew, Sarphati would probably have achieved much more, but sadly he died in his early fifties. He was widely mourned — the statesman Johan Rudolph Thorbecke wrote that 'Amsterdam and the country have lost one of their most useful citizens'. The slogan on Sarphati's bust in the park now bears one of his nicknames: 'Founder of the New Amsterdam'.

I leave the park and walk west along Govert Flinckstraat, heading towards the area of Amsterdam where many of the big museums are, which is innovatively known as the Museum Quarter. Many of the apartment buildings I pass on the way are modern and plasticky, but — as is often the case in Amsterdam — they are of a similar style and slender shape to the older buildings, meaning the overall streetscape remains quite pleasant even if individual buildings are ugly. Not everything is so discreet, though. To my surprise, at the end of the residential street there's a cluster of red-lit windows, with sex workers posing in their underwear just yards from a café where a group of young mothers sit drinking coffee while their kids play nearby. As a small girl wobbles past on a bike with stabilisers, a man approaches and sheepishly examines 'Jessica' through the glass, while she stands pouting in a bikini next to a poster advertising 'soft and hard s&m'. All cities are exercises in contrasts, but Amsterdam often feels particularly so.

Perhaps fifteen minutes after leaving the Sarphatipark, I arrive at the Museumplein; the large area of grassy parkland behind the Rijksmuseum. On a sunny Friday afternoon, it's packed with people: tourists taking a break from sightseeing,

Dutch teens eating Pringles and listening to portable speakers, and ordinary Amsterdammers walking dogs, reading newspapers, or having lunch in the sun. I think of a line from the novelist H.M. van den Brink, who wrote that in sunny weather, the city's inhabitants come out 'as if the sun were on special offer, an exceptional bargain in the sales that would never be seen again'.[22]

A pair of policemen on bikes do their best to discourage some young boys from playing football dangerously close to a road, and fail. Three men stumble past me looking very drunk and I hear a mother tell her children, in Dutch, 'those men have been drinking special orange juice and now they're very happy'.

The Museumplein has long been one of the most popular public spaces in the city. In 1883, for instance, the green fields here hosted the 1883 International Colonial and Export Exhibition, a sort of grand world fair organised while the Rijksmuseum was still under construction. The Dutch pavilion featured a group of people from Suriname who were displayed as if they were animals in a zoo. The Dutch Queen visited for more than an hour and (according to newspapers) much enjoyed learning about the 'primitive households'.[23] A few years later, on Boxing Day 1887, the Museumplein also hosted (according to *Ons Amsterdam*) the city's first football match between an Amsterdam and a Rotterdam club. At the time, the sport was so new that a reporter didn't know quite what to make of it. 'The game of football is one of many good things which we have taken from the English, and which, if the initial success be taken as an omen, will soon be native here,' the report began. 'So it's full of excitement ... [and] attractive to both the players and the spectators.' Their overall verdict was positive: 'In a word, the game of football is one of the nicest, most cheerful games imaginable.' Amsterdam beat Rotterdam 1-0.[24]

I am tempted to sit in the sun for a while but head across the grass towards one of the museums. My next objective is to learn more about another Dutchman who had a big impact on this part of the city, albeit in a very different way to Heineken and Sarphati: Vincent van Gogh. Flashing my museum membership card, I enter the Van Gogh Museum, which looks like a paper coffee cup half-sunk in the grass. I haven't been here for years, but the museum is largely as I remember it: big, bright, modern, and absolutely packed with art by both van Gogh and the artists who inspired him. Rounding a corner on the first floor I find one of van Gogh's famous bright, prickly self-portraits, followed by a Monet, a Pissarro, a Toulouse-Lautrec, and a Degas. There's so much to look at that it's a bit overwhelming, and I feel like a child in a toy shop who doesn't know where to look. 'This is not the way I remember it,' an American woman says. 'There are just too many paintings!' Crowds of visitors flood the staircases and hallways, all invariably pronouncing the artist's name 'van go' rather than in the proper Dutch way, which sounds like someone coughing up a hairball. In the galleries, it's so busy that someone accidentally sticking an elbow through a painting feels like a real possibility. At one point a man standing next to me even reaches out and runs his fingers across the surface of a painting, commenting on how it feels 'bumpy' and nearly giving a security guard a heart attack. Nearby, a Canadian woman loudly explains to someone that she is going on 'the cheese tour' tomorrow. 'I want to find out how they make the holes,' she says.

One thing that surprises me about the museum is that there's almost no mention of Amsterdam itself. A big timeline painted on the wall that summarises the places van Gogh lived and worked doesn't mention the city, and the only depiction of Amsterdam which I can find on display is a waterfront scene by Claude Monet. This seems odd, given that van Gogh spent a formative period of his life in Amsterdam, and knew the city well.

Van Gogh moved to Amsterdam at an exciting time, in the spring of 1877, just a few months after the North Sea Canal opened, when everything was booming. The young artist was at that time a bit lost, with plenty of ambitious ideas but a poor record of following through on them. By moving here, he hoped to find new focus, and 'put my hand to the plough', as he wrote.[25] With that goal in mind, he moved in with an uncle of his, Rear Admiral Johannes van Gogh, who lived near the docks and was a quintessential Dutch naval man who had (as one biographer put it) 'commanded men and ships in war … navigated unknown seas … [and] sailed the navy's first steamships at a time when steam was still a wild and fickle force'.[26] Young Vincent seems to have been blown away by the beautiful chaos of the city's harbours;* frequently interrupting his studies of Latin, Greek, and geometry to wander the waterfronts and watch thousands of workers marching to the shipyards with their feet rapping the pavement 'like the roaring of the sea'.[27]

As he tried to find his feet, van Gogh — like me! — set out on a series of long walks through and around the city, often

---

*   If you look closely, you can find a plaque marking the spot where
     Vincent lived with his uncle, on a corner north of the Maritime
     Museum, just past the bike racks.

with a book in hand. He walked to the sea at Zeeburg, along the dikes of the Zuiderzee, through farms and meadows, and out to the Jewish cemeteries on the edge of the city. 'Every day I go for a long walk,' he wrote to his brother Theo in 1877. 'I recently came across a very nice part when I walked all the way down … [to] the IJ, and I walked along all kinds of narrow little streets with gardens full of ivy. It was somehow similar to Ramsgate.'[28] Van Gogh also visited Amsterdam's brothels and had some fun there. 'I would sooner be with a common whore than be alone,' he once wrote.[29]

Van Gogh's studies in Amsterdam seem to have gone poorly. As his mental health deteriorated, he took to staying up all night, and despaired at his own lack of direction, begging God to 'let me complete one significant work in my life'. Yet Amsterdam also provided him with a great education. Within days of moving to the city, van Gogh began making regular visits to the Trippenhuis, the forerunner to the modern Rijksmuseum, and was inspired by what he saw there. In particular, the young artist seems to have been deeply moved by the works of Rembrandt and Hals, whose vibrant styles made him think, 'my studies are too black'.[30] Thereafter he began working in more vivid oranges and ochre, layering the paint on in thick ridges and waves rather than thin, muddy layers; and producing what he called 'pictures full of painting'. Noting that many of the old Dutch Masters worked quickly, van Gogh resolved to work faster himself, and soon managed to dash off three quick snapshots of Amsterdam in bad weather, 'done in a tearing hurry'.[31] Once, when a friend arrived at the central train station, he found Vincent in a waiting room feverishly painting a picture while 'surrounded by a crowd of conductors, workmen, tourists'.[32] Van Gogh ended up staying in Amsterdam only about four hundred days, but it was in many ways the making of him.

Leaving the Van Gogh Museum, I amble a short distance across the grass to the Rijksmuseum. It's mid-afternoon by now, and the Museumplein is even busier than before; filled with people basking like seals in the sun. Music plays, hotdogs are eaten, and souvenir stands do a brisk trade in every conceivable item emblazoned with the works of Rembrandt and van Gogh. On the cycle path that cuts through the base of the museum, I see a smartly dressed older cyclist remove his jacket, fold it neatly in half, and stow it in the rear pannier of his bike — all without slowing down at all.

I've been to the Rijksmuseum countless times before, but it still has the power to awe. It's a vast, palatial building that looks a bit like London's neo-Gothic Natural History Museum, with added bikes. (By one count, 13,000 cyclists pass through the museum tunnel every day.)[33] Flashing my membership card again, I descend into the central atrium under the bike path, then ascend a wide stone staircase into the galleries proper. The windows above the stairs are richly coloured, and the floor underfoot is dappled like snakeskin by the sunlight streaming through. It feels nothing at all like the modern Van Gogh Museum next door, and a lot like an unusually busy cathedral.*

---

*   It's easy to forget that the bike tunnel wasn't originally popular. When it opened in 2013, a column in the NRC described it as 'incomprehensible tyranny', while Trouw compared it to 'bird droppings on a shining windshield' and wrote that 'only one thing needs to happen: the bike tunnel must be closed'. (Fietsersbond, '10 jaar Onderdoorgang Rijksmuseum', 2023)

The Rijksmuseum is, of course, another relic of Amsterdam's second Golden Age; also built in the years after Heineken started messing about with hops and yeast. Pierre Cuypers was still in his thirties when he produced the design for the museum. He came up with six different designs to fill the space before settling on one that (like his central train station) resembled the old city gates, with tall towers on either side and a tunnel through the base (cars were allowed to drive through it until the 1930s.) Augustus Pugin, who'd designed parts of London's Houses of Parliament, was one of Cuypers' inspirations. Famously, Cuypers was a Catholic, known for building churches, and many prominent Protestants were outraged that he'd designed the museum in a style that looked so suspiciously like a cathedral. Invited to the museum opening in 1885, even the King refused to visit 'that monastery'.[34] Some early reviews of the museum's contents were also poor. One newspaper complained that *The Night Watch* was shown in a space that suffered from 'insufficient light'.[35] 'It is such a pity that this great building turned out to be such a disappointment,' one acquaintance of van Gogh's wrote when he visited. 'There it stands for all eternity, to the annoyance of future generations.'[36]

As we all know by now, the cranky reviewers were wrong, and the museum was an incredible success. Immediately after opening, the corridors were clogged with visitors, and people sometimes had to wait patiently to catch a glimpse of *The Night Watch* over the heads of the crowd. In early October 1885, van Gogh visited, wearing a soggy coat and hat that made him look 'like a drowned tomcat'.[37] He reportedly stood in front of some paintings for hours as the crowds seethed around him, gasping with amazement at works by Vermeer,

Hals, and Ruisdael and occasionally crying: 'My God, look at that!'[38] Vincent himself later wrote to his brother: 'I should be happy to give ten years of my life if I could go on sitting here in front of this picture for a fortnight, with only a crust of dry bread for food.'[39] Better still was Frans Hals's *The Night Watch*-esque *The Meagre Company*. 'I stood there literally rooted to the spot,' he later wrote to his brother. 'That painting alone makes the trip to Amsterdam well worth while.'[40]

I walk back under the Rijksmuseum heading south towards the Concertgebouw concert hall, which looks like a cross between a Dutch railway station and a Greek temple. It was built in the 1880s after the magazine *De Amsterdammer* denounced the shameful state of musical life in the capital.[41] Unfortunately, efforts at rejuvenating the city's cultural life were sometimes hit and miss: when Brahms visited in 1883 to introduce his own 'Piano Concerto No. 2', he was unimpressed by a squabble between the cellists. 'You are friendly people,' Brahms said of Amsterdammers, 'but bad musicians.'[42]

For many years, Amsterdam had seemed hesitant to build grand civic structures like this. Many felt that it was, as Steven Naifeh and Gregory White Smith put it, 'neither good business nor good symbolism to build grandly on sand'.[43] However, by the late 1800s, as trade boomed and the population grew, grand civic monuments came back in vogue. Impressive new buildings sprouted up all over the place like buttercups in bloom. One neighbourhood that was transformed was the Leidseplein, just north of the Rijksmuseum. The Leidseplein was once a so-called *wagonplein* — a car park where horse-drawn wagons could be left outside the city gates after arriving from the direction of Leiden. But in the second Golden Age the gate itself was demolished and replaced by landmarks including the Stadsschouwburg theatre and the American Hotel (where the dancer and spy Mata Hari spent her honeymoon). Inevitably, progress sometimes came at a heavy cost. In the rush to build shiny new things, some beautiful old buildings were pulled down and many canals were filled in. However, some new buildings swiftly became indispensable parts of the cityscape, such as the 1903 Beurs van Beurlage stock exchange near Dam Square and the 1915 De Bijenkorf department store. By the early 1900s, Amsterdam was a glittering destination city where the wealthy could view great art, go to the opera or a play, and hope they didn't fall in a canal after one too many cocktails. A cultural renaissance also helped foster a new generation of writers, artists, and playwrights. In the early 1900s alone, three Amsterdam scientists won Nobel prizes. Even World War I wouldn't really knock the city off its stride. 'The untravelled Englishman's idea of Holland as a country where the people ... walk in wooden shoes is not altogether correct,' one traveller reported in 1920. 'The Dutch girls ... are often as up to date as any London flapper.'[44]

I walk west, following the busy Van Baerlestraat. After ten minutes or so, I reach the Vondelbrug, a solid stone bridge that passes over the famous Vondelpark and is graffitied with the words 'FREE PALESTINE'. In the park down below are walkers, cyclists, mothers with prams, several dogs, and a gang of hungry ducks chasing a toddler with a sandwich. An elderly man in a tracksuit looks at his smart watch, punches the air and shouts 'Yes! Three thousand!'

I turn left down the Vondelstraat, a wide, leafy avenue

lined with large, handsome front gardens. Behind the houses, to my left, the Vondelpark is near enough to toss a ball into. After a hundred metres or so, I come to the Vondelkerk, a church whose rust-coloured brick façade is paired with an unusual number of pointy little turrets and sharply angled roofs. A sign next to the front door reads: 'YES, IT LOOKS LIKE A CHURCH BUT IT'S AN OFFICE!' Just across the street stands another building that looks like a church but isn't, with sharply sloping tiled roofs. I've only ever seen the house (the Nieuw Leyerhoven) in books before, but its style looks immediately familiar, and for good reason: it is another brainchild of Pierre Cuypers, who designed it for himself to live in. The tiled façade still includes a not-too-subtle jab at some of his critics: a depiction of three men accompanied by the text: '*Jan bedenckt et, Piet volbrengt et, Claesgen laeckt et. Och, wat maeckt et*', which roughly translates as 'Jan invents it, Piet completes it, Claesgen laughs at it. Oh, what does it matter'. In Cuypers' mind, some of the city authorities would always be like the fool Claesgen, mocking and opposing his work even as it put Amsterdam back on the map.

Rounding the Cuypers' house, I enter the Vondelpark. Before shattering my leg, I jogged in the park quite often after work and, like many Amsterdammers, have a real fondness for it. The Vondelpark isn't huge — by my calculations it's about a seventh the size of New York's Central Park and a third the size of London's Hyde Park — yet it always strikes me as everything a city park should be: grassy, scenic, surrounded by pleasant buildings, and well-equipped with places to get a coffee or something stronger. There's even a Picasso sculpture on display: an ugly upright slab of reinforced concrete shaped like the head of a bull. It's always busy here; packed with walkers, runners, cyclists, lovers, fighters, drinkers, dogs, and ducks; all jockeying for space on the gravel paths that wind between the lakes and trees. I walk past a man trying to ride a unicycle, and a busker with a truly horrendous voice mangling a U2 song. For passers-by, it is not a 'Beautiful Day'.

The Vondelpark is yet another product of Amsterdam's second Golden Age. Until the 1850s, Amsterdammers were able to enjoy walking in the Plantage, a string of fifteen or so gardens linked by pathways in the north-east of the city. In 1858, however, the city sold the land which the Plantage stood on and permitted people to build on parts of it, leaving Amsterdam's park-lovers suddenly park-less. ('People's love for money exceeds their love for parks,' the mayor explained.) A group of prominent Amsterdammers started a campaign to build a 'Riding and Walking Park' and placed adverts in local newspapers seeking support. A paper that I found from 1864 included a letter declaring:

> One of the main jewels of our city may be the new
> walking park. But for this it is necessary that the
> whole bourgeoisie should take the matter seriously
> ... Everyone, even the lowest citizen, must be able to
> contribute ... Let a shopkeeper give his dollar and
> a cleaning woman her quarter — but everyone who
> visits the park must be able to say: this is MY park.[45]

The park's champions were motivated partly by honourable social aims, but also knew that having a big park here would raise property values in the adjacent streets. Yet their public appeals clearly worked, as nearly a thousand donors chipped in for the first land purchase and a ten-hectare patch of park was soon open, with more to be added later as funds allowed. In June 1866, newspapers reported that 'the board of the Association for Construction ... has the honour to announce that the first part of the Park will be opened to the public on Thursday, June 15 ... and will be open until further notice, every day from 7 a.m. to 10 p.m.'[46] This was followed by a list of ground rules, including a stipulation that 'loose horses, donkeys, cattle, etc. are banned' and another saying 'Beggars and people who are apparently intoxicated are not allowed in'.

After about forty minutes dawdling through the park, I reach its south-western tip, where a pair of green iron gates open onto the busy Amstelveenseweg. I pass a dogwalker expertly walking no fewer than eleven dogs, followed by a man carrying an inflatable stork and a sign that says, 'It's A Boy!' I leave the park and turn left, stopping briefly to take a photo of the beautiful OCCII cultural centre, with its colourful wooden façade which makes it look like a Tibetan temple. As I keep heading south, I gradually get the feeling I'm leaving Amsterdam proper, and entering the suburbs. The roads get wider and busier, the nice old buildings are replaced by sterile modern blocks, and the bistros and boutiques are replaced by real estate agencies and insurance companies.

Rounding a corner, I arrive at perhaps the ultimate symbol of Amsterdam's increased confidence and status in the early 20th century: the Olympic Stadium, which hosted the 1928 Olympic Games. Standing on a large open area next to a busy road, it's a doughnut-shaped structure of red brick, with a ring of red flags flying around the top of its roof. Today, the Amsterdam Games are mainly remembered for being the first at which track and field and gymnastics events were open to female competitors. Old habits of misogyny died hard, though: when, during the women's 800-metre run, several female competitors collapsed from exhaustion, officials decided 800 metres was just too far for women to run, and banned every female running event of more than 200 metres for the next three decades. Somewhat less controversial was the behaviour of the Australian rower Henry Pearce, who stopped paddling midway through his quarter-final race to let a family of ducks pass, but still went on to win the race and eventually the gold medal. The relatively far-flung location of the shiny new stadium created some headaches for the organisers, including how to deal with all the visitors who wanted to travel there in their new-fangled motor cars. When competitions had finished, how would enthusiastic sports fans find their way back to their cars? A solution was found in the form of blue signs that had a white letter 'P' in the middle. And so it was that the international traffic sign for parking was born.

Looping around the back of the stadium, I walk south on a cycle path leading to Aalsmeer. The scenery is nondescript — office blocks, concrete bridges, car parks — and as the temperature drops, I begin to regret leaving the bistros and cafés of the city centre behind. I plough on though, and soon arrive at my final destination for the day: the Amsterdamse Bos, or Amsterdam Forest; a large wedge of parkland tucked under the A10 motorway. I've never been here before and am pleasantly surprised to find an attractive shady woodland, an enormous lake with rowers on it, and a waterfront café that looks like a big trilby hat made of wood. Birds sing in the trees, clouds scud slowly across the sky, and the bustle of the

Museumplein and Vondelpark feels very far away.

The Bos was famously created in the 1930s as a make-work scheme for unemployed Amsterdammers, at a time when a global economic crisis meant that (by some estimates) nearly one in four people were unemployed.[47] Thousands of job-seekers spent years planting trees, sowing seeds, and digging lakes. For people who were used to working in offices or shops, the manual labour could be brutal: *Ons Amsterdam* reported one worker saying:

> You sometimes worked with people in a team who
> had never worked with their hands [before] ... You
> smeared your hands with Vaseline and then that
> healed a bit in the evening and at night. But then
> you would come in the morning and if it was cold at
> all, your hands would burst, then the blood would
> run down them. I saw them cry in pain, that was a
> terrible thing.[48]

Sadly, the Bos has never quite captured the public imagination in the way Vondelpark has, probably for the simple reason that it's much further away from the city centre. It's loved by many Amsterdammers, though, offering a precious semi-wild space in a city where nature often feels far away. In her memoir of an Amsterdam childhood, Patricia Wessels writes of idyllic times in the Bos:

> Where, depending on the weather, we swam in the
> canoe pond, made daisy chains, flew kites in the field,
> or threw stones and grass from the bridge to watch
> the greedy carp nibble. Of course, my mother also

used those trips to pick food. Nettle tops for a soup in the spring, elderberries for a vitamin-rich dessert in the autumn. 'All gifts from the forest', [my mother] said.[49]

Later, the park also served as a training ground for Ajax football club, who have their stadium nearby. In his memoir, the Amsterdam hero Johan Cruijff laughs about other players faking coughing fits to get out of running laps there.[50]

It's early evening now, and the sky is turning the glowing golden-blue colour of a week-old bruise. After wandering in a big loop through the forest I go back to the trilby-shaped café, sit on the deck outside, and order a coffee. Out on the lake, rowers knife their way through the water. On the adjacent grass, two big dogs gallop up and down like racehorses, ignoring their owner as he calls them. I sip my drink slowly and watch the sun sink behind the trees.

CHAPTER SEVEN

The Jewish Quarter, the Plantage, and the Holocaust Monuments

The war, Anne Frank, and the city's darkest days

It's a perfect winter's day in the city: bright blue skies, golden sunshine, and clear, cold air in which my breath hangs like cigar smoke. The leafless winter trees cast strong shadows on the rows of townhouses, and canalside churches stand on top of their own perfect reflections. On a day like this, the city would normally be fizzing with life; bustling with people walking and jogging and cycling and talking in the sunshine. But here on the Jonas Daniël Meijerplein, a gravelly square just east of Amsterdam's old city centre, it's quiet enough to hear a pin drop. Hundreds of people stand gathered on the stones in silence, forming a respectful circle around a bronze statue of a man in baggy clothes. The only sound is the faint rumble of traffic, and the occasional trill of a passing bicycle bell.

Today is the anniversary of the so-called *Februaristaking*, or February Strike — the occasion when, at the height of

World War II, thousands of Amsterdammers rose up against Nazi tyranny, and gifted the city what may have been its finest hour. Perhaps three hundred people have gathered on the Jonas Daniël Meijerplein to pay their respects and listen to worthy speeches, right in the shadow of the city's largest synagogue. One of the old houses flanking the synagogue is flying a huge Amsterdam XXX flag, and at the centre of the circle of spectators, next to the bronze statue, flies an enormous white flag bearing the motto '*Heldhaftig, Vastberaden, Barmhartig*' ('Valiant, Resolute, Merciful'). I shuffle carefully through the crowd, trying to get a better view. The people in attendance aren't exactly representative of the city at large — every single person I can see is white — but the attendees are still demographically varied: amid the crowd I spy a pair of dreadlocked hippies, a tattooed old teddy boy with lots of earrings, and a pair of baffled Danish tourists wondering what's going on. Many people are carrying bunches of flowers or wearing red scarves. One young man carries a big poster on a stick denouncing the Dutch far-right leader and conspiracy theorist Thierry Baudet. '*Nooit Meer Fascisme*', it reads; 'Never Again Fascism'.

It's late afternoon now, and as the sun sinks, the sky begins to turn a lovely dusky violet colour. The keynote speaker steps up to a wooden lectern: a Dutch trade union leader wearing a red scarf, whose greyed pomade and strident tone remind me of the British Prime Minister Keir Starmer. In a clear, powerful voice he begins to speak, in Dutch:

> How brave do you have to be to stand up for
> someone else when your freedom is not respected,
> resistance is regarded as high treason and violence

> against demonstrators is not shunned? And while you
> know it could cost you your life? … Real heroes are
> often ordinary people.

The speaker is standing in front of a statue known as the *Dokwerker*, or Dock Worker, a stout bronze of a man in overalls with his arms outstretched, and he gestures towards it now.

> The *Dokwerker* appeals to us. Speak up when
> freedom is in danger. Speak up when our democratic
> rights are under threat. When freedom is abused
> by one to restrict the freedom of another. When
> democratic rights of minorities are curtailed. Speak
> out against dehumanisation, against injustice.

He stops speaking, and the crowd bursts into applause.

I almost didn't come to this event today. I've attended similar commemorations in Rotterdam in the past, and Amsterdam's wartime history also often feels more than a little overexposed: there seems to be a new book published about it almost every month. However, there's little doubt that the war was a transformative episode in the city's history, reshaping not just its built environment but its sense of itself. Without the war there'd quite possibly be no Red Light District, no cannabis-vending cafés, and no reputation as The Most Liberal City In The World™. And so I've decided to come and spend an evening walking around some of the city's hallowed memorial sites, and see what I can learn.

The memorial ceremony draws to a close. One of the many delights of living in the Netherlands is the long evenings in the summertime: it's not unusual for it to still be light enough at 11.00 pm to read a book outdoors. In February, though, the nights draw in early, and we're still a long way from the annual tipping point where people stop complaining it's too cold and start complaining it's too hot. I zip up my coat and regret not having brought a hat or gloves.

I start walking west along the Jodenbreestraat, towards the city centre. I passed this way during my long walk in search of Rembrandt, and found the neighbourhood marred by horrible plasticky apartment blocks. However, there are also still a few architectural gems hidden away, if you know where to look. A few minutes after leaving the Jonas Daniël Meijerplein, I come to one: the *Huis de Pinto*, or Pinto House; a whitewashed building that looks like a bank or an embassy, squeezed improbably between a florist's shop and the Bluebird 'coffee' shop.

The house was built in the early 17th century for a VOC executive and subsequently renamed after the Pinto family of Portuguese-Jewish bankers who lived there. The front door is ajar and so I duck inside and am surprised to find myself in a space that resembles a small library, with bookshelves on the walls and big wooden tables surrounded by friendly old men reading *De Groene Amsterdammer* and *The Economist*. What's really extraordinary though, is the ceiling: richly frescoed with wood panels painted with dozens of flying cherubs, creeping vines, and crescent moons against a bright blue sky. It reminds me of the Sistine Chapel.

The Pinto House serves as a helpful reminder that this area was once the beating heart of Amsterdam's Jewish community. From the early 1600s onwards, Jews found they were able to practise their religion in greater freedom in Amsterdam than in many other cities, and migrated here in large numbers from the Iberian peninsula and Central and Eastern Europe. Many were so-called 'New Christians' who had left the Jewish faith, but returned to it after their arrival here. Associations were created to care for the poor, invalid, and orphaned, and gradually there emerged (in the words of the city's Jewish Museum) 'a melting pot of Iberian, Jewish and Dutch culture'. In other Dutch cities Jews were often subject to harsh restrictions — the authorities in Utrecht, for example, forbade Ashkenazi Jews from staying in the city overnight. In Amsterdam, though, the restrictions were milder, partly because the city's leaders realised Jewish networks in Spain and Portugal could be good for business. Andrew Marvell wrote a short poem about the city's religious diversity in 1653:

Hence Amsterdam, Turk-Christian-Pagan-Jew
staple of sects, and mint of schism grew
that Bank of Conscience, where not one so strange
Opinion but finds Credit, and Exchange.[1]

In time, Amsterdam became the world's unrivalled centre of Hebrew and Yiddish book printing, and the Ashkenazi Great Synagogue and Portuguese Synagogue here were considered the finest (and probably the largest) synagogues in Europe. By the beginning of the 20th century there were about 60,000 Jews living here, in a veritable Jerusalem on the Amstel.[2] 'Mokum', many Jews called the city, from the Hebrew for 'the place' — a name that stuck, and which you still sometimes see on posters and stickers around the city.*

After marvelling at the painted ceiling for ten minutes, I leave the Pinto house and turn left down the Nieuwe Hoogstraat towards Dam Square. I'm close to the Red Light District and it shows: the streets are lined with shops selling falafel and fries, T-shirts and phone cases, Belgian waffles and postcards of Banksy paintings. At the end of the Damstraat, I pass the grand Hotel Krasnapolsky, whose *wintertuin* (winter garden) is a nice place to have a coffee away from the crowds. It's said that a man called Gerard Philips visited here in the early 1890s and was so impressed with the new electric lights on display that he decided to set up a new firm producing light bulbs. The business was a success and became world famous: Philips.

Dam Square is busy, as always. Dozens of smart phone cameras point towards the Royal Palace and the Nieuwe Kerk, but my attention is focused in the other direction, towards the big white war memorial on the eastern side of the square. As I noted during my very first walk through the city, there's something about the monument that has always struck me as a little off — the giant white pillar looks as if it was designed by a man who had sensitivities about a certain part of his anatomy. However, as I slowly circle the base, I can see that the design is more thought-provoking than I had appreciated. The monument actually consists of two distinct

---

*   Some other Hebrew words also entered the local lingo, including *kalletje* (prostitute), which comes from *kallah*, the Hebrew word for a bride; and *penose* (criminal gang), which comes from *parnasa*, meaning livelihood.

parts: the tall not-compensating-for-anything column, and a lowish wall of polished white granite that curves around the column's base like a sea wall. The wall has a series of niches carved into it, and I remember reading that each niche contains an urn of soil taken from somewhere Dutch people were murdered or tortured during the war. The column itself also has figures engraved on its surface: some men in chains and, at the centre, a large Christ-like figure with outstretched arms. Atop it all stands a woman holding a child, symbolising rebirth after the conflict, and at the back are a series of doves representing peace. The monument was unveiled by the Queen in 1956, accompanied by children who'd lost their fathers during the war.

World War II took many Amsterdammers by surprise. The Netherlands had been fortunate to escape World War I almost completely unscathed, and Amsterdam's main role in that conflict was a place of sanctuary for refugees. In an odd echo of the 16th century, many refugees fleeing World War I arrived in the city from Antwerp, including many children. One young Dutch woman told reporters she wanted to look after a baby 'but there are not enough to go round'.[3]

Some sensed that tragedy was looming — in September 1939, Rembrandt's *Night Watch* and about thirty thousand other artworks were taken from the Rijksmuseum and hidden in bunkers along the North Sea coast. However, as war came to Europe a second time, many Dutch people naturally hoped to repeat the trick of remaining neutral and staying out of the war altogether. Hitler's rise to power was facilitated by a young Dutchman, Marinus van der Lubbe, who is said to have started the fire at the Reichstag in 1933, but the Netherlands' immunity to fascism seemed strong. Some in the city even joked about it: at one Purim in the late 1930s, a Jewish man living in south Amsterdam sparked hilarity when he turned up at a friend's house and rang the bell dressed as Hitler.

For a while it looked as if the optimists and jokers assuming Amsterdam would be spared the conflagration were right. Even as late as the beginning of 1940, while the rest of Europe tipped into terrible conflict, Amsterdam again found itself serving as a place of refuge. The thousands who fled here from the Nazis included the writer Joseph Roth, who stayed in Amsterdam's Eden Hotel writing forlorn letters to Stefan Zweig hoping he could 'find a rich man who can help me out for a couple of months'. 'I'm sick and no one will give me an advance,' Roth wrote from the Eden. 'My heart is as empty as a desert ... but the people here are kind to me.'[4]

Sadly, Amsterdam's status as an island of tranquillity couldn't last long. For Hitler, the Netherlands was an important piece of a bigger strategic puzzle: the outlet for the Rivers Ruhr and Rhine, and a stepping stone towards the eventual invasion of England. In May 1940, the city of Rotterdam, forty miles south of Amsterdam, was hit by a terrifying wave of bombing, which left its once-beautiful city centre looking as if had been wiped clean by a giant hand. Fearing Amsterdam and other cities might soon get the same treatment, the Dutch government swiftly surrendered. On 15 May 1940 the Nazis arrived in Amsterdam in a wave of trucks and jeeps. Some locals were happy to see them. In the words of the Anne Frank Foundation: 'Along the route of the German soldiers there were many Dutch people who enthusiastically gave the Nazi salute [and] when the Germans arrived at the city hall, they were welcomed by an official with a map of the city.'[5] Nazis who approached the city from the southeast, meanwhile, were welcomed at Duivendrecht by the deputy mayor, who expressed a hope that the city's Jews would not be harmed. A Nazi leader reassured him: 'If the Jews don't want to see us, we don't see the Jews.'[6]

After taking a few photographs of the war memorial, I leave the Dam and continue walking west, along Paleisstraat, towards the setting sun. There's a chill in the air now, and I walk faster to keep warm. On the right, I pass the Naaldenmakersgang, a tiny alleyway whose near-unpronounceable name points charmingly to its historic use: Needle-makers Way. I add it to the list of other odd Amsterdam street names in my notebook, alongside Mosterdpotsteeg (Mustard Pot Lane), Dubbeleworststeeg (Double Sausage Lane), Oude Nieuwstraat (Old New Street) and Nieuwe Nieuwstraat (New New Street). A man passes me on a bicycle carrying a stepladder, as if it's the most natural thing in the world, followed by a young English woman on foot who says to her friend: 'This is me at stage one of being cold. When I get to stage two, I'll turn from white to blue.'

My next destination is probably the most famous address in the city: Prinsengracht 263, better known as Anne Frank's house. I haven't visited for years, but it's not hard to find: round the back of the Westerkerk snakes a long line of tourists, all waiting to enter the house. I join the back of the queue, behind a young woman who snaps a selfie with an exaggerated pouting sad face and posts it online with the caption '#annefrank #sad'. Behind me, I hear an Irish woman loudly ask her teenage daughter: 'Go on then, do you know who Anne Frank was?' To which comes the amazing reply: 'Something to do with the war, I think. A Nazi, maybe?'

The Anne Frank Museum is an odd structure these days. In order to handle the 1.2 million visitors who traipse through it each year it's been extended into neighbouring buildings, and the entrance now looks like that of a discreet luxury hotel, all white concrete and glass. Beyond that, though, the house itself is remarkably well-preserved; a crooked, creaking old building which feels as if it hasn't changed a bit in decades. After collecting my ticket, I shuffle respectfully through it, reading displays and peering at relics under glass. Like many people, I already know the story of Anne Frank's life quite well, but still find the simple displays deeply moving. On one wall a screen plays some remarkable video footage of Anne leaning over a balcony as a young child — the only known moving image of her, captured on a neighbour's wedding film in 1941. I've only ever seen still photographs of Anne before and for a moment am stopped in my tracks by the unexpected sight of her in motion. I look around and see other visitors have a similar reaction. A dozen or so of us stand there in silence for a minute, mesmerised by a few seconds of footage playing in an endless loop.

The Frank family were among the many German Jewish refugees who moved to this city in the early 1930s. Anne's father Otto was a member of a wealthy family in Frankfurt, and after marrying Edith Holländer he fathered two daughters: Margot, born in 1926 and Annelies Marie in 1929. For a while the family lived happily in Germany but in the early 1930s, after Hitler rose to power, they joined the crowds seeking sanctuary in Amsterdam, moving into a home at

Merwedeplein 37, in the Rivierenbuurt. The area was at that time already home to a bustling community of German Jews, and Anne in particular seems to have quickly felt at home, learning to speak fluent Dutch and attending a local school. She blossomed into an outgoing, precocious child, known for speaking her mind and acting older than her age. 'God knows everything,' one of her friend's mothers once said, 'but Anne knows everything better.'[7]

After the Nazis invaded in 1940, life in Amsterdam at first continued largely as normal. Arthur Seyss-Inquart, the Austrian fascist who the Nazis had tasked with running the Netherlands, promised: 'We are not coming here to oppress and destroy a national character and to deprive a country of its freedom.'[8] Trams ran on time, shops were well-stocked, children ran to school, and parents gossiped over coffee. Teade Sysling, in his memoir of an Amsterdam childhood, recalled the early days of the occupation:

> Other than the sound of a few distant explosions,
> the war action was not much noticed in Amsterdam.
> People were still very innocent in their view of war
> and most went on with their regular daily routine as
> if nothing was happening. I still have a vivid image
> in my mind of the dairyman making his rounds
> delivering milk, butter and eggs ... [and saying] he
> hoped that the war would be over soon.[9]

BBC reports that Polish Jews had been executed were dismissed by one of the presidents of Amsterdam's Jewish Council as 'nothing but English propaganda'.[10]

In late 1940 and early 1941, however, the situation began

to change. The Dutch fascist party — the NSB — recruited more than ten thousand members in the city and the streets echoed with the sound of Nazi soldiers on parade. Benches were labelled 'Not for Jews' and some streets were crudely renamed, with the Nieuwe Kerkstraat (New Church Street) becoming Joodschestraat (Jew Street). Swastika flags hung from the palace on Dam Square. There were also reports of looting. One day Reichsmarschall Hermann Göring, one of the most senior figures in the Nazi Party, appeared at the premises of the art dealer J. Goudstikker on the Herengracht, wearing a white uniform and clutching a baton. An eyewitness reported: 'Huge lorries and barges drew up outside, and were soon filled to overflowing with valuable paintings and antiques. Goudstikker's was left empty. Everything went to Germany.'[11]

Otto and Edith Frank did what they could to shield their children from the horror enveloping the city. In the summer of 1942, Anne celebrated her thirteenth birthday, and received as a gift a red-and-white plaid diary. Her diary entries started out how you'd imagine a teenage girl's diary would: 'Rob Cohen used to be in love with me too, but I can't stand him anymore'; 'This morning I lay in the bathtub thinking how wonderful it would be if I had a dog.'[12] However, they quickly turned much darker as she recounted the myriad hardships and absurdities of life in Nazi-occupied Amsterdam. In one entry, in June 1942, she summarised some of the restrictions Jews faced in the city:

> Jews were required to wear a yellow star: Jews
> were required to turn in their bicycles! Jews were
> forbidden to use street-cars! Jews were forbidden
> to ride in cars, even their own! Jews were required

to do their shopping between 3 and 5 P.M. ...
Jews were forbidden to take part in any athletic
activity in public; Jews were forbidden to sit in their
gardens or those of their friends after 8 P.M.; Jews
were forbidden to visit Christians in their homes;
Jews were required to attend Jewish schools ...
Jacque always said to me, 'I don't dare do anything
anymore, 'cause I'm afraid it's not allowed'. [13]

Continuing through the Anne Frank house, I find the small
rooms crowded with visitors. I assume I may have crossed
paths with some of them before at the Rijksmuseum or
Heineken Experience, but the mood here is very different.
Everyone shuffles in muted silence, listening diligently
to audio guides and carefully studying photographs and
documents displayed on the walls. For the most part, the
rooms are stripped bare, with a modern linoleum floor and
bright lighting overhead, and I find it hard to picture how it
must have been in the 1940s. Some of the relics on display are
arresting, though. On one wall hangs a framed yellow star of
fabric, about the size of a tennis ball, embroidered with the
word '*Jood*'. Opposite it hangs a carefully typed list of names
of students from the Municipal Lyceum '*van joodsche bloede*',
or 'of Jewish blood', with Anne's name halfway down the first
page.

By the summer of 1942, the situation had grown so
desperate that the Frank family began making plans to go
into hiding in an empty annex above the soap and perfume
company where Otto worked. The move didn't happen
overnight: weeks were spent installing bathroom equipment,

cooking equipment, and furniture; the Franks' friend Miep Gies carried so many sacks of food to the annex that Anne said she looked like a mule. But the hiding place was still not finished when, early in July 1942 a messenger arrived with a letter ordering Anne's sister Margot to report to the train station for deportation. The family rushed into hiding the next morning, telling anyone who asked that they were on their way to Switzerland. Anne wrote in her diary that as the family walked to their hiding place:

> The four of us were wrapped in so many layers of clothes it looked as if we were going off to spend the night in a refrigerator, and all that just so we could take more clothes with us ... The stripped beds, the breakfast things on the table, the pound of meat for the cat in the kitchen — all of these created the impression that we'd left in a hurry. But we weren't interested in impressions. We just wanted to get out of there, to get away and reach our destination in safety. Nothing else mattered. [14]

I climb a creaking staircase to the next floor, where a small *overloop* (landing) leads to a thick bookcase standing ajar from the wall on stout hinges. It's only when the people around me start surreptitiously taking photos that I realise what it is: the famous door to the secret annex, behind which Anne and her family remained hidden for more than two years. Beyond the door, the lighting is dim and the floorboards creaky. It is, again, the smaller details that are most arresting: the cut-out pictures of movie stars stuck on the wall of the small bedroom which Anne shared with Fritz Pfeffer; the pencil marks on the wallpaper showing how much Anne and Margot had grown during their time in hiding. The Frank family would remain hidden in the annex for 761 days.

Sooner than expected, I reach the end of the tour and find myself back in the gleaming lobby. I step out onto the pavement, inhale deeply, and look up at the darkening sky, relieved to be out in the fresh air again. All around me stand young tourists in varying degrees of shell shock, depressed by what they've just seen. 'Fuck, man, that was heavy,' a young man who exited just before me says.

'Yeah,' I reply with a sigh. 'Heavy.'

Walking away from the house and circling the Westerkerk, I pause to take a photo of a lovely little statue of Anne Frank, looking like a plaintive ballerina, which is perched on the cobbles in front of a cheese shop. It was made by Mari Andriessen, who also made the *Dokwerker* statue I saw at the memorial ceremony earlier. Then, just a few steps away, comes the *Homomonument*; the low-key 'gay monument', which stands right on the bank of the Keizersgracht canal. This was designed by the Amsterdam-born artist Karin Daan in the late 1970s and was supposedly the first monument of its kind anywhere in the world, although others have now sprung up across Europe. It's often forgotten that as well as persecuting Jews, the disabled, and other minorities, the Nazis sent an estimated fifteen thousand gay men to concentration camps, of whom about 60 per cent died.[15] Despite its rather odd name (in English), the *Homomonument* is a poignant, if low-key, memorial to them, comprising three salmon-coloured triangles of stone, one of which points into the canal like the bow of a boat. On one triangle is engraved a quotation from the gay Jewish poet Jacob Israël de Haan: '*Naar Vriendschap Zulk een Mateloos Verlangen*', or 'Such an endless desire for friendship'. Today the monument is covered in flowers and rainbow ribbons and candles. 'Axe!' one little rainbow placard reads, in Dutch, 'So sweet. So beautiful. I miss you xxx'.

I walk north along the Prinsengracht, skirting the edge of the Jordaan. As I move away from Anne Frank's house the crowds quickly thin out, and I enjoy glorious, stereotypical scenery: narrow 17th-century townhouses, pretty humpbacked bridges, thousands of parked bicycles, and every other Amsterdam cliché you can think of. Looking left, I'm also treated to a truly lovely sunset, with the sky to the west turning a floral pink and then a brilliant Dutch orange. There might be prettier urban landscapes than this, but I haven't seen them.

I soon arrive at the Noorderkerk. Compared with some nearby churches this one is a little bland: the tower is stubby rather than soaring, and the roof a dull mass of smooth grey slate. However, the church does have an interesting shape — it was originally built in the form of a Greek cross, with four arms of equal length, but shops and houses were soon added to fill the gaps between the arms, meaning that from above it now looks like an octagon. One of the grand church doorways is being used as the backdrop for a fashion shoot. A young woman in a long blue overcoat and glittery heels stalks across the cobbles like a panther as a camera flashes away.

I circle the church slowly, dodging prancing models and photographers as I go. After a minute or two I find what I've come to see: a chocolate-coloured bronze plaque, about the size of a tabloid newspaper, mounted on a wall of the church. The text on it reads, in Dutch:

> MONDAY FEBRUARY 24, 1941
> IN THE EVENING AT 6 PM
> MEMBERS OF THE THEN-PROHIBITED
> COMMUNIST PARTY OF THE NETHERLANDS
> SPOKE HERE TO 250 FELLOW CITIZENS
>
> THEY CALLED FOR A PROTEST STRIKE
> AGAINST THE REMOVAL OF 400 JEWISH
> AMSTERDAMMERS BY THE GERMAN OCCUPIERS.
> THE NEXT MORNING
> THE FEBRUARY STRIKE BROKE OUT

The plaque refers, of course, to the same February Strike that was being commemorated in the memorial ceremony I attended a couple of hours ago.

The strike was triggered by a series of incidents in early 1941, including a fight between Nazi thugs and Jewish customers at the popular Koco ice cream parlour. The Nazis had been waiting for a pretext to take drastic action against the city's Jews and now they had it. On 22 February 1941, a roundup of Jewish men began. Ies Dikker, a haberdasher, wrote to his sister-in-law about what he saw:

> Suddenly the lorries came rushing in … The bridges
> [over the canals] were drawn up and everybody was
> trapped. The streets were closed off and … soon
> screams of frightened girls and women were heard
> [and] the streets were filled with running men, who

thought they could escape ... Boys were torn away
from their girlfriends and taken along; some people
tried to hide in their houses, but were caught there
and sometimes dragged down from the attics. Doors
were kicked in and young people taken out. They
were all taken to the Jonas Daniël Meijerplein, where
they had to line up in front of the synagogue ... At
the smallest movement or the slightest sound a guard
came and hit the offender violently with his rifle or
dropped its butt onto his feet. The lorries were on the
other side of the square and the brutes had the boys
crawl to them on their knees.[16]

There are, remarkably, photos of the roundup that are
easy to find online, showing helmeted Nazis wielding rifles as
rows of young men kneel on the cobbles with their hands in
the air, the looks on their faces somewhere between shock and
despair. The men were loaded onto trucks and driven away;
first to Kamp Schoorl in the northern Netherlands, where
a handful were released, and then on to the concentration
camps. Of the nearly four hundred men moved from the Jonas
Daniël Meijerplein to the camps, only two survived.

To their everlasting credit, the people of Amsterdam didn't
take this persecution of their Jewish neighbours lying down.
A few days after the roundup, the strike began. One observer
reported:

Something incredible happened! The tram drivers
took their trams to the depot and went home. The
shopkeepers of Amsterdam let down their shutters as
a sign of mourning. The factory workers abandoned

their machines and refused to work in a city so full
of injustice and suffering ... The streets went quiet.
Amsterdam went quiet. It was as if everyone held
their breath.[17]

'Just about every business was closed,' Teade Sysling
recalled. 'The doors of the schools were locked and streetcars
stayed in their garages. Normally lively Amsterdam had come
to a complete standstill.'[18]

Inevitably, the Nazis did not take the rebellion lightly.
One Nazi officer wrote in his diary: 'we must show this gang
of Jews just how big and sharp our teeth are'.[19] There was
shooting in the streets and arrests, and some strikers were
swiftly executed. The City of Amsterdam was forced to make
hefty 'reparations' payments to the occupiers and its mayor
and chief of police were replaced by Nazi sympathisers.
Given that the strike had lasted barely forty-eight hours,
some historians would later view the whole episode as a futile
gesture — one called it 'a fiasco'.[20] Yet its emotional impact
was enormous. The February Strike entered Amsterdam
legend as a sort of Dutch version of the Warsaw Ghetto
uprising, commemorated in statues, museum exhibitions,
songs, and poems. Even under the cruel boot of occupation,
the city still retained some of its old tolerance and liberalism
— and a willingness to fight to defend them.

I leave the Noorderkerk and head north, then turn east along
the beautiful Brouwersgracht (Brewers' Canal). A dog sleeps
happily on a balcony, and a young man below engages in
that timeless Dutch pursuit: trying to find your own parked

bike amid a sea of dozens of near-identical ones. Crossing the Singel, I look south and spy the famous *Poezenboot*, or Cats Boat – a waterborne cat sanctuary which looks like a floating batting cage. I could wander happily here for hours but press on, navigating myself towards the tower of the Zuiderkerk, which I glimpse occasionally over the rooftops. It's now dark enough that the lamps outside and inside houses have started to come on. Many cities are thrilling at night, but I've always thought there's something especially wonderful about central Amsterdam after sunset, when all those slender houses light up and the old street lamps begin to glow. If Paris is the city of light, filled with wide-open squares and wide plazas flooded with dazzling sunlight, Amsterdam is perhaps the city of darkness — not the gloomy kind, but a close, cosy, embracing darkness, when every street looks like a model from a nativity display.

After about half an hour of zigzagging, I find myself back where I began, on the Jonas Daniël Meierplein. It's almost completely dark now, and with the memorial ceremony long finished, all that remains is a ring of flowers encircling the *Dokwerker* statue like a colourful halo. I walk a short way across the gravel to where a row of beautiful tall townhouses stands overlooking the statue. There I find three square brass plaques, each about the size of a pack of playing cards, set neatly into the cobbled pavement. They are engraved with the names Ephraim Izaäk Levie Rosenbaum, Johanna Frederika Suzanna Rosenbaum-Zion, and Izak Michel Max Rosenbaum. There are other similar plaques nearby, outside other houses. They are, I quickly realise, *Stolpersteine*, 'stumbling stones', small memorial plaques that have been proliferating in Amsterdam in recent years, laid outside the places from where Jewish people were deported to their deaths. As the name suggests, *Stolpersteine* are not a Dutch invention — they were initiated by a German painter called Gunter Demnig, who began laying them in Germany in 1995. Every plaque is stamped by hand and there are now more than fifty thousand of them scattered across Europe. 'I never imagined that there would be so many,' Demnig once said. 'There's no end.'[21] The power of the stones lies in their simplicity and ubiquity, and the stark stories that the names and dates convey. Izak Rosenbaum, for example, was born in 1943, arrested in 1943, and murdered at Sobibor in 1943. A baby, sent from Amsterdam to the camps like cattle.

I approach the synagogue on the northern side of the square. This was once the largest synagogue in the world, and it's still an imposing structure: a giant cuboid of dark red brick that looks more like a power station or pumping house than a place of worship. Security is tight today, with no fewer than five burly policemen hanging around outside the front door, and an airlock of sliding doors to pass through if you want to get inside. When I stop to take a few photos of the exterior and scribble in my notebook, one of the policemen quickly walks over and hovers at my shoulder, anxious to see what I'm doing. I can't blame him for being a little suspicious, but it's sad such security is necessary.

After borrowing a little blue kippah, I walk through the airlock, across a courtyard and into the synagogue itself. It's a large, murky, squarish space, with a high wooden ceiling and rows of empty pews. It's beautiful but austere, and echoingly empty. I find something rather haunting about it — the building's grandeur testifies to the importance of Amsterdam's

Jewish community in the past, yet its quietness and emptiness also serves as a reminder that the city's Jewish community is not what it once was, and probably never will be again.

After the February Strike of 1941, life in Amsterdam quickly got harder. Early in 1941, Arthur Seyss-Inquart, the fascist who'd previously pledged not to oppress people, gave another speech in which he added a crucial caveat to his earlier pledges of tolerance, declaring:

> My statement that 'we do not want to oppress the Dutch people and force them to accept our convictions' remains valid, but it applies only to the Dutch people ... We do not see the Jews as Dutch citizens... and anyone who takes their side will suffer the consequences.[22]

From April 1942, Jews in the city would have to start wearing a badge on their clothes: a six-pointed yellow Star of David with the word 'Jew' in the middle, with failure to wear one punishable by a one-way trip to a concentration camp. Jews were forced to pay for their own badges. Some non-Jewish Amsterdammers protested by wearing homemade stars with the words 'Catholic' or 'Aryan' on. In South Amsterdam, reported Miep Gies, so many non-Jewish people wore yellow stars in solidarity that the neighbourhood was referred to as 'the Milky Way'.[23]

Other measures were even more serious. In January 1942, top Nazis met at a lakeside villa on the Wannsee, just outside Berlin, and prepared a detailed plan for fixing the

Jewish 'problem' once and for all. The notes of the meeting included figures summarising the size of the 'problem' in the Netherlands: 160,800 people, the majority of whom lived in Amsterdam.[24] Soon afterwards, the Nazis started deporting large numbers of Jews from the Netherlands to death camps in Eastern Europe. Hundreds of people were rounded up at gunpoint in Amsterdam and herded to the Central, Amstel, and Muiderpoort train stations; marched to their deaths through the same hallways where commuters now shop for snacks and magazines. By late 1942, thousands of Jews had been sent to the camps. Thousands more would follow. 'Countless friends and acquaintances have been taken off to a dreadful fate,' Anne Frank wrote in her diary. 'Night after night, green and gray military vehicles cruise the streets. They knock on every door, asking whether any Jews live there ... No one is spared. The sick, the elderly, children, babies and pregnant women — all are marched to their death.'[25]

I leave the synagogue and walk southeast a short distance along the busy Weesperstraat, before turning left into a small park tucked in next to the city's botanical gardens. Here stands another memorial; a touching little statue of black marble paying tribute to 'the Jewish deaf victims of the Nazi regime'. '*De wereld bleef doof*', the enscription reads: 'the world stayed deaf'. Then just through the Wertheimpark comes yet another: the Auschwitz Memorial, consisting of six big panes of greenish glass set in the gravel floor like the skylights of an underground car park. The big glass panes are deliberately cracked and broken, and another piece of glass propped upright nearby bears the engraving '*NOOIT MEER AUSCHWITZ*' — 'Never Again Auschwitz'. This memorial is somewhat famous in Amsterdam — it was designed by the beloved writer Jan Wolkers, author of the novel *Turks Fruit*, who said:

> Designing a memorial for the spot where the urn
> containing the ashes of victims of Auschwitz rests
> in Dutch soil, seems an impossible task ... You rack
> your brains to conceive of an image that might
> convey the ignominy and suffering. You look up
> at the sky and can't understand how that blue
> firmament could have stretched up serenely and
> indifferently above such horror ... That is what gave
> me the idea of placing broken mirrors on that small
> patch of earth above the urn of ashes. Never again,
> on this spot, will the sky be whole.[26]

By early 1944, most Jews had been removed from Amsterdam and the Franks were still in hiding. On the streets the mood was increasingly anarchic. Yet there was also hope that the end of the war was in sight. 'I'm finally getting optimistic,' Anne wrote in July 1944. 'Now, at last, things are going well! They really are.'[27] Sadly, her optimism was misplaced. On the morning of Friday 4 August 1944, a car pulled up outside the Franks' hiding place, and a man climbed the stairs to utter the words everyone had been dreading for more than two years: 'The Gestapo is here.' 'The door flew open and a man stood before us holding his pistol,' Otto said. 'No one wept. Anne was very quiet and composed, only just as dispirited as the rest of us.

Perhaps that was why she did not think to take her notebooks.'[28]
The Frank family was taken to the Gestapo headquarters in
Euterpestraat, and then to a prison on Weteringschans. On 8
August they were moved on by train to the transit camp at
Westerbork and, a few weeks later, to Auschwitz, on the very
last transport to go between the two. There were a little over a
thousand people on their train and upon arrival about half of
them were gassed immediately, including the younger children.
Anne, at fifteen, and eighteen-year-old Margot were spared for
labour. Anne had her head shaved and was tattooed with a
number on her forearm. In October 1944, with the Russian
army approaching, Anne and Margot were transferred again,
to Bergen-Belsen, near Hanover; 'a hell of chaos and squalor'.[29]
Someone who met Anne there soon after her arrival described
her as 'a broken girl'. [30] Rachel van Amerongen-Frankfoorder
wrote that in Bergen-Belsen the starving, sickly Frank girls 'had
little squabbles, caused by their illness … They were terribly
cold. They had the least desirable place in the barracks, below,
near the door, which was constantly opened and closed. You
heard them constantly screaming, "Close the door, close the
door", and the voices became weaker every day.'[31] Another
survivor recalled that Margot was the first to go, 'falling dead
to the ground from the wooden slab on which she lay'.[32] Anne,
heartbroken and skeletal, died a day or two later. The precise
date of her death has never been determined, but we know she
nearly made it out: only a few weeks later, Bergen-Belsen was
liberated.

Feeling sad to the bones, I walk southeast out of the
Wertheimpark and find myself on the Plantage Middenlaan, a

wide, busy street with trams running down the middle. I follow the tram tracks towards the National Holocaust Museum, which opened in 2024 after many years of campaigning and fundraising. It's closed now, but I visited a few days ago and found it impressive, if rather modest in scale. As always, the exhibits I found most powerful were the small ones: the dainty china teacups emblazoned with swastikas; the tiny pink girl's jacket bearing a yellow star reading 'Jude'; the video interview with a Jewish descendant of Holocaust survivors who says he'd never think of getting a tattoo.

At number 24 I pass the site of the *Hollandsche Schouwburg*, or Dutch Theatre. It's not much to look at now, but beyond the façade is a nice memorial designed by Gabriel Lester, consisting of a life-sized metal sculpture of a tree that has shed its leaves onto the white marble floor around it. The theatre has been described as 'one of the most emotionally charged, contested, and meaningful sites in the Netherlands'.[33] Between July 1942 and November 1943 alone, nearly fifty thousand Jews were interned here before being deported to concentration and extermination camps.[34] The theatre, once a place of joy and entertainment, became, in one observer's words, 'a gateway to terror and death'.[35] However, there were also stories of hope. Across the street from the theatre, I spot a nondescript building that once housed a nursery. This nursery served as a kind of holding centre for children who were about to be sent to the camps, but several staff members were part of the resistance and smuggled many children to safety, hidden in bags, suitcases, milk churns or between the dirty laundry. Hundreds were saved in this way. One of those rescued, Ed van Thijn, went on to become mayor of Amsterdam.

The war had arrived late in Amsterdam, and it was late leaving, too. In early September 1944, Brussels and Antwerp were liberated by the allies, and rumours spread that Amsterdam would follow. But for weeks, no one came. Long after the liberation had been expected, there were still Nazis everywhere, and the skies were still filled with bombers at night. In late September, parts of Amsterdam were ablaze again. 'The old town is trembling on its foundations,' the writer Bert Voeten recorded in his diary, as he watched warehouses and cranes toppling like 'constructions of reed'. 'The barbarians revelled in the destruction of what has been the source of prosperity for this merchant city for centuries,' he wrote.[36]

Worse was to come. As an unusually cold winter set in, canals and rivers froze, and the IJjsselmeer — the huge body of water to Amsterdam's east — became impassable, making it hard to keep the city supplied by boat. Much of the city's gas and electricity was shut off, and Amsterdammers resorted to cutting down hundreds of trees for firewood, burning park benches and even the doors and staircases from inside their own houses. The Vondelpark was closed to the public 'because of wood theft and major destruction'. 'The de-greening of Amsterdam', one newspaper called it.[37] Worse still, the food began to run out. By early 1945, many people were eating less in a week than doctors recommended eating in a day. Central kitchens were set up offering food to the starving, including one on the Spuistraat, and people roamed rural areas around the city in search of produce to buy or even dead horses to cut meat from. North of the IJ, Shell grew vegetables in the garden for its staff, pretending it was conducting research into pesticides. It wasn't enough. By early 1945, the death toll in Amsterdam had climbed well past a thousand a month.[38] The Zuiderkerk temporarily served as a 'municipal repository for the dead' and one visitor reported seeing corpses stacked outside the ancient churches like firewood. Just about the only people doing good business were the gravediggers, although fuel was now so scarce that top-hatted undertakers were forced to ferry cardboard coffins to the cemetery by tricycle. A correspondent from *The New Yorker* reported:

> Women's ankles and wrists were so swollen from starvation that they could hardly walk to the distant fields and dig the sugar beets to feed their families … The Concertgebouw [concert hall] head porter recently said that it normally takes six of his men to move a concert grand piano but that by April of 1944 the average weight of his assistants had dropped … and it took ten of them to move a piano. When the other hungry western Europeans were liberated, newspaper headlines pictured them as starving [but] only the Dutch were really starving.[39]

'For the last eight months of the war,' the *New Yorker* reporter said, 'the Dutch lived on tulip bulbs … usually made into *tulpen pannenkoeken* or tulip pancakes, fried and browned in cabbage-seed oil. They were sickening, unnourishing, but filling, and they were swallowed with gratitude.' Even by the standards of the 1940s, it was an unprecedented event: a full-blown famine in what had been one of the richest countries in Europe.* As Stephen Devereux

---

* Among the survivors of the Hunger Winter: the mother of the former Prime Minister, Mark Rutte.

later wrote, 'those who suffered during the famine were probably the wealthiest, best educated and most mobile victims of any famine in history'.[40]

Eventually the war did end, of course. Hitler committed suicide in Berlin on 30 April 1945, and a week later the Nazis surrendered. The front-page headline in *Trouw* the next day was succinct: '*God Dank*'. After five terrible years, the Netherlands was free. In Amsterdam, however, there was a bitter coda: on 7 May, when thousands gathered on Dam Square to celebrate, a group of Nazis opened fire on the crowd. Astonishing photos, which you can find online, show people running for cover in terror — one, being Dutch, is carrying his bicycle. When the shooting stopped, dozens of people lay dead. Eventually, though, the last pockets of Nazi resistance were mopped up and the celebrations started in earnest. Throughout the city people danced and sang, kissed and cheered, waved flags. Harry Mulisch described the atmosphere well in his seminal novel *The Assault*:

> Amsterdam looked like a dying man who suddenly flushes, opens his eyes, and miraculously comes back to life. Everywhere flags at windowsills in need of paint, everywhere music and dancing and crowds rejoicing in the streets where grass and thistles grew between the pavement. Pale, starved people laughingly crowded about fat Canadians … Jeeps and armoured cars were being patted like holy objects. Whoever could speak English not only became part of the heavenly kingdom that had come down to earth, but perhaps even received a cigarette.[41]

Along the Kalverstraat, swastika flags were replaced by dozens of tricolored Dutch flags. Canadian and British liberators were showered with flowers, and handed out chewing gum and chocolate in return. One group of young Dutch women went to the edge of the city, where a sign said AMSTERDAM, and posed for a photo alongside it, arm in arm with some grinning Canadian soldiers. 'This is May 10', they scrawled on the white sign, 'and it ain't 1940'. In many other ways, however, Amsterdammers had little reason to celebrate. Parts of the city looked desolate: on the Museumplein, *Het Vrije Volk* reported, 'what remained ... was a trampled, battered, plundered terrain ... like a wide-open, ragged mouth in despair.'[42] According to Hannah Arendt, 103,000 Jews were deported from the Netherlands to the death camps, the majority of them from Amsterdam, and only five hundred and nineteen returned.[43] Overall, about one tenth of the city's population had died. After five years of horror, Amsterdam was free, but it was a city of ghosts.

Leaving the Schouwburg, I circle back to the Weesperstraat, and quickly reach the final memorial I'll see today: the National Holocaust Names Monument. This is one of the newest and biggest memorials in the city, and it's certainly striking: a zigzagging labyrinth of high walls made of small orange bricks, topped with large boxy mirrors. (Viewed from above, the walls spell out in Hebrew the words 'in memoriam'.) Inscribed on each of the more than 100,000 bricks is the name, date of birth and age at death of someone from the Netherlands who died in the Holocaust. The memorial was designed by Daniel Libeskind, a Polish-American son of

Holocaust survivors who's best known for designing the 9/11 memorial in Manhattan. The obvious comparison is with the more famous Holocaust memorial in Berlin, which also uses a maze-like format to disorient the visitor. I have to say, though, I find Berlin's version more effective: there's something about the German memorial's simplicity and bleakness that encourages silence and introspection. This Dutch one is busier and more prescriptive, and I personally find the whole thing mildly interesting rather than deeply moving. However, in this opinion I may be alone: Libeskind's memorial has won several awards and been widely praised by many in Amsterdam's Jewish community, who feel it has filled an important gap in the city's memorial landscape. 'This is exactly what we need,' one Holocaust survivor said.[44]

It's getting late and I'm getting tired — tired of walking, and tired of war memorials. Does Amsterdam really need so many of them? The answer to that question is sensitive, but one reason so many memorials have sprung up is that some of the early ones had important failings or omissions. The main monument on the Dam, for instance, is now a beloved focal point for national remembrance, but also has clear Christian overtones — doves, cruciform figures — which have always struck some as odd, given that not everyone in the Netherlands was or is Christian. The Dam Square monument remains not a monument to the horrors of the Holocaust, but to the suffering of the *Dutch people*. Ian Buruma once called it the place 'where the nation feels most sorry for itself'.[45]

Unfortunately, memorial-builders were not the only ones to have problems with the way the war is remembered in the Netherlands. After the war ended, some 300,000 Dutch people were investigated for crimes of collaboration, with thousands ending up in prison and about forty executed.[46] Yet despite these efforts to secure justice, many surviving Jews found returning to Amsterdam a heartbreaking experience. In the rush to rebuild the city, many Amsterdammers preferred to focus on promoting the idea that all Dutch people were equally victims, or on the idea that the whole city had heroically resisted the Nazis. 'Such a myth suited almost everyone,' one historian later wrote, 'from former collaborators who wanted a chance to be brought back into the fold, to an exhausted public that was eager to put the war behind them.'[47] Yet the truth was more complex: many Dutch people, and many Amsterdammers, had collaborated with the Nazis quite enthusiastically. 'Concerning the Jewish Question, the Dutch police behave outstandingly and catch hundreds of Jews, day and night,' the Nazi in charge of Amsterdam's police once wrote to Heinrich Himmler.[48] Even the Royal Family wasn't innocent: in 2023, proof of the late Prince Bernhard's membership card from the Nazi party NSDAP was found in his archives.[49] The Prince — grandfather of the current King — had previously told *de Volkskrant* 'I swear on the Bible: I was never a Nazi. I never paid party dues. I never had a membership card.'[50]

When Jewish people returned to Amsterdam from the camps, they often got a rough reception. One Jewish returnee, Rita Boas-Koopman, was told upon her return: 'Quite a lot of you came back. Just be happy you weren't here – how we suffered from hunger!'[51] Another was denied an advance from his employer on the grounds that in Auschwitz, 'You had a roof over your head and food the whole time!'[52] Incredibly, the Dutch government even fined some returning Jews for not having paid their taxes.

Among those who came back, in June 1945, was Anne Frank's father Otto. After being freed from a concentration camp, he arrived in Amsterdam knowing his wife was dead but hoping his daughters were alive. In August 1945 he placed an advert in *Het Vrije Volk*, appealing for information. However, a month or so after his return he was told Anne and Margot were dead. Janny Brandes-Brilleslijper, who helped break the news, recalled:

> [Otto] stood on the porch and rang the bell. He said, 'Are you Janny Brandes?' Because he was a very polite gentleman, he came into the hallway and remained standing there and said, 'I am Otto'. I could hardly speak, because it was very difficult to tell someone that his children were not alive anymore. I said, 'They are no more.' He turned deathly pale and slumped down into a chair. I just put my arm around him.[53]

The news of his daughters' deaths understandably crushed Otto. According to Francine Prose: 'People who encountered Otto Frank during this period recall a handsome, distinguished man with the bearing and reserve of a Prussian officer — but whose eyes were perpetually red from weeping. He carried the manuscript [of Anne's diary] with him wherever he went, and, at times, tears flowed down his face as he read a few pages aloud.'[54] Of the eight people who had been in hiding in the annex on the Prinsengracht, only Otto had survived.[55]

Otto began trying to get Anne's diary published, but it was widely rejected by nearly every major publishing house in the United States. Alfred A. Knopf, Inc. described it as 'very dull' and a 'dreary record of typical family bickering'.[56] The diary was also censored, with Otto carefully editing out bits of Anne's writing which he found upsetting. ('The little hole underneath is so terribly small that I simply can't imagine how a man could get in there,' Anne had written about her genitalia, 'let alone how a whole baby can get out'). [57] Also edited away were a few prominent references to Jewish religious practice, which might have put off non-Jews.

In 1947 the diary was finally published in the Netherlands. Early reviews weren't always good — *Het Parool* dismissed the book as a 'diary by a child ... stammered out in a child's voice'.[58] In time, though, it became the ultimate example of what publishers might call a sleeper hit, eventually translated into more than sixty-five languages and selling well over 35 million copies. A play and a film based on the book were both also hugely successful and were shown all over the world — including in Germany, where (Alvin Rosenfeld reported) 'the theatre reviews of the time tell of audiences sitting in stunned silence at the play and leaving the performance unable to speak or to look one another in the eye.' In Japan, the book even became an odd kind of cultural meme, with girls referring to the day when they had their first period as their 'Anne Frank day', because she'd mentioned menstruation in her diary. [59]

In Amsterdam, Anne became, after Rembrandt, perhaps the closest thing the city has to a patron saint. In the early 1950s, the building containing the Franks' hiding place was almost razed to enable construction of a modern office block, but following a campaign to protect it, developers withdrew their plans. In 1957 the Anne Frank Foundation was established and three years later, the annex opened as a museum. It was soon attracting tens of thousands of visitors each year. Not everyone was happy: *The Jerusalem Post* once reported that one of Anne's childhood friends wrote in the guest book: 'Anne Frank didn't want this.'[60] Others were uncomfortable with the way a tragic figure had been refashioned as a beacon of hope and optimism. In a 1997 essay, Cynthia Ozick noted that many editions of the diary are adorned with phrases like 'a song to life' or 'a poignant delight in the infinite human spirit', and do not dwell on the fact that the protagonist died shaven-headed and skeletal in a Nazi death camp. 'Because the end is missing,' Ozick wrote, 'the story of Anne Frank … has been bowdlerized, distorted, transmuted, traduced, reduced; it has been infantilized, Americanized, homogenized, sentimentalized; falsified, kitschified,' with the annex and other memorial sites reduced to mere cogs in 'the Anne Frank industry'.[61] That seems a little harsh to me — any discomfort caused by the commercialisation of Anne's legacy is surely outweighed by the benefit of educating young people about the Holocaust. (When I visited the secret annex, almost everyone there seemed to be under the age of thirty). However, it's hard not to feel uncomfortable at the way the war is remembered in Amsterdam sometimes. It is true that many Amsterdammers bravely resisted the Nazis. But it's also sadly true that many more either were guilty of atrocities or participated in what's sometimes called *het grote wegkijken* — the big look away. As several historians have noted, the Nazis never felt it necessary to post many officers in Amsterdam, even at the height of the persecution of the Jews, because much of the heavy lifting was done by the Dutch themselves. At one point, city authorities even diligently prepared a map for the Nazis showing where all the Jews lived, to make rounding them up for execution just that little bit easier. The Dutch national railway, NS, charged the Nazis a fee for each Jew they deported, plus another fee to cover the cost of constructing a new railway line to the camps. The mayor of a village that the new track passed through objected on the grounds of 'potential destruction of the natural beauty'.[62]

In the years after the war, questions of guilt and responsibility would cast a long shadow over Dutch society. These tensions were often captured in Dutch literature, which in the years after the war was dominated by several great writers — W.F. Hermans, Harry Mulisch, Anna Blaman — who specialised in writing about moral complexity and spiritual disillusionment; producing works that were (in the words of one newspaper reviewer) 'drenched in an intensely phobic atmosphere that must surely be the legacy of war'.[63] Yet the horrors of the war also spurred a new determination to refashion Amsterdam into the most liberal city on earth; a place where no one much cared if you were Jewish or gay or communist, where drugs were sold freely, and where sex workers had a trade union.

It's been an emotionally grinding evening, and after visiting so many places of sorrow and remembrance I feel a sudden urge to be somewhere filled with life. I walk quickly back through the Jewish Quarter, past the Waag and into the Wallen; the warren of streets and alleyways that is better known as the Red Light District. It's about 9.00 pm by now and the streets are a riot of life and colour. Women behind red-lit windows wink and smile at passing men, and people crowd the doorways of kebab shops and burger joints. At one point, I pass a man dressed as a bishop, complete with a diamond-studded crook and tall mitre, drinking vodka from a bottle. Nearby, a woman in a green wig is puking into a bin, while her back is rubbed by a man in a hoody which reads: 'AMSTERDAM: Stoned Again, Horny Again'. It all feels horribly seedy — a slice of the worst of Bangkok imported to northern Europe. But at the same time, it also feels completely safe. There's not a hint of malice or insecurity in the air. Despite the cold, the open-air terraces are bustling. The 17th-century houses are beautifully lit. The streets are cleanly swept and there are even several families with young children happily walking around, bemused by the chaos. A lot of the story of Amsterdam at war is utterly depressing, of course — humanity at its worst. Yet as I look at the modern city around me, I think there's also something indisputably wonderful about the fact that it has recovered from the war so thoroughly. Will Ukraine and Syria and Yemen look like this in another seventy years? I hope so. Despite all the monuments and memorials I've seen today, I think this might be the greatest of them: that Amsterdam has turned into everything the Nazis would have hated it to be.

CHAPTER EIGHT

NDSM, the North, and the River IJ

How Amsterdam's industry collapsed, and how the hipsters took over

London has red buses. Venice has gondolas, San Francisco has streetcars, and New York has yellow taxis. And Amsterdam has its sturdy little blue-and-white ferries, chugging determinedly back and forth across the River IJ, free of charge, whatever the weather. In a city that has (unusually) not a single bridge spanning the river at its heart, these little boats are an institution, and one of the nicest ways to get around the city — especially on days when the rain isn't coming in horizontally.

My plan for today is to cross the river to the area known as NDSM, a few miles west of Central Station, walk for an hour or two through some of Amsterdam's northern suburbs, and then catch another ferry back across the river to the KNSM island, east of the station. NDSM to KNSM: it's a route fit for Scrabble addicts. Along the way, I hope to visit some less touristy parts of the city, learn more about the heavy industry that shaped the north of it, and see how a wave of gentrification is now changing it.

I begin at the rear of the central train station. Until a few years ago, this side of the station — and indeed this whole area of Amsterdam — felt rather neglected and overlooked; a victim of the city's decision to shut itself off from the IJ when building the railways more than a century ago. Recently, however, the area has undergone a belated revival, with new office buildings and cafés opening, a new waterfront promenade leading pedestrians and cyclists towards the Houthavens, a new terminus where Rhine cruise boats can unload their pensioners, and a gleaming Shard-like tower called the IJdock, which juts from the riverbank like a splinter of broken glass. Next to the station, there's also a lovely foot/bike tunnel linking the riverbank with the city centre, which has walls decorated with blue-and-white tiles forming a stunning enlarged version of an 18th-century tableau by Cornelis Bouwmeester. The naval scenes on the tiles are beautifully rendered but did cause some hilarity among Amsterdammers when they were revealed to be portraying a ship that was actually from Rotterdam.[1]

A ferry arrives. The front ramp lowers to meet the pontoon and dozens of cyclists and pedestrians pour out like soldiers storming a beach on D-Day. After letting them pass, I board and find a spot to stand at the rear of the ferry, out on the open deck. The other passengers are a delightful cross-section of modern Amsterdam: a trio of fashionable young men in deliberately ill-fitting clothes, a pair of young mothers with children affixed to various appendages of their bicycles, a woman in a yellow beret carrying an enormous bunch of yellow flowers, and a delivery guy skilfully manoeuvring a cargo bike full of parcels. I'm the only passenger without a bike.

The ferry lurches forward, away from the shore, and the deck falls silent as my fellow passengers disappear into their smart phones. I leave mine in my pocket and focus on the scenery. As we reach the middle of the river, I begin to see clearly how the two banks differ. To the south, towards the city centre, the landscape looks fairly quaint and historic; dominated by low-rise buildings, with slender church spires peeping over the horizon. To the north, the riverbanks look much more modern and industrial, dominated by glassy tower blocks, cranes, pylons, chimneys, and wind turbines. Further off to the west lies the large port and industrial area that stretches to IJmuiden; a dark underbelly of the city which remains hidden from most visitors, but still makes a huge contribution to the region's economy.

Directly across from the train station I see a couple of prominent landmarks. First comes the distinctive offset tower of the horribly branded A'DAM Toren. This was built in the 1960s as an office for Shell but is now a tourist attraction featuring what's supposed to be Europe's highest swing, on which brave visitors can dangle 100 metres above the ground. In old photos, the tower sticks out of the surrounding wasteland like the proverbial sore thumb, but it's now rapidly being overshadowed by the new towers shooting up around it, like a tall man getting lost in a group of lanky Dutchmen. Just out of sight to the right of the tower is the Tolhuistuin, the site of a tollbooth where ships would pay a fee to enter Amsterdam in the Middle Ages. A little further to the east lies another landmark: the Eye Filmmuseum, a sort of Dutch version of Sydney's Opera House, which dominates the skyline on this stretch of river. The museum, which opened in 2012, is certainly striking: a giant, angular, gleaming white structure that rests on 348 pillars and seems to defy all the usual rules of architecture.[2] It's sometimes described as an eye, winking at the city across the water, or (by the architect Cees Dam) as a 'liberating building' that looks like a feather.[3] To me, it's always looked more like a giant white paper plane, crisply folded and crash-landed on the riverbank.

Records show ferries were plying the route across the IJ as early as 1300. For centuries, the north side of the river was the wrong side of the tracks, used mostly for activities considered too ugly or unpleasant to be done closer to the centre. This included the aftermath of executions. A criminal sentenced to death in the city centre in the 17th century was likely to be hanged on the Dam or one of the other central squares, and then have their body taken across the water to Volewijck, near where the Eye Filmmuseum is today, where it would be displayed for the birds to feast on. (The name Volewijck may in fact come from the Dutch word for bird: *vogel*.) One villain — or perhaps victim — disposed of in this way was an eighteen-year-old Danish woman called Elsje Christiaens. She came to Amsterdam from Jutland looking for work in 1664, struggled to pay the rent and had a dispute with her landlady which ended with the landlady lying dead from axe wounds at the bottom of the stairs. Young Elsje told her neighbours all the blood was from a nosebleed, fled the scene, and jumped into the Damrak. However, she was swiftly captured, garroted, and displayed on the Volewijck with her feet dangling in the wind. Rembrandt himself made the journey across the water to draw her, producing two quick, sad, slightly gruesome sketches (now in the Met Museum in

New York) of a young woman slumped like a marionette with cut strings. Looking at the pictures now, it's hard to believe such things ever happened here — the biggest danger you're likely to face these days is being run over by a speeding bicycle.

In Rembrandt's day, and for centuries thereafter, the IJ here would have been busy with farmers rowing over to the city to sell milk, eggs, and cheese. Today there are no farmers, but the river is still teeming with life: bulky barges hauling goods towards the Rhine, small container ships loaded with colourful cuboids, little sailing boats bobbing their way towards the city centre, and cruise ships just arrived from Köln and Koblenz. To the south I see the former warehouses of the Houthavens, where wood used to be processed after arriving from Scandinavia.*

As we continue chugging west, the view to the south is dominated by the giant 'Pontsteiger' apartment building, a colossal structure shaped like a squared-off horseshoe, which epitomises the modern Dutch belief that buildings can be any shape an architect wants as long as they're not rectangular. In 2016, local media reported that a penthouse here was the most expensive apartment in the country, having sold for an estimated sixteen million euros, or €11,000 per square metre.[4] The lucky buyer, a restaurateur called Won Yip, was said to have beaten Brad Pitt in a bidding war.[5] Not all the residents may be so upstanding, though. A few years ago, armed police arrested two suspected gangsters in the car park who had

---

* There are plans to build a new bridge across the IJ from the Azartplein to the Hamerkwartier, and perhaps another from the Houthavens to NDSM, but the plans have been debated for years, and at the time of writing they look unlikely to be built before the mid-2030s. The city's transport chief has pledged to deliver 'a bridge with attitude', whatever that means.

hundreds of thousands of euros in their car. I sometimes come for a swim in the IJ near here after work — the water tastes awful, but on warm evenings every pontoon and harbour wall is packed with young kids joyfully flinging themselves into the river.

There's a loud thunk as the ferry bangs into the north bank. We've arrived at NDSM, which sounds like a questionable sexual predilection but is in fact the name of this neighbourhood of Amsterdam, derived from the *Nederlandsche Dok en Scheepsbouw Maatschappij* (Netherlands Dock and Shipbuilding Company), which used to be based here. There was a time when I visited NDSM often and knew it well, but I haven't been for three or four years now, and I'm immediately astonished by how much it's changed. The area around the ferry dock, which I remember as a neglected wasteland with just one hotel oddly marooned in the middle of it, is now filled with half a dozen shiny new apartment buildings, shops and eateries. A coach is dropping a load of tourists outside a towering hotel. A gleaming hipster café and bakery sells kimchi toasties and lentil stew sandwiches, and signs advertise other establishments with hipster-parodic names like Brooklyn and Cannibale Royale. I count seven Teslas in the adjacent car park. 'I'm just going to get a chai latte,' a passing hipster says to his girlfriend; a cliché made real. I stop to buy a croissant at a bakery and realise with a start that it's a branch of the same small chain which I used to buy bread from when I lived in Uganda. The world can seem very small sometimes. Then, a little further inland, comes another familiar sight: an enormous, much-photographed mural of the original rebellious proto-hipster Anne Frank, covering much of one side of the huge old warehouse. Inside is the STRAAT street art museum — an overpriced but impressive gallery where the artworks on display are often the size of houses. On the surrounding walls are dozens of other pieces of street art. Some are just scribbles but others are astonishingly well done. On one wall I see a black-and-white spray painting of a bewigged gentleman in a ruff collar, looking like a subject for Rembrandt. On another is a portrait of Amy Winehouse looking defiant in a Statue of Liberty crown. Round the corner, an enormous brick wall is dominated by a big portrait of Rembrandt himself, done in the style of Banksy, with Rembrandt looking back over his shoulder with a spray can in hand and a guilty look on his face. Like everyone else walking past, I snap a few photos for social media. A note scribbled on one wall reads: 'Artist at work? Buy them a beer!' Nearby, I spy a group of schoolchildren with a teacher, all wearing plastic aprons and receiving a lesson in how to do graffiti on a warehouse wall. School trips in the Netherlands are not like those elsewhere.

Needless to say, this whole area used to look very different. As I learned on a previous walk, during the 17th-century Golden Age, one of the biggest shipyards in the world lay at Oostenburg, behind where the Maritime Museum is today. However, during the 19th-century second Golden Age, Oostenburg struggled to accommodate a new generation of larger steamships. When one great ship was launched in 1906, the *Leeuwarder Courant* reported that 'Due to the abnormally high water level before the *SS Rembrandt* was discharged through the Oosterdok lock, water pipes burst in thirteen streets of Amsterdam ... Cellars and basements were flooded with wet bedding, and many people had to seek refuge'.[6] Thankfully, a solution to such problems presented itself here, on the north side of the IJ, where there was ample empty space. In 1920 the *Nederlandsche Dok Maatschappij* (Netherlands Dock Company, or NDM) opened a ship repair yard, and two years later came the *Nederlandsche Scheepsbouw Maatschappij* (Netherlands Shipbuilding Company, or NSM). Within a few years, the area had grown to be the biggest shipyard in Europe, with thousands of men toiling to build or repair massive ships which, when finished, slid down the huge ramps into the IJ like whales seeking freedom.

Today, any signs of industrial prosperity have sadly vanished. Rounding a corner, I'm confronted by another enormous red-brick building, as big as an aircraft hangar, emblazoned with the English words 'NETHERLANDS SHIPBUILDING COMPANY'. An enormous concrete slipway leads from the building's massive sliding doors down to the waterline. I climb up to the top of the ramp and am rewarded with a nice view back across the river towards the city centre. I wander slowly down the ramp to the water, taking photographs as I go. A man in a tracksuit walks past listening to the radio in Russian, and a wrecked small motorboat is filled with litter. There's graffiti everywhere, lots of litter, and tall weeds growing from cracks in the concrete. The whole area feels like somewhere a gin-soaked Scottish detective might find a body in a gritty police drama.

World War II hit this area hard. Amsterdam may have been spared the kind of carpet bombing that razed Rotterdam, but the shipyards were first bombed by the Allies during the Nazi occupation, and then sabotaged by the Nazis as they fled. And it wasn't just shipbuilders who were suffering. Between 1940 and 1945, Dutch real GDP almost halved.[7] One American

journalist who visited Amsterdam soon after the war reported
that:

> [while] the Dutch of all classes have always been
> heavy eaters, the war and its resulting shortages
> have pulled their egalitarianism askew ... The Dutch
> workingman, sitting in his single cozy room, is
> entitled, according to his ration cards, to only the
> equivalent of three meatballs and two eggs a week ...
> [plus] one new suit a year, and no Holland gin ever.[8]

The Dutch foreign minister's view was even bleaker.
'The outlook for Holland seems blacker than for any other
country,' he wrote. 'Poverty will be universal.'[9]

Thankfully, that Dutch foreign minister couldn't have
been more wrong. In the space of only a decade or so after
the war, the Dutch not only patched up the holes in their
economy but set it sailing swiftly off on a bold new course.
The Netherlands received over a billion dollars of aid from
the post-war Marshall Plan — roughly ten times as much per
person as the Belgians did — which paid for damaged harbours
to be dredged, cities cleared of rubble, and factories rebuilt.[10]
(Legend has it that when two American officials visited Prime
Minister Willem Drees to discuss the aid plan, Mrs Drees
served them tea and biscuits. The visitors responded by saying
that any country where the first lady served the biscuits herself
deserved everything it wanted.) North Sea gas also brought
huge wealth — over a few decades, the Groningen gas field
generated revenues (in today's money) of over four hundred
billion euros.[11] Also of huge consequence was the way the
Dutch chose to run their economy. The famous Polder Model

is somewhat difficult to define, but essentially aims to split the difference between full-blooded capitalism and full-soya socialism, taking a consensual approach to tackling difficult problems that means no one ever gets exactly what they want, but no one is really unhappy.

Between 1945 and 1950, the Dutch economy grew by almost 20 per cent a year.[12] This growth was of course starting from a low base — if you're at rock bottom, the only way is up. However, rapid growth was maintained for decades, and the country would end up setting a world record for economic growth, going a remarkable 103 quarters (or twenty-six years)[13] without tipping into recession.* Companies like Royal Dutch Shell, Unilever, Philips, P&O, Heineken, and Douwe Egberts grew to become international brands. In 1960, the Netherlands' GDP per capita** was (in constant dollar terms) about one third of the level of the United States, but by the late 1970s they were equal, and by the early 2000s the Dutch had actually pulled ahead of the Americans.[14] By the 2020s, the Netherlands' GDP per capita was about a sixth higher than those of Germany or Belgium, and a third higher than France.[15] The average Amsterdammer currently earns more in four months than the average Greek does in a year.[16] A country devastated by conflict rose from the ashes to become one of the wealthiest places in the world.

The most obvious beneficiary of all this was Rotterdam, rebuilt post-war to be Europe's biggest container port.

---

* The Netherlands' growth record was later broken by Australia, which passed the 104 quarters mark in 2017.

** For the non-economists among us: GDP per capita is the total value of all goods and services in an economy, adjusted for the size of the population. It's essentially a simple measure of how productive or successful a country is.

However, the booming Dutch economy also meant good times for Amsterdam. In 1952, the new Amsterdam-Rhine canal opened, linking the city more directly to the industrial hubs of West Germany, eastern France, and Switzerland. Around the same time, the North Sea Canal was also widened and deepened, and the harbour mouth at IJmuiden was expanded to accommodate larger ships. North of the IJ, the post-war years were a period of unprecedented prosperity. In 1946, the shipbuilding and ship repair firms NSM and NDM merged, forming a new entity called — you guessed it — NDSM. Between 1951 and 1957 Dutch ship production doubled. Many workers at NDSM assumed they had a job for life. 'I saw the dramas in the [collapsing] textile industry in Twente on television,' an employee called Arie de Ridde once told *Ons Amsterdam*, 'and I thought, luckily, that won't happen to us. There is no such thing as Amsterdam without shipbuilding.'[17] 'Once you worked at the yard, you never left,' one historian recorded. '40-year company anniversaries were commonplace, and a few reached 50 years.'[18] For local residents, the launch of a new ship was a major event, with brass bands playing and children cheering as huge vessels slid into the water. 'The smell of a ship!' an NDSM welder told *Ons Amsterdam*. 'Such a mixture of smells, of the cargo, the galley, the ship itself. Every ship smells different. Even when I see a boat passing by, I can smell the smell.'[19] North Amsterdammers took real pride in being part of a thriving industry which was putting their city back on the global map. Half a century after its second Golden Age, Amsterdam was experiencing a third.

At NDSM, the glory years didn't last. In 1945, the end of World War II sparked an ugly battle in Indonesia, with Dutch forces fighting brutally against guerilla forces headed by Sukarno, fighting for independence. After several years of bloody conflict, the Dutch essentially gave up the fight in 1949, and Indonesia became independent. In Amsterdam, the loss of the Netherlands' Asian colony dealt a blow to companies that had grown rich trading, building or repairing colonial ships. As the size of container ships and oil tankers continued to grow, Amsterdam — with its narrow canals and harbours, and locks limiting its access to the sea — struggled to compete. A series of bailouts and restructurings attempted to keep the show on the road, but to little avail. In 1957 Dutch shipbuilders produced more than 170 oceangoing vessels, but by the mid-1980s this had fallen to fewer than 30 per year.[20]

In Amsterdam's north, the shipbuilders didn't go down without a fight. In 1960, four thousand workers at NDSM went on strike, calling for a shorter working week and paid travel expenses. They won after just a few days, encouraging them to repeat the trick, and throughout the 1960s and 70s there were regular strikes in Amsterdam involving thousands of workers. However, all the uproar only delayed the inevitable. By the early 2000s, Amsterdam shipbuilding had mostly gone the way of British coalmining.* For workers who'd built their whole lives around the shipyards, the collapse was devastating. In 1994 *Het Parool* reported:

> The employees who ended up on the street overnight
> still have the aftertaste of this bitter pill in their
> mouths ... For many people, the bankruptcy of
> the [shipyards] was a huge blow, requiring the use

---

*   There are still some smaller firms that do good business making specialist vessels such as dredgers and cable-layers. One firm sells a line of superyachts with prices starting at €50 million.

of psychiatrists and pills. Marriages broke down, people had to move because the rent for housing became too high. Some are still having a hard time with it. 'The future you had in mind was completely gone,' one said.[21]

Another NDSM worker, Flip Waldram, told a historian: 'I saw the closure coming, so I could prepare for it. And I thought: enough hobbies, I'll manage. Still, the blow hit hard ... Shipbuilding had become part of our identity. It was incomprehensible that it suddenly disappeared. I had just completed my fortieth company anniversary.'[22] North Amsterdam would never be the same again.

I leave NDSM and walk inland, away from the river, heading northwest. Further from the waterfront, the landscape quickly turns drearily suburban: wide modern roads, glassy tower blocks, and a big bell-shaped building called The Curve. A few kids mess about on skateboards on a concrete ramp which is graffitied: '*NOORD WORDT STEEDS MINDER GROF*' — 'North [Amsterdam] is getting less rough'. After five minutes or so, I turn north onto a smaller road and find myself in a neighbourhood of neat little two-storey houses with red tile roofs, squeezed alongside one another like matchboxes on a supermarket shelf. It looks a lot like a post-war council housing estate in Britain, but with more bikes parked outside. A couple of homes are flying upside-down Dutch flags — a provocative sign of support for anti-government protestors who oppose the climate policies of their leaders in The Hague. Going one better, one house is proudly flying the flag of Rotterdam's Feyenoord football club — a suicidally brave move, in this Ajax-supporting city. Some of the houses are a little scruffy and when I later check the statistics, I find that 80 per cent of the homes in this area are social housing and the average income here is only €22,500 per person – meaning the average resident could afford to buy a penthouse at the Pontsteiger after working more than 700 years.[23]

Fifteen minutes after leaving the ruined shipyards, I arrive at a pleasant grassy triangle, the size of a couple of football pitches, tucked in between Pomonastraat and the prettily named Perenpad (Pears Path). Some boys are playing football, and a young woman is trying to teach a cute black puppy to sit, although he just wants to chew her shoes. Walking towards the rear of the triangle, I find a big six-chimneyed medical centre with distinctive architecture: a curved entrance like a watchtower, a steeply sloping tile roof, and a façade dressed in rippled red tiles. It's an example, I think, of the famous Amsterdam School of architecture pioneered in this city between the world wars by architects including Michel de Klerk and Joseph Crouwel. They used Art Deco influences to construct affordable buildings that were enlivened with swooping brick walls, colourful windows, wrought-iron railings, and turret-like towers. (Walk near Zaanstraat today and you can still see the most famous example: de Klerk's Het Schip apartment building, with its red-brick façade and swooping curves like the inside of a seashell.)

I walk across the grass and find, under a great weeping willow tree, something I've been looking out for: a handsome bronze bust of a man called Arie Keppler, looking dapper in a trilby and bow tie. Keppler isn't exactly a household name these days, but he did a huge amount to shape the way

Amsterdam looks today. Born in the 1870s, Keppler served as the city's Director of Municipal Housing from mid-World War I until just before World War II. One Amsterdam alderman described him as 'a difficult man, but also a genius', who stopped at nothing in his quest to deliver 'a dignified home for every worker'.[24] It's been estimated that on Keppler's watch, a total of 11,000 municipal homes and 21,000 association homes were built, giving tens of thousands of lower-income Amsterdammers the chance to live happy, comfortable lives — including many north of the IJ.[25]

World War I may have largely passed the Netherlands by, but it did have a large political effect, in that from about 1918 onwards, Dutch leaders became nervous about the risk of a communist uprising against the established order. Such fears were probably overblown — when Karl Marx visited Amsterdam in 1872, his speech arguing for 'the elevation of the worker and the destruction of capital' attracted only about a hundred people and, a journalist reported, 'came to a very quiet end'.[26] But there were some signs of unrest: in 1916 there were riots over the price of food in the city, and in 1917 a potato shortage sparked an attack on police in the Jordaan 'by 200 women from the Kattenburg district, armed with bayonets, revolvers and stones'. [27]

Housing was the biggest problem. During the second Golden Age, the supply of homes had failed to keep up with the growth of the population, and in places like the Jordaan, many families were squeezed into small spaces with terrible sanitation. Under these circumstances, it was no surprise that the Spanish Flu pandemic of 1918–19 hit the city hard. Well over twenty thousand people in the Netherlands died during the pandemic, including perhaps two thousand Amsterdammers. Some Dutch cities closed schools and other services but Amsterdam, worried about the social effects of lockdown, opted to remain largely open. National newspapers carried headlines that would be eerily familiar to readers a century or so later: 'Closure of public schools extended another week', 'On orders of the mayor the carnival is cancelled', 'Doctors are not yet sure whether schools are infection hubs – children might spread the sickness more'. 'In every neighbourhood one sees funeral processions passing from morning until late into the afternoon,' *Het Volk* reported, 'and on the roads leading to the cemeteries there are constantly funerals coming and going'.[28]

After the pandemic, the Dutch authorities finally began tackling some deep-rooted social problems. In the 1920s thousands of new low-cost homes were built as part of a push led by the socialist F.M. Wibaut, who got rich in the timber trade and then joined the city council. Several parts of Amsterdam were transformed by new developments, but the area north of the IJ was one of those most affected. 'The director of the Municipal Housing Service, Mr A. Keppler, has drawn up an expansion plan for the area north of the IJ, which has now been finalised', one newspaper reported in 1926. 'The starting point for [future growth] must be the IJ, which provides many jobs through its port facilities ... Spacious, hygienic, industrial buildings can arise, and those who want to enjoy the pleasure of the perfect country life will be able to obtain it in the vicinity of the big city. More joy in life, more peace, can be achieved for many with the realisation of the plan.'[29]

In 1919 construction of the first new suburb near NDSM, Tuindorp Oostzaan, started; by 1924, it was almost finished, and construction of the neighbouring Tuindorp Nieuwendam and Tuindorp Watergraafsmeer (later known as Betondorp) was well underway. By the mid-1920s, something resembling a whole new town had been created north of the IJ, including over a thousand houses, more than three dozen shops and one especially grand house allocated to the local doctor. The new neighbourhoods had much in common with England's Garden Cities, aiming to combine the best features of both the city and the countryside, with lots of fresh air and space, plenty of grass and trees, and good civic amenities like schools, libraries and doctors' surgeries. The writer Jan Donkers, who grew up in Tuindorp Nieuwendam, described the homes there as 'the pinnacle of luxury at the time, [with] a shower cubicle and three bedrooms on the top floor. A wonderful place to grow up, so close to Waterland that in the summer you could hear the croaking frog orchestra through the open window'.[30] Competition for houses here was fierce and those working in the docks nearby were bumped to the top of the list. There was one big disadvantage to living here, though: pubs were banned.

Thanks in part to all the new housing, Amsterdam's population kept climbing. Yet for the city planners, this wasn't enough. Amsterdam had to keep evolving. In the mid-1930s, the expansionist impulse reached its zenith with the famous *Algemeen Uitbreidingsplan*, or AUP or General Expansion Plan; an official proposal to expand Amsterdam radically in the coming decades, masterminded by Cornelis van Eesteren. Van Eesteren had studied architecture and planning in Rotterdam and Paris, and subsequently made his name with a bold design for Berlin's Unter den Linden. In Amsterdam, his ambitious vision called for high-density housing to be packed into the countryside towards Haarlem and Schiphol, interspersed with wide boulevards, parks, and sports fields. To some it all seemed like an impossible pipe dream, but eventually a surprising proportion of the plan was implemented. Five new neighbourhoods were established to the west of the old city centre, at Slotermeer, Slotervaart, Overtoomse Veld, Geuzenveld, and Osdorp. Low-cost housing was the priority, but other daring projects were also allowed. In 1932 the first Dutch skyscraper had been built, in the Rivierenbuurt. Designed by J.F. Staal, it was an ugly apartment building that had a whopping twelve storeys and innovative facilities including a lift, rubbish chutes, central heating, hot water, and an electric bell system. Known simply as the *Wolkenkrabber* (Cloud-scraper), Staal's tower was about a tenth the height of the Empire State Building, which was built around the same time. Visitors found the views from the top floor — forty metres above street level — dizzying.

World War II put a serious dampener on Amsterdam's expansion. However, when the conflict ended and the authorities raced to rebuild, they dusted off pre-war plans for expanding the city. 'There was nothing in my office save two copies of the General Expansion Plan of 1935', the new Alderman of Public works said of his first day at work in 1948. 'I knew nothing of urban development, but I read it in one go, throughout the night. I then called my chief of Public Works and told him to start working right away.'[31] A frenzy of construction ensued, with new homes and office blocks springing up all over the city. In some cases, things moved so fast that constructors began driving massive pilings into the ground before they'd received official permission to build. If anyone asked, they sometimes got out of trouble by arguing the poles had been 'vertically stored'.

I wander around for a while, zigzagging my way up and down narrow residential streets until I find myself on the Meteorenweg, a wide road of terraced houses. The homes here are chintzy, with lots of gardens adorned with stone buddhas, colourful plastic butterflies, concrete gnomes, and little signs pontificating on the importance of family and home. However, the neighbourhood is far from unpleasant. Every home is neat and tidy, and most have expensive-looking cars parked outside. After consulting my map a few times, I eventually arrive at a modest terraced house that stands out from the others, thanks to a big blue flag hanging above the front windows. I've heard this home is opened a handful of times a year for people curious to see inside a pre-war home. I pull a handle next to the red front door, a bell rings, and I am invited inside by the fellow who runs the place; a cheerful, chatty man of about sixty with a shaved head and stubbly grey beard. He swiftly explains that the long-time resident of this house had kept the interior unchanged since the 1930s or 40s, and when she died, the decision was made to keep the house exactly as it was, as a time capsule showing what life was like in this area nearly a century ago. The man then asks what brought me here. I mumble something about working nearby and he swiftly asks, as if by reflex, whether I work at Damen — a shipyard near here. I tell him no, I'm just passing through, and I don't think many people work at the shipyards these days, anyway. 'Yes,' he replies. 'The area around NDSM, it's developing so fast. If I don't ride my bike there for two weeks, then when I go again I see that everything's changed! There are new buildings everywhere!'

The man is distracted by the arrival of another visitor, and I begin exploring the house. It won't take long: the building is what Brits might call a 'two-up, two-down', with just a couple of adjoining rooms and a small kitchen downstairs, and two bedrooms and a bathroom upstairs. The décor reminds me of my late grandparents' house — spotlessly clean but also musty and cluttered, with every available surface filled with knick-knacks, framed photographs, and ornaments. In the dining room there's an ancient gramophone in a dark wooden cabinet and three sewing machines standing by the window. In the kitchen, I nosily open a cupboard and find several glass jars of home-pickled green beans, each with a handwritten label reading '1968'. Leaning against one wall is an old, framed poster warning that:

MALARIA ravages Tuindorp Oostzaan
MALARIA undermines your workforce
MALARIA costs you money
MALARIA spoils your holiday ...
MALARIA must disappear[*]

---

[*] Thanks to the swampy terrain, malaria was common around Amsterdam until surprisingly recently. In 1826 alone, 2,400 Amsterdammers died of 'malarial disease'. In the 1930s, doctors' practices displayed posters bearing poems: *Ziet ge muggen, lang van poot/Aarzel niet, maar sla ze dood/Klein is de mug, maar groot het leed/Veroorzaakt door een muggebeet! (A mosquito is neither friend nor pet/So don't hesitate and kill him dead/Small the bug but big the blight/Caused by a mosquito bite!)* As temperatures rise due to climate change, some have speculated that the disease may make a comeback. (Rachel Schats, 'Malaise and mosquitos: Osteoarchaeological evidence for malaria in the medieval Netherlands', Analecta Praehistorica Leidensia, 2015)

I'm not the only person poking around. The upstairs is filled with people, most of whom are a good thirty or forty years older than me. For many of them, coming to a house like this offers a trip down memory lane. 'I remember my mother washing my clothes in one of these!' a woman of about seventy excitedly tells her husband, gesturing to a decrepit-looking mangle and metal washtub. Twice in three minutes I hear a telephone alarm going off reminding someone to take their medication. Above the stairs, framed pictures show NDSM in its heyday, with giant ships being pecked at by cranes, *Titanic*-style ocean liners heading out to sea, and propellers the size of houses being fixed to ships in dry dock. In one bedroom there's also a video playing of the great *dijkdoorbraak* (dike break-through) of 1960; an event as firmly etched on the memories of older people in this area as the Blitz was on a certain generation of Londoners. The film shows cars floating in the streets as people are rescued by boat, fleeing residents putting their bikes on their roofs before they leave, and children being passed over the dikes to safety. Once the floodwaters receded, the government provided residents with compensation. According to local legend, the payouts were so generous that for years afterwards, locals prayed before going to sleep: 'Lord, give us today our daily bread — and a flood every year.'

I'm already behind schedule so, after twenty minutes, I leave the museum house and continue walking briskly along the Meteorenweg and then into a maze of small residential streets. Many homes look a good deal newer than the original houses of the interwar years, but all follow similar principles: two storeys, cheap prefab or brick construction, small gardens cluttered with trinkets and children's bicycles. In several places, residents have decorated the walls of their garden sheds with huge blown-up photographs, including tropical scenes: a Greek island surrounded by a turquoise sea here, a beach of pure white sand there. I'm tickled by the thought of people sitting in their chilly gardens and basking in Mediterranean views.

At first the names of the streets I walk past are pleasingly astronautical: Nieuwe Maanstraat (New Moon Street), Poolsterstraat (Pole Star Street), Kometensingel (Comet Canal), Uranusstraat (Uranus Street). After a while, though, I notice them becoming fruitier: Ananasplein (Pineapple Square), Pruimenstraat (Plums Street), Abrikozenstraat (Apricots Street), Citroenenstraat (Lemons Street), Mandarijnenstraat (Mandarins Street). Studying my map, I belatedly realise where I am — an area of Tuindorp Oostzaan named, on account of its colourful street names, Tuttifruttidorp (Tutti Frutti Village). The vitamin-filled nomenclature isn't an accident. Amsterdam's planners long took the view that shipyard workers were a bit like pet rabbits or budgies — if you gave them enough light and fresh air, they'd live longer and have fewer health problems. People who lived here were in many ways fulfilling the Dutch dream: home ownership, steady employment, happy children. Yet the social pressures to conform could be intense, and Dutch society between and after the wars was still permeated by conservative religious values. The new suburbs' odd mix of freedom and pressure to conform was captured well by H.M. van den Brink in his novel *On the Water*, in which he describes an antebellum neighbourhood that:

had been planned in the depression by the city's
strong men, patriarchs with a social conscience who
saw it as their sacred duty to give the population
four walls and a roof over their heads ... subjecting
us to a geometrically pure street plan, a succession
of squares, shops, bath houses and doorways which
one could traverse in only one direction and a house
design that was so compelling that not so much as a
chair, let alone a table or a city, could be placed in
a spot which the powers that be considered socially
irresponsible.[32]

Despite its anarchic reputation, much of Amsterdam has
always been as orderly and well-organised as an accountants'
convention.

Not all post-war developments have been so successful,
though. One development in particular — the Bijlmer, which
lies a few miles southeast of the city centre — has become
rather notorious among Dutch people, and among urban
planners around the world. The Bijlmer sprang up quite
quickly in the decades after World War II.* Between 1968 and
1975 alone, about thirteen thousand high-rise homes were
built here, spread across more than thirty big tower blocks.[33]
At the time it was built, the development was considered
innovative and attractive. Tall towers were set between green
parks and ponds, and roads and railways were elevated above
street level. In April 1968, the *Algemeen Dagblad* reported

---

* The area is technically called the 'Bijlmermeer', but many
  Amsterdammers call it just 'the Bijlmer'. For simplicity, I've used
  the latter name throughout. It's pronounced Bye-ma. For more
  information on this area, see the final chapter.

excitedly that 'the residential area of the future' was nearly complete. The Bijlmer was, the paper said, getting a '*bosachtig karakter*' — a 'forested character', thanks to forty thousand trees being planted between the towers.[34] By November 1968, papers were reporting the arrival of the 'first resident of Amsterdam's newest city area ... the family R.J. Copray, father, mother and six children'.[35] Mayor Gijs van Hall said the Bijlmer would be 'more beautiful and modern' than any other city in the world.[36]

In time, however, the Bijlmer became not famous, but infamous. The development's designers had imagined the small apartments here would suit young families, but demand was low, and many apartments remained empty or were illegally inhabited by squatters. Others provided cheap homes for immigrants, including many from Suriname, which had gained its independence from the Netherlands in 1975, soon after the towers opened. A remarkable one-third of Suriname's population moved to the Netherlands after independence,[37] and many found themselves living in the towers there — so many, in fact, that planes which flew from Suriname to Amsterdam were sometimes jokingly called 'the Bijlmer Express'. On the ground, meanwhile, social problems multiplied. As an article by the academic F.A.G. Wassenberg explained:

> Vacancies arose, turnover rates were high, there were enormous quality-of-life problems and the financial situation was deplorable ... Surveys held among residents uncovered the same grievances time after time: degradation, vandalism, crime and a lack of safety ... The combination of high unemployment

rates, high crime rates ... and the large number of
single-parent families ... provided a very negative
stigma, certainly among outsiders ... More and more
problems arose, which all spiralled together into
decay.[38]

In the 1980s, the area began to improve somewhat,
thanks in part to the opening of the Ajax football stadium
and several other entertainment venues in the area. But still,
in 1985 around a quarter of apartments remained empty.[39]
For many Dutch people, 'Bijlmer' became a byword for urban
poverty. One expert described the area as 'an object lesson in
"how not to do it" as regards town planning'.[40]

Sadly, the Bijlmer was not the only part of the city to
experience social and economic problems as its immigrant
population grew. As the Dutch economy boomed after the
war, labour shortages arose, and the government began
encouraging the recruitment of 'guest workers' from Morocco
and Turkey. The first Moroccan migrant arrived in 1961, and
by 2012 Amsterdam had 34,000 first-generation Moroccan
migrants who had been born abroad, and another 34,000
second-generation migrants whose parents were born
abroad.[41] These 'guest workers' and their children were
joined by other migrants from former Dutch colonies, from
within the European Union, and from places like Bosnia
and Somalia. Together, these new arrivals brought about a
profound shift in the demographics of the city. At the time
of writing, the city council says Amsterdam is home to no
fewer than 174 different nationalities, including about 13,000
Italians, 12,000 Turks, 11,000 Brits, 11,000 Germans, 9,000
French and 8,000 Americans.[42] More than half (59 per cent)

of the city's residents now have a 'migration background',[43] with one or both parents born abroad.*

Shifting demographics sometimes caused social problems. Many immigrants came from former Dutch colonies and arrived with a good knowledge of the local language and culture. In the book *Ethnic Amsterdam*, Daphne Laberga said of her arrival from Curaçao:

> When I arrived in Amsterdam in 1952, to begin my training as a library assistant, I did not have the feeling ... that I was in a strange land. I had heard about the Leidseplein and the Leidsestraat and knew also that I must go past the first three canals to come to the famous Kalverstraat ... In Curaçao where I was born, we learned so much about the Netherlands in school, sometimes even more than we knew about our own island.[44]

However, 'guest workers' from Morocco and Turkey usually lacked such advantages. Interestingly, it seems that Amsterdam took a different approach to integration than some other parts of the country. Scholars drew a contrast between the migration policy adopted by Rotterdam, which emphasised law and order and effectively tried to force

---

*   One reason this country is a popular destination: the fact that over 90 per cent of Dutch people can speak good English, with most Dutch people able to 'read advanced texts with ease' and 'negotiate a contract with a native English speaker' (although interestingly, proficiency is higher in Groningen and Utrecht than in Amsterdam). (Education First, 'English Proficiency Index', 2023). For a Zambian, Iraqi or Syrian who speaks English, the language barriers are much lower here than in, say, Rome.

integration, and the gentler approach taken by Amsterdam, which emphasised the benefits of multiculturalism. The latter approach is generally seen as having been less effective, as it led to many minorities living in their own segregated communities. A 2009 study found that 73 per cent of Moroccan men living in Amsterdam had 'difficulties' speaking Dutch, and 79 per cent of Turkish men had difficulties. Fifty per cent of all Moroccan and Turkish immigrants said they rarely used the Dutch language and had difficulty speaking it when they had to.[45] The Moroccan-born poet Mohammed Chacha wrote a verse that movingly expressed the alienation some migrants felt:

Before Mhand left he'd been taught one important thing:
'Do your work and stay away from extremists!'
He worked in the factories. He cleaned the toilets.
He washed dishes. He made beds.
He began to see that he would stay.
He sent for his wife.
He produced children who grew up and went to school.
They forgot how to speak Berber.
Dutch flowed from their mouths like water.
...
His children break his heart.
One son is behind bars, the other wants to change his passport.
The bread sticks in his throat.
He has reunited his family.
He himself, however, is nowhere to be found.[46]

There are of course many migrants in Amsterdam (and elsewhere) who integrate well and feel at home in their new country. The 150-seat Dutch parliament includes numerous people of Moroccan and Turkish descent,[47] and at the time of writing, one of the most powerful politicians in the country is Dilan Yeşilgöz, who was born in Turkey to a Kurdish father and moved to the Netherlands as a refugee when she was still a small child.* However, there are many others who struggle to find their place, and who seem poorly served by the government's approach to integration. I'm often struck by the fact that if you visit a doctor, pharmacist or an accountant in London, there's a reasonable chance they'll be someone with a migration background. But do the same in Amsterdam, and there's little chance their family will be from Morocco. And while a Brit of immigrant descent will generally be accepted as 'British', any Dutch citizen with Moroccan parents will almost always be called 'Moroccan', as if their Dutch citizenship is conditional or even meaningless.

For many years, debates about asylum and immigration were mainly the preserve of academics and policymakers, but after 9/11, they suddenly became front-page news. Outspoken critics of Islam — including Pim Fortuyn, Geert Wilders, Ayaan Hirsi Ali, and Theo van Gogh — called on the Dutch government to abandon its 'failed' policy of multiculturalism and curb immigration. In 2002, Fortuyn was shot and killed by a radical left-winger, just before elections in which he might well have become prime minister. Two years later, Theo van Gogh was brutally murdered while cycling near

---

* Amusingly, the two most prominent politicians on the anti-immigrant right, Geert Wilders and Thierry Baudet, both have Indonesian ancestry. Another, Caroline van der Plas, is half Irish.

the Oosterpark. His killer was an Islamic extremist called Mohammed Bouyeri, who shot van Gogh several times and nearly decapitated him with a knife, before pinning a note to van Gogh's body which threatened to also kill Hirsi Ali. Bouyeri fled, but was quickly shot in the leg by police and apprehended.**

Van Gogh's murder would have been shocking if it happened anywhere, but it was perhaps particularly so in a city that had long prided itself on its tolerance of outspoken eccentrics and provocateurs. After the murder, Amsterdam's integration policy took heavy fire from politicians and commentators. 'We've been too naïve,' the hardline immigration minister Rita Verdonk said.[48] At the spot where van Gogh was murdered, one member of the public placed a toy monkey with two plasters crossed over its mouth and a sign reading: 'The Netherlands died here on 2 November. I'm suddenly a total stranger in my own country.'[49] Mohammed Bouyeri, meanwhile, was chillingly unrepentant. 'I don't feel your pain. I don't have any sympathy for you,' he told van Gogh's family during his trial. 'I did what I did purely out of my beliefs … If I ever get free, I would do it again.'[50]

Thankfully, the vast majority of Amsterdam's Muslims have no truck with such beliefs. But deep divides remain, and the murder of van Gogh continues to cast a long shadow. Today, he's memorialised in Amsterdam in a low-key way. There is an official monument to him in the Oosterpark; a rather underwhelming steel profile of a man's face called *De Schreeuw*, or *The Scream*. But if you visit the spot where

---

** If you're interested in Dutch politics and the assassinations of the early 2000s, I highly recommend a book called *Why the Dutch Are Different*, which goes into more detail. It was written by me.

he was killed, on the Linnaeusstraat, you find no plaque or memorial stone, just a shop with the improbable name 'All the Luck in the World'. The last time I visited, the pavement close to the spot where van Gogh died was partly blocked by a big black advertising board, reading: 'GET INSPIRED AND FIND YOUR LUCK!' As an absurdist provocateur, van Gogh would probably have appreciated the irony.

I continue walking east, and cross a small canal at the Bongerdkade which is lined with houseboats like floating garden sheds. To my left, a patch of wasteland is filled with half-finished apartment buildings. The streets are quiet and there's almost no one around, apart from a father walking home with a tired boy in a football strip, and a black cat walking proudly along the pavement with a dead mouse in its mouth. I turn south for a block or two and then continue east, following the Klaprozenweg parallel to the river. I've left the twee suburbs behind now and am again astonished by the number of new buildings which have appeared since I last visited a couple of years ago. An area that I remember as patchily inhabited now contains many modern towers of gleaming glass and concrete, more reminiscent of lower Manhattan than old Amsterdam. There seems to be a big building site on every corner, with pile drivers hammering long poles into the ground and pumps draining water from boggy ground. 'Nova Zembla lofts' one new apartment building is called, in an unlikely tribute to Arctic explorers of old. I stop to take a picture and a little white dog that looks like a miniature polar bear flings itself violently at the glass balustrade of a balcony, yapping furiously. It's hard not to be impressed by the pace of change: I can practically feel the neighbourhood becoming more prosperous by the minute. Yet I also wonder if something important is being lost as this part of the city gentrifies. How long will communities like Tuindorp Oostzaan last, before ordinary working families are squeezed out by overpaid expats and professionals? The average house price in this area has nearly doubled in the last ten years.

Just when I'm beginning to get bored of the scenery, it changes again. I turn off the main road and within moments find myself on a delightful brick-paved country lane — the Buiksloterdijk — which curves along the top of a dike next to a pretty little waterway. Down off the dike to my left, I see a sweet little church, the Buiksloterkerk, which reminds me of the ones you see in old Dutch towns in upstate New York, which were built around the same time. The road is lined on one side with nice old cottages, many of them built partly from red brick and partly from brightly painted wood. Some have traditional Dutch wooden shutters next to the windows, with a diamond red and white pattern; others have handsome bell-shaped gables.

A ginger cat comes and rubs his head playfully against my ankles, then runs off when I try to pet him. On one doorstep, a pair of women are delightedly reading a toddler a book about a bear; on another, an older woman sits with her eyes closed, blissfully basking in the bright midday sun. I feel as if I've suddenly stepped through a magical portal and been transported from lower Manhattan to a village in the 1950s. My English obsession with house prices kicks in again, and I turn to Google: €990,000 for a neat little family home.

Consulting my notebook and map, I realise there's a good reason why this place feels like a village separate from the rest of Amsterdam — that is, until quite recently, exactly what it was: one of several small rural towns and villages which were enveloped by Amsterdam, in much the same way as London has absorbed places like Greenwich and Richmond. On New Year's Day 1921, Amsterdam more than doubled in size as it formally annexed the surrounding municipalities of Nieuwendam, Ransdorp, Watergraafsmeer, Sloten, and Buiksloot, collectively home to tens of thousands of people.[51] Some residents were delighted to see their municipalities absorbed by their bigger neighbour. The local newspaper *De Waterlander* wrote: 'Everyone knows that the future ... is very dark ... [but] what a bright vista suddenly opens up in that darkness when we think of Nieuwendam as incorporated into Amsterdam!'[52] Others, though, were angry to see their communities being swallowed up by the growing city. 'We are a rural municipality on the border of Amsterdam, built to stay green,' one villager told a reporter.[53] The Mayor of Broek in Waterland, H.G.M. te Boekhorst, was even firmer: 'Grass is sacred to us, I always say. Our construction volume is about five new homes per year ... Instead of building the new, we should focus on restoring the old!'[54] The city's boundaries have continued to shift, though: in 2022 the municipality of Weesp, about fifteen kilometres southeast of the city centre, was formally swallowed up by Amsterdam, following a ceremony where the Weesp mayor solemnly removed his chains at midnight. 'I am and remain a Weesper,' he said. 'If we can't have our own mayor any more, so be it.'[55]

I continue walking east. Outside one house, there's what the Dutch call a *straatbieb* — a little cupboard of books that functions as a free lending library, provided by local volunteers. I happily pick up a Hella Haasse novella and make a mental note to come back and donate a few books to the collection later in the week. A pair of young men walk past loudly discussing the latest Dutch political party to have risen rapidly to national prominence by promising to represent the interests of real people against the elites. I can't help but recall a line from Mark Twain that seems apt in this country: politicians and diapers must be changed often, and for the same reason.

I cross a bridge over the unpronounceable Noordhollandschkanaaldijk and soon find myself back on a busy residential road, with lots of cars driving too fast. I pass a chip shop with the unlikely name of Pont Neuf, and kebab shop called Great Sandwich House. Peeking down the side streets I can see many homes have been boarded up and are presumably slated for demolition. There's litter in the streets, and I see several parked bicycles that have had almost every component apart from the frame stolen. The traffic is relentless, but I see only one other person walking past: a man who impassively watches his mean-looking dog do a massive shit on the pavement. My head once again spins from the contrasts: the NSDM hipsters, the twee suburbs of Tuindorp, the village-like Buiksloterdijk, and this rather bleak place are all within about forty minutes' walk of each other. Yet even here, there are signs of gentrification. Amid the litter and social housing and petrol stations, I see a gourmet pizza restaurant, a tapas place, and a 'design gallery and event space' called VANMOKUM, which has distressed metal furniture and antique typewriters on display. A little further along the road there's even an old warehouse that has been painted pink and now contains a roller disco. Further still, an old warehouse contains a pop-up pizzeria, which is packed with male hipsters with Freddie Mercury moustaches. A sign explains that this area was once dominated by the Draka wire and cable factory, which in 1960 employed 1,400 people but has now been converted into 'a sustainable urban district', whatever that means. Give it a few years, I think, and this place will be crawling with vintage clothing shops, craft breweries, and artisan bakeries.

I reach the IJ again, just in time to hear the siren that sounds when an Amsterdam ferry's ramp is descending. I break into a jog and make it on board just before the boat departs, heading south across the IJ back towards the city centre. It's getting chilly, so I hunker inside out of the wind, next to a woman in thigh-high snakeskin boots who can't stop yawning. There are, as always, dozens of cyclists on the ferry but only three or four pedestrians, sticking carefully to the edges of the boat lest they be swept away by a tide of disembarking bikes. I can spot the expats a mile off: they're the only cyclists wearing helmets.*

A few minutes after leaving the north shore of the IJ, the ferry passes a little grassy lump in the middle of the river, sticking out of the water like a muddy little iceberg. I realise this must be the *Kompaseiland*, or Compass Island — so called because it was once the place where ships leaving Amsterdam stopped to calibrate their compasses. There's been talk of building houses on the island, but they haven't materialised yet. Moments later, the ferry clanks into its

---

*   Surveys show that about a third of Dutch people own a bike helmet, but only 2 per cent always wear one when cycling. (SWOV, 'Hoe vaak wordt in Nederland een fietshelm gedragen?', 2019)

destination: the island known as KNSM, which is shaped like a battleship and lies east of Central Station, just south of the Kompaseiland. Cyclists pour out of the front of the ferry and I follow them onto the quayside, where there's an impressively hideous fountain, consisting of a charging horse with water spouting out of his nostrils. I walk a short distance west into Java Island, which neighbours KNSM and is connected to it by several small bridges, and then loop back onto KNSM again. There's not much to see here — dozens of modern apartment buildings, small areas of parkland and a few shops and restaurants. Only the street names point to a more exotic past: Sumatrakade, Javakade, Levantkade. A sign scrawled on a sheet of metal reads: 'THANK YOU FOR STEALING MY STUFF YOU MOTHERFUCKER.'

Like NDSM, this area was once one of the most important centres for industry in the city. Its history dates back to the late 1800s, when shipowners began complaining to the municipality that their operations on the IJ were hindered by wind and waves. In the 1890s the authorities built a new breakwater jutting into the IJ, which was later raised and widened to form the island. In 1903, parts of it were taken over by the *Koninklijke Nederlandsche Stoomboot-Maatschappij* (the Royal Dutch Steamship Company, or KNSM), which specialised in trading coffee, tobacco, cocoa, and wood. By 1910, 1,600 ships from the East Indies and Americas were mooring there annually,[56] making it one of the busiest spots in town and a key node in the Dutch colonial empire. However, as at NDSM, the glory days didn't last. The shift to containerised shipping killed off a lot of the island's business, and in 1977, the KNSM company packed up and moved out. Left empty, the old warehouses soon degenerated, and by the 1980s, the area was being described in the press as an 'industrial wasteland', filled with only 'strange buildings [and] drug trade'.[57] High cranes were dismantled and grass grew between the rails of the train tracks. However, the island was not completely deserted. After the shipping companies left, squatters moved in. For a while, there was a large hippy camp on KNSM, along with the legendary bar in a bus known as the Busbar, run by some lads from Bradford. Police largely avoided the area, and the camp became a sort of scruffier, poorer version of the famous Christiania commune in Copenhagen. In September 1988, the Surinamekade hosted Amsterdam's first ever 'house party', when two thousand people gathered in an abandoned warehouse to listen to a new style of dance music with a rhythm of 120 beats per minute. 'Sometimes I had the impression that I had ended up with some sort of African tribe,' the DJ at that first party, Eddy de Clercq, told the writer Job de Wit. 'All those people were dancing and moving, very violently ... not not for two or three songs, but non-stop, five or six hours in a row.'[58]

These days, the KNSM and Java islands are more likely to host a toddlers' play group than an all-night rave. In the 1990s, the islands saw some of the most frenzied housing development in Amsterdam, with thousands of new homes added. The architect Rem Koolhaas proposed putting a highway along the waterfront like the one in Manhattan — an idea that city officials liked, but which was eventually abandoned for financial reasons, to locals' relief. The city decided instead to focus on building what planners call 'compact, sustainable communities'.[59] Some warehouses were demolished, and others were converted into galleries, architects' studios, and designer furniture shops. (One now houses a ceramics shop with the remarkable name of *Pols Potten* — Pol's Pots.) In their industrial heyday, the islands were poorly connected to the city centre, because authorities were reluctant to build bridges that would obstruct freight traffic. Now, though, bridges enable cyclists to reach the city centre in about ten minutes. According to the geographer Kimberley Kinder, one of the designers behind the development read a book on Japanese hillside villages and decided the rejuvenated neighbourhood should be constructed such that a walk through it would feel like a 'thrilling mountain walk', passing between distinct small communities.[60]

Unfortunately, I'm not sure the plan to build a Japanese utopia here has succeeded. Perhaps it's just the grey weather, but to me, the Java and KNSM islands feel rather lifeless. Early in the afternoon there are very few people around and at one point I walk for ten minutes along the northern edge of the islands without seeing another soul: almost unheard of in a city as busy as Amsterdam. Some of the modern apartment buildings are remarkably ugly, and remind me of those in Beijing or Moscow. One monolithic grey block with the vaguely sci-fi name of Skydome is a strong contender for the ugliest building in Amsterdam. In other places, however, the islands do feel like the epitome of modern urban planning: largely car-free, child-safe, and bicycle-friendly, with hundreds of families living in comfortable apartments with nice views across the water. I could imagine living here with children and loving it.

After walking through KNSM for about ten minutes I reach the eastern tip of the island, where there's a huge circular apartment building that looks like a football stadium. Behind it there's a cobbled little plaza on the water's edge, where an older man with wild hair and a giant moustache is enthusiastically using some public exercise machines, cross-country skiing on the spot like an athletic Burt Reynolds. I nod hello and climb a few steps onto a concrete viewing platform that juts out over the water. It begins to rain a little, but I don't mind much: this is a fun place to be. Seagulls glide overhead and big barges pass by on the river; the wind carries a salty tingle from the sea. I have the palpable sense of being on the very edge of the city, with water on three sides of me. A map on the balustrade confirms it: I am standing close to the point where the IJ meets the Outer IJ and the Amsterdam Rhine Canal. Across the water, cranes are putting the finishing touches to yet another big new apartment block, on land that was recently underwater. The city is always changing, and always growing.

CHAPTER NINE

West, the Sloterplas, and the Red Light District

*How Amsterdam became famous
for sex and drugs — and then tried
to push them away*

The end is in sight, and I can put it off no longer. It's time to get stoned. I have until now managed to avoid the ultimate Amsterdam cliché, but as my series of walks nears an end, I'm forced to admit that not smoking weed would represent a grave dereliction of authorial duty, and that writing a book about modern Amsterdam without consuming cannabis would be a bit like writing a book about France which doesn't mention the food. And so it is that I find myself standing outside a 'coffee' shop on a rainy Friday afternoon, plucking up the courage to go inside.

I have never actually been to a coffeeshop* before, despite living in the Netherlands for years — my experience

---

*   For the uninitiated: in the Netherlands a 'café' sells coffee, but a 'coffeeshop' specialises in something stronger.

of smoking weed consists largely of taking an occasional puff of whatever's being passed around at a party. I've therefore chosen this particular coffeeshop not on the basis of any insider knowledge, but because of its positive reviews on Google. ('Good spot to escape the tourists. Made to feel very welcome by the locals'; 'Delicious and strong space cakes, I recommend the chocolate cookie.') From the outside it's an unremarkable place, hidden behind frosted windows on the ground floor of a residential building in the west of Amsterdam. The name is a little off-putting, though: it's called Ruthless. I can't help but feel as if I'm doing something wrong by coming here, and that any moment my mother will appear and tell me she's not angry, just very disappointed.

This is the first stop on a walk that will take me through the western side of the city, to places like the Overtoomse Veld, and then back to the Red Light District at sundown. On the way, I hope to learn a bit more about how Amsterdam gained a reputation for allowing anyone to do anything — and how it might well lose that reputation in the future. But first, some smoking.

I take a deep breath, open the door and step inside Ruthless. The space I walk into is small and dingy, with a compact bar to my left and a red leather bench running along the wall to my right. To my surprise, the place is packed, with people leaning on the counter, sitting on the bench, and lying sprawled on various chairs and benches. At the till, a man who looks old enough to know better is carefully chopping a heap of cannabis into neat lines, as if it's cocaine. Europop dance music plays quietly in the background. Most customers look as if they're relaxing after a day of hard work; one man who's puffing on a monster joint still has a hammer hanging from his tool belt. It doesn't look like any tourist has been here for a long time. The atmosphere isn't unfriendly, but the vibe is definitely more Albanian gangster hangout than 1960s San Francisco. The air is unbelievably smoky — I think you could probably get stoned just peeping through the letterbox.

A burly bouncer in a wool cap welcomes me and then steers me firmly towards the bar, where a man in a white hoody is waiting to take my order. Speaking English with an East European accent, he briskly asks me a series of questions. 'Weed or hash?' 'To get stoned or high?' 'Flavoured or plain?' I get flustered for a while and then point at one of the options on the menu: White Widow, which the barman assures me is not too strong and 'will get you stoned, not high; nice and chilled'. He hands me a little cone-shaped plastic tube with a joint inside. Still associating drugs with something illicit, I am astonished by how cheap it is: €3 for a fat joint; cheaper, in this city, than a cup of coffee. I sit on the leather bench, remove the joint from its casing and light it. I take a tentative puff, lie back in my seat, and wait for it to take effect.

In a city built on misconceptions, cannabis may be the biggest one. Outsiders often assume that Amsterdam is awash with drugs, and that many Dutch people smoke weed the way other people drink cups of coffee. (When I was growing up in England, the sum total of my knowledge about this city came from a long-running comedy sketch on the *Harry Enfield and Chums* BBC show, in which a pair of Amsterdam policemen smoke 'some really excellent blow' in their squad car, share a girlfriend, and explain that they have solved the problem of burglary by legalising burglary.)

It's true that the Netherlands has a long history when it comes to cannabis. In 2012, a group of workers who were digging a new rail line in Hattemerbroek, about sixty miles east of Amsterdam, uncovered traces of cannabis pollen alongside a body that was buried some 4,200 years ago.[1] Dutch cannabis consumption is therefore approximately as old as the pyramids of Egypt. In the 17th century, the VOC was a major player in the opium trade. In the early 20th century there was even a cocaine factory — the *Nederlandsche Cocaïnefabriek*, or Dutch Cocaine Factory — located on the Duivendrechtsekade, which produced around a thousand kilograms of cocaine per year. One of the factory's main customers was a British firm producing a potion called Forced March, which included cocaine and caffeine and promised to boost endurance 'when undergoing continued mental strain or physical exertion'.[2] British soldiers consumed litres of the stuff during World War I, and Ernest Shackleton took some on his ill-fated expedition to Antarctica.

Despite these early bad habits, however, for much of its history Amsterdam was not known for its tolerant approach to drug use. If anything, the opposite was true. According to a paper by Jean-Paul Grund and Joost Breeksema, the Dutch were among the first signatories of the International Opium Convention in 1912 and 'the use, possession, cultivation and trade of cannabis were criminalised in 1953, in some cases leading to strict sentences. Illicit drug use was rare.'[3]

In a way, there's no great surprise here. Although we now think of the Netherlands (and Amsterdam in particular) as a liberal paradise, for much of the 20th century it was still pretty conservative. The church played a big role in society and most Amsterdammers were about as likely to use drugs as they were to fly to Burkina Faso. In the years after World War II, however, the established order began to crumble. Welfare spending was seen (in Tony Judt's words) as 'a prophylactic against political upheaval',[4] and the rise of the welfare state, rapid economic growth, and weakening religious institutions all helped drive the so-called *nivellering*, or levelling, of Dutch society. As incomes rose, a new consumerism swept the nation: the Netherlands had a total of just seven supermarkets in 1961, but a decade later there were more than five hundred.[5] Perhaps most significantly, there was a post-war baby boom, with no fewer than 2.4 million babies born between 1946 and 1955 alone. In the words of the national statistics authority CBS: 'Dutch postwar population growth was unique in western Europe ... nowhere was [the birth rate] as high as in the Netherlands.'[6] By 1960, a third of the Dutch population was under fifteen years old.[7]

The combined effect of these trends was a sea change in the values that people lived by. In Amsterdam, many young people rapidly cast aside traditional values such as chastity, patriarchy, and monogamy. The city became (as in the first Golden Age) a magnet for rebels. The war memorial on Dam Square became one of the most popular places in Europe to smoke weed, while the Vondelpark was filled with young campers playing guitars, making art, and swimming naked in the murky ponds. The national airline KLM even advertised its services with the slogan 'Fly KLM, sleep in the Vondelpark'.

One sign of how Amsterdam was changing came in June 1964, when the city hosted the hippy equivalent of a royal visit: an appearance by the Beatles. Thousands of people turned out to see the Fab Four explore the city, and when the band took a tour of the canals in a glass-ceilinged boat, dozens of fans dived in and swam behind them. The Beatles themselves enjoyed spotting unusual local fashions. George Harrison later explained:

> In Amsterdam, somehow, we were boating along the canals waving and being fab and we saw this bloke standing in the crowd with a groovy-looking cloak on. We sent [road manager] Mal to find out where he got it from. Mal jumped off or swam off the boat and about three hours later turned up at our hotel with the cloak, which he'd bought from the guy.[8]

The cloaks the Beatles had spontaneously purchased inspired the styling of the 'Help!' album cover, on which the band are sporting fetching blue ponchos.

Five years later, John Lennon came back to the city with Yoko Ono, arriving in a white Rolls Royce to stay in room 902 at the Amsterdam Hilton. John and Yoko apparently liked it there, for not long after arriving they announced they would hold a 'bed-in' for peace; seeking to solve all the world's problems by having a long lie-in. The stunt garnered huge media attention but after seven days the couple gave up and left, reportedly without paying their bill. If you go to the Hilton today, you can still stay in the John and Yoko

Suite for about €2,000 per night.*

John and Yoko's antics were fleeting, and could easily be dismissed as a daft publicity stunt. A more profound influence on Amsterdam's politics and culture came from the movement known as 'Provo'. The movement started as a series of regular protests held on the Spui from 1964, and included both political demonstrations and music, and a lot of weed smoking. The gatherings grew in size. Alarmed by the lawless nature of the happenings, the Dutch government commissioned an official report that branded the participants as 'provocateurs'. The name stuck, in shortened form, and the protestors would forever more be known as 'Provos'.

The politics of Provo were not always well defined: according to one observer, participants were against 'capitalism, consumerism, sugar consumption, fascism, Nazism, Catholicism, Calvinism, bureaucracy, dictatorship, snobbism, racism, colonialism, militarism, the use of atomic weapons, the war in Vietnam, and ... the marriage of Queen Beatrix'.[9] But it was essentially a radical left-wing movement that opposed consumerism and Cold War militarism. The

---

*   John and Yoko weren't the only celebrities enamoured of Amsterdam's chilled-out vibe. Nina Simone also lived here towards the end of her life, while more recently, the film director Quentin Tarantino lived here while writing *Pulp Fiction*. 'I just had this cool writing existence,' Tarantino later said. 'I would get up and walk around Amsterdam, and then drink, like, twelve cups of coffee, spending my entire morning writing.' The writer Irvine Welsh also moved here in search of a quieter life after the success of *Trainspotting*; the British film director Steve McQueen is a current resident, and pop icon Justin Bieber reportedly bought a three-floor penthouse overlooking Dam Square for a rumoured €25 million. Angelina Jolie also came for a while. 'I was in Amsterdam and got a little crazy, dropping my pants at a tattoo parlour and woke up the next morning and saw this really funny dragon ... I realized I made a mistake.'

group's unimprovable motto was 'Better long haired than short sighted'.[10] The radicals aimed to change society not through direct political action but by staging stunts and provocations; much like modern-day activists who throw paint over famous paintings to get attention. One early 'happening' saw the painter Fred Wessels block the drains at his house in the Jordaan during freezing weather and turn on all the taps, creating an indoor ice rink.*

For a while, Amsterdammers seemed willing to protest almost anything. In the autumn of 1969, an angry crowd of artists even turned up to protest the driving of the first pile of the new Van Gogh Museum, complaining it was too expensive and did nothing to support local artists. They threw potatoes at bemused construction workers and paraded a huge plaster ear covered in fake blood. Around the same time, protestors also occupied the Rijksmuseum, protesting cuts to art subsidies. An hour before closing, approximately 250 protestors marched into the room containing *The Night Watch* and refused to leave until they got a meeting with a government minister. The minister refused to come, and perhaps seventy invaders ended up staying overnight, dozing under the watchful eye of Frans Banning Cocq. They were, according to news reports, 'awakened the next morning by the guards with coffee and shortbread, after which they made way for a new horde of museum visitors'.[11] The authorities were annoyed by the protest, but things could have been worse: rumour had it that an alternative plan was to put LSD in Amsterdam's water supply.

---

* Later, a Provo called Bernhard de Vries managed to win a seat on the city council after campaigning with another great slogan: 'Vote Provo for Better Weather'.

Provo's most famous stunt came in 1966, when Princess Beatrix (mother of the current King) married Claus van Amsberg, a former member of the German army and Hitler Youth. The public reaction was understandably prickly, given that the country had been occupied by Nazis barely two decades previously. However, the authorities seemed oddly tone deaf: faced with protests over the Nazi past of the prospective royal husband, the Amsterdam police reportedly asked if they could monitor the protests from a temporary base in the Anne Frank House. On the couple's wedding day, Amsterdam's streets echoed with the sound of protestors shouting *'Claus raus!'* ('Claus out!') and *'Republiek, Republiek, Republiek!'*. Some protestors wore yellow stars like those forced on Jewish people during the war, and carried signs referring to 'Clauschwitz'. As Beatrix and Claus rode in the royal Golden Coach over the Herengracht, one protestor tossed a white chicken into the path of the coach, nearly causing the horses to bolt. (According to some sources, the chicken-thrower then had to be rescued by police after an angry monarchist threw him into a canal.) The wedding eventually went ahead as planned, but the next day, newspapers around the world carried photographs of Amsterdam cloaked in white smoke from the anarchists' smoke bombs.

The Provo movement disbanded in 1967, after holding a funeral ceremony for itself in the Vondelpark. However, the movement did have two lasting effects on the city. Firstly, the Provos and their allies helped transform the way Amsterdam was perceived abroad, and perhaps perceived itself. As Martin van Schaik once wrote:

> Provo marked the coming-of-age of the Dutch
> welfare state and the rapid transformation of a rather
> sedate and traditional country into what [to] the
> outside world began to look like a nation of pot-
> smoking progressives.[12]

Secondly, and perhaps more importantly, the Provos and their allies also helped preserve the physical landscape of the city. As Amsterdam continued to grow after World War II, designers proposed developments that would have made it look like Los Angeles. Most notoriously, a 1966 book called *Op Zoek Naar Leefruimte* (*In Search of Living Space*) by twins Rudolf and Robbert Das envisaged the Stadhouderskade — the road the Heineken Museum and Rijksmuseum now sit on — being replaced by a futuristic highway with high flyovers, skyscrapers and a monorail. That proposal thankfully got laughed out of town, but others came much closer to fruition. In the early 1970s, the authorities planned to demolish a large part of the old Jewish Quarter (around the Rembrandt House Museum) to make way for a new highway, metro station, and office buildings. Historic properties, including the Pinto Huis, would have been levelled. To their great credit, local campaigners — including many of the same left-wingers involved with Provo — protested fiercely against the plans, fighting with police and squatting in buildings to prevent their destruction. The odds seemed stacked against them, but the campaigners were ultimately successful. The city council voted narrowly in favour of a metro line being built in the area, but scrapped the plans to build a highway. Some old buildings around the Nieuwmarkt were flattened, but not nearly as many as planned, and the Pinto Huis stayed standing.* Ironically, one of the revolutionaries' greatest legacies was that they helped keep the city centre much as it always had been.

Back in Coffeeshop Ruthless, I've smoked half a joint and feel as if I've drunk a whole bottle of wine and had a long bath. All around me other men are smoking furiously; lighting and relighting joints and blowing out great plumes of grey smoke that swiftly dissolve into the fug which fills the room. It's smokier than a forest fire in here. There's no alcohol in sight but almost everyone has a can of Fanta or Red Bull next to their ashtray, which seems a little odd — I'd have thought Red Bull and a joint would somewhat cancel each other out. I puff contentedly and type notes on my phone that will make no sense when I read them back later. ('Man hads big headf thats pGood.')

Given the great liberalising wave that swept the Netherlands after the war, it's unsurprising that attitudes towards cannabis also began to diverge from international norms. As Jean-Paul Grund and Joost Breeksema have written, in the late 1960s the Dutch authorities began shifting their focus from prosecuting the *consumption* of cannabis to prosecuting the *supply* of it, and in 1976 the law began to make a clear distinction between 'soft' and 'hard' drugs. Today, Dutch drug policy is often misunderstood. Cannabis is not, technically speaking, legal in the Netherlands. It is instead

---

* Today, the point where the city lost the argument and gave up its roadbuilding plans is marked by a statue of a tortoise with a big column on its back — you can see it in front of the Rembrandt house. If you go down to the platforms in the Nieuwmarkt metro station, you can also see photos of the protests that helped save the area.

gedoogd, or tolerated, with authorities essentially choosing not to prosecute minor drug offences in the same way that police in another country might choose not to prosecute drivers who slightly break the speed limit. In the words of the Dutch government's official public advice on the law:

> It is against the law to possess, sell or produce drugs. However, the Netherlands has a policy of toleration regarding soft drugs. This means that the sale of small quantities of soft drugs in coffeeshops is a criminal offence, but the Public Prosecution Service does not prosecute coffeeshops for this offence. Neither does the Public Prosecution Service prosecute members of the public for possession of … no more than five grams of cannabis [or] no more than five cannabis plants.[13]

The policy is a masterpiece of Dutch difference-splitting: unable to decide whether to make drugs legal or illegal, the government has done both.

In much of the Netherlands you're about as likely to find a coffeeshop as you are a mountain. However, in Amsterdam the liberal approach to drugs has transformed the way the city looks and smells. Last time I checked, there were more than 150 coffeeshops in the city. Surveys show that locals aren't especially fond of cannabis — about one in six young Dutch adults say they've smoked it in the last year, compared with about one in five French, Spanish, and Italian young people. However, tourists who visit Amsterdam are mad for the stuff. One survey found that more than 80 per cent of Brits who come to Amsterdam end up in a coffeeshop at some point.

One in three British tourists say coffeeshops are their main reason for visiting Amsterdam, compared with about one in fourteen who say museums.[14] 'Maybe,' a Dutch friend suggested to me, 'they just really like coffee?'

The *gedoogbeleid* (tolerance policy) has in many ways been a great success. Because the Dutch police don't prosecute minor drug offences, they have more time to focus on serious crimes, and the taxes paid by coffeeshops bring in valuable revenue for the state. There's also not much evidence that liberal drug laws have led to an epidemic of other kinds of crime: the Dutch murder rate, for example, is one of the lowest in Europe, and nearly halved between the early 2000s and early 2020s.[15] The policy also seems not to have led to increased drug use by locals: only one in four Dutch people say they've ever tried cannabis in their life, compared with one in three Brits.[16] Tellingly, when I asked Dutch friends to recommend a coffeeshop in Amsterdam, most of them had no idea, having not been to one in years. In a city where a joint is almost as easy to buy as a loaf of bread, most people never touch the stuff.

Viewed from another angle, however, the *gedoogbeleid* has serious flaws. The most obvious is that commercial cannabis growing remains illegal, so coffeeshop owners who need to restock their shelves have to buy weed from suppliers who have broken the law. 'You are allowed to buy the milk, but you can't know anything about the cow,' was how one politician once put it.[17] This contradiction might seem like an amusing quirk, but has helped make Amsterdam a global hub for the narcotics trade. The crime writer Roberto Saviano, best known for uncovering the activities of the Italian Camorra network, once told *de Volkskrant* that he believed mafia influence in Amsterdam might be even worse than in Italy. 'Whoever controls the Netherlands has one of the arteries of the global drug market,' he said.[18] Remarkably, Dutch police officials have even claimed that some individuals involved in drug networks centred on Amsterdam have become billionaires. Not millionaires, but *billionaires*.[19] Politicians in neighbouring Belgium have started complaining that Amsterdam-linked cocaine traffickers are causing havoc across Europe. ('When even the Belgians tell you you're running things badly, you know you've really screwed up,' a Dutch friend of mine replied.) I once spoke to a senior Dutch police officer who claimed to have found an enormous stash of cocaine hidden inside a shipment of cheese. "It was a difficult case to crack', he said, 'but the cheese tasted good!'

For many years, the Dutch authorities turned a blind eye to these problems. To many people, a few gangs seemed a small price to pay in exchange for maintaining Amsterdam's liberal identity and huge revenues from tourism. However, in the last decade or so, drug crime has burst into the open in shocking fashion. Perhaps the most high-profile example of this was the shooting of Peter R. de Vries. A household name in the Netherlands, de Vries was a crime reporter known for bravely holding drugs cartels to account. In 2021 he was shot near the Leidseplein in broad daylight, minutes after appearing on a TV chat show. He died in hospital a little over a week later. In 2019, a lawyer called Derk Wiersum, who was representing a key witness in a drug crime trial, was also shot dead outside his home near the Amstelpark. He left behind two young children.*

---

*   In 2024, three men were jailed for up to twenty-eight years for involvement in the murder of Peter R. de Vries, and in 2021 two men were jailed for up to thirty years for involvement in the murder of Derk Wiersum.

Other events were perhaps even more gruesome. In 2016 the severed head of an alleged gang member was found outside a waterpipe lounge on the Amstelveenseweg. 'It seemed to have been placed in such a way that the head was staring in through the windows of the café, like a kind of signal,' a neighbour told *Het Parool*.[20]

Even to people who are used to dealing with violent crime, it sometimes feels that things have spun out of control. 'We have crossed a new boundary again,' Amsterdam's police chief said after the de Vries assassination. 'Look at Pim Fortuyn, Theo van Gogh, Derk Wiersum ... We are not naïve, [but] the boundary is being stretched further and further.'[21] 'Sure, we're not Mexico,' Jan Struijs, the chairman of a Dutch police union said in 2019. 'But if you look at the infrastructure, the big money earned by organised crime, the parallel economy. Yes, we have a narco-state.'[22] Behind some of those charming little coffeeshops lies a ruthless drug-trafficking operation.

Sitting in Coffeeshop Ruthless, the idea that Amsterdam is a de facto narco-state overrun by gangsters and hitmen is hard to believe. Everyone seems half asleep, and after most of a joint, I am too. I've been to reggae parties on the beach that were more stressful than this. I'm tempted to just stay here all day, but after an hour or so I reluctantly haul myself into a vertical position and gather my things to leave. I don't feel massively stoned, but my legs are soft, and I sway gently as I walk out of the door, like a sailor just starting his shore leave.

Outside Ruthless, I spend far too long looking at the map on my phone before eventually figuring out exactly where I am: the neighbourhood known as the Baarsjes, in Amsterdam

West. Just a few days before my walk, West was chosen by *Time Out* magazine as the ninth coolest neighbourhood in the world, ahead of Fort Green in New York and Neukölln in Berlin. Amsterdam West is, *Time Out* says, 'Hip, cosy and creative, [with] a unique blend of Dutch heritage and international energy.'[23] That sounds a bit like hyperbole to me, but it's certainly very pleasant here. The streets are wide and liberally sprinkled with big beech trees, with trams running down the middle and cycle lanes down the sides. I stumble happily along past bike shops, wine shops, cafés, dry cleaners, and small restaurants serving various international cuisines. A sticker on a lamp post reads, in Dutch: 'People who love cheese prefer to date offline.' I am stoned enough to find this hilarious and take several photos.

After walking south for a few blocks, I arrive at another local highlight: the Mercatorplein; a big square encircled by café terraces. Near the centre stands a huge slab of vertical concrete, like a mislaid chunk of the Berlin Wall. On it is a wonderful street painting of Eberhard van der Laan, a much-loved former mayor of Amsterdam who died of cancer in 2017. Next to him are printed words from his farewell letter to the city he adored, which have become an unofficial Amsterdam motto: '*Zorg goed voor onze stad en voor elkaar*' — 'Take good care of our city and of each other'.

Turning west, I cross the road and come incredibly close to being hit by a tram, leaping out of the way just in time to avoid being flattened. Moments later, I have to jump aside again to make way for a hurtling *bakfiets* loaded with children, and then spring the other way to avoid a pair of speeding teens on bicycles. In retrospect, I probably should have waited for the weed to wear off before I braved the Amsterdam traffic.

Amsterdam's love of bicycles is largely a post-war phenomenon. People began cycling here in the 19th century and by 1921, the *Algemeen Handelsblad* was already complaining that 'The endless row of three or four cyclists next to each other ... makes crossing the road ... perilous'.[24] As the 20th century progressed, however, bikes rapidly began to be squeezed out of the city. Car ownership became a marker of status, and after World War II, the number of cars in Amsterdam exploded, rising from around 200,000 in the early 1950s to 500,000 in 1960, a million by the mid-60s and two million by 1970.[25] Several beautiful old squares, including the Noordermarkt and the Spui, were partly converted to parking, with city authorities literally paving over paradise to put up a car park.

For Amsterdam's cyclists, the consequences of increasing motor traffic were disastrous. According to Fred Feddes and Marjolein de Lange, between 1957 and 1967 the number of bicycle movements during rush hour in Amsterdam halved, while car use doubled.[26] Worst of all, city planners had little interest in turning things around. The city's urban development plan of 1968 ran to more than 400 pages but contained 'not a single chapter, or even paragraph, about the bicycle'.[27] Remarkably, in the 1960s the authorities even banned bicycles on some of Amsterdam's streets, including around the Nieuwezijds Voorburgwal, while leaving them open for cars. In 1964, Mayor Gijs van Hall boasted that he had used a bike only once in the previous seventeen years.

So far, so depressing. But then, from about the early 1970s onwards, things rapidly began to change. Amsterdam, on the verge of capitulating to the car for good, instead became a cyclists' paradise. Why? There was no single cause, but it obviously helped that the Netherlands in general, and Amsterdam in particular, were remarkably flat and also rather small, making bikes a much more practical way of getting about here than in bigger or hillier metropolises. It also perhaps helped that Amsterdammers valued what Giselinde Kuipers called 'conspicuous non-consumption',[28] embracing the humility of bike travel rather than being put off by it. A turning point came in 1973, when an Arab oil embargo quadrupled the price of oil, which led to the Dutch government banning the use of cars on Sundays. Amsterdammers liked having car-free streets and began pushing to make the closures permanent. A *Stop de Kindermoord* (Stop the Child Murder) anti-car campaign, run by a journalist whose young daughter had been killed by a speeding driver, was also hugely influential. In 1977, some nine thousand cyclists staged a protest on the Museumplein, lying on the grass next to their bikes to protest road deaths and then blocking the road near the Vondelpark. Not everyone was supportive: motorists leant on their horns and shouted insults. 'You bastards, you'll be asking for a lift again tonight!'[29] Yet in the long run, the campaign helped deliver a profound change in the way Amsterdammers moved around. By the late 1970s, a city that had scorned cyclists was working to make them feel at home, building a dense network of dedicated cycle routes, often separated from other road users by curbs or buffer strips. New bike bridges were built across rivers and canals, and huge bike parks installed at major train stations. Amsterdam became a 'fifteen-minute city' decades before fifteen-minute cities were a thing.

More recently, the changes have continued: in the last few years Ferdinand Bolstraat has gone car-free, Haarlemmerstraat and the Nieuwezijds Voorburgwal have been upgraded with wider cycle lanes and footpaths, and an enormous new bike parking at Central Station has opened. Cars have not been pushed out of Amsterdam altogether, but they are relatively rare: in the city centre there's currently about one car for every three households.[30] Forty per cent of Amsterdammers say a bicycle is their main mode of transport, compared to 12 per cent of people in Brussels, 14 per cent in Paris, and 17 per cent in Berlin.[31] Amsterdam becoming a paradise for cyclists wasn't automatic, or just due to the city's size or flatness — it was the result of deliberate policy choices that other cities could also make if they wanted to.[*]

The health benefits of cycling are well known, but I also often think that in this city, it helps foster a sort of no-nonsense robustness. After years of pedalling everywhere, the Dutch are unafraid of wind and rain, raise their kids free range, and think antibiotics are for wusses. Cycling also, I think, helps reinforce the egalitarian, democratic nature of the country at large. Here cycling is not a political act, and owning a bike is not a signifier of liberal bona fides, athleticism, or status. If cleaners and CEOs both turn up at work by bike with sweaty hair and damp trousers, it's somewhat harder for one to feel superior to the other. The guy who empties your bins probably cycles to work in the morning, and so does the Defence Secretary, and so does the brain surgeon at your local hospital. As one writer put it, 'the city is owned by cyclists'[32]

---

[*] Data also shows that all this cycling infrastructure means cycling is safer in the Netherlands than in almost any other country – the number of cyclist fatalities per kilometre cycled is about one-third that of the UK, and less than a quarter that of the USA. Fatalities here are, however, rising – primarily due to the spread of fast e-bikes. (OECD, 'Cycling, Health and Safety', 2013)

— and pedestrians had better watch out if they don't cross the road quickly enough. In London you need balls of steel to ride a bike through the city; in Amsterdam you need balls of steel not to.

Not long after leaving the coffeeshop, I arrive at a leafy park, the Rembrandtpark. Three girls in hijabs sit gossiping on a bench, and a man with a henna-dyed beard speeds past on a bike which is too small for him. Compared to the Vondelpark, the Rembrandtpark feels quiet, but there are an extraordinary number of dogs running around on the grass. Atop a bridge in the middle of the park there's even a pair of plastic ones: giant red fibreglass canines, each about the size of a car. The Netherlands seems to have a particular love of public art like this — it's hard to visit a park or even drive along a motorway without being accosted by an oversized garden gnome or a giant paper clip or a house-sized concrete traffic cone. Jeff Koons would feel right at home.

The Rembrandtpark isn't big, and I soon find myself leaving it, passing under a busy road bridge and into another residential area, along the Piet Mondriaanstraat. The Dutch like naming all the streets in an area according to a theme — flowers, trees, athletes' names — and in this part of Amsterdam many streets are named after painters. I check my map and realise I'm now in the Overtoomse Veld. The streetscape is what my mother would call 'pretty grim': ageing tower blocks, graffiti, litter. One of the ground-floor spaces under an apartment block holds a childcare centre, and as I stumble past, a door bursts open. A little boy runs out, wearing red pyjamas and cackling like a cartoon villain. I freeze for a moment, too dozy to decide whether to intervene, but then a young woman dashes out and grabs him. '*Neeeee!*' the boy cries as he's carried back inside.

A few minutes after leaving the Rembrandtpark I reach a large mosque, the Moskee el Oumma, which has an attractive coppery dome and tall minaret. A group of bearded old men stand outside chatting in Arabic, and the young boys who run past with a football are also speaking Arabic rather than Dutch. Just past the mosque, I walk through a small shopping precinct towards the August Allebéplein; a concrete plaza surrounded by low-rise apartment blocks. Many of the shop signs are in Arabic and almost all the women who pass me are wearing Islamic head coverings. The supermarket Ummah and the Berrak kebab house both offer halal food, and a fading poster in a shop window solicits donations to help earthquake victims in Morocco. At the centre of the square a Henry Moore-type bulging statue is decorated with 'Free Palestine' stickers, and up on the balcony of a nearby apartment I see a Palestinian flag flying.

I'm tempted here to describe this part of Amsterdam as feeling 'like another country'. That would, however, be a crude exaggeration. Amsterdammers these days come in all shapes, sizes, colours, and religions, and someone who wears a robe and supports Fenerbahçe or Raja Casablanca is no less authentically Dutch than someone who supports Ajax and wears G-Star Raw. However, it's also clear that this place has a very different culture from some other parts of the city. I'm struck by the fact that in several months of walking all over the old centre of Amsterdam, I've hardly ever seen someone wearing clear indications of Muslim identity, while here on the outskirts, perhaps 80 per cent of the people I pass are wearing either a *djellaba* robe or some form of headscarf. When I get home later, I check the statistics and see this shouldn't come as a surprise: in Amsterdam's Museumkwartier (the wealthy neighbourhood where the Rijksmuseum is), about 75 per cent of all residents come from a 'Western' background, and only 1 per cent are of Moroccan background and 2 per cent Turkish. In the Overtoomse Veld-Zuid, meanwhile, 74 per cent come from a 'non-Western migration background', including 10 per cent who are Turkish and 35 per cent who are Moroccan.[33] Any book about Amsterdam is inevitably a tale of two cities.

A few years ago, this area was a popular stop for pundits and politicians pontificating about the problems of Islam in Europe. Mohammed Bouyeri, who murdered Theo van Gogh, attended the El Tawheed Mosque in West, lived in the Slotervaart and worked for a while on the August Allebéplein. Thankfully, by the time of my walk, racial and religious tensions seem to have eased somewhat. However, there are still some issues that remain contentious, including the wearing of burqas and other Islamic facial coverings, which the government banned in many public places a few years ago.* Anti-immigrant parties also regularly do well in elections. In 2006 the party led by Geert Wilders (who has pledged to close mosques and deport Muslims) won less than one-sixteenth of the vote nationwide, but by the early 2020s this had risen to almost a quarter.[34] (In Amsterdam, the far-right typically receives less than 10 per cent of the vote, and the city remains a Green/Labour stronghold.) Predictably, some politicians describe the city as a delightfully

---

*   The attention given to the issue is disproportionate to the size of the problem: in 2009, Annelies Moors estimated that only about 400 women in the Netherlands wear a face covering — equivalent to 0.002 per cent of the population.

colourful multicultural melting pot where the nasi goreng is as good as the injera, while others claim it's a sewer of extremism where every other person is plotting to flatten Tel Aviv. They're both wrong, but it does often feel as if the country is just one terror attack away from a major rift.

Interestingly, tolerance of Islam is one area where that famous Dutch open-mindedness seems to be in short supply. Surveys have found that 70 per cent of Dutch people say they have a favourable opinion of Muslims living in their country, compared to 72 per cent in France, 78 per cent in Britain, 54 per cent in Spain, and 41 per cent in Italy.[35] When it comes to ethnic diversity, the Dutch are also not as progressive as you might presume: in 2021 only 62 per cent of people thought that having many different 'ethnic groups, religions and races' was a good thing for the country,** compared to 71 per cent of Germans and 85 per cent of Brits.[36] The reasons for this are complex, but Dutch debates about immigration and integration often boil down to a single issue: housing. For years, the Netherlands has failed to build enough new homes, and in Amsterdam there's now a critical shortage of affordable homes for younger people — particularly given that about half of the city's residents are aged between 18 and 45 (compared to a national average of about a third).[37] Immigrants often get the blame for 'stealing' homes from 'real' Dutch people, and populist politicians find it profitable to whip up a frenzy. But those who complain they're being priced out of the city do have a point. If there were just a few hundred thousand more affordable homes in Holland,

---

** There is one exception to this: attitudes to Judaism. When surveyed, the Dutch seem to view Jewish people more positively than other European populations, with 92 per cent of them saying they view Jewish people favourably, compared to 86 per cent of Germans.

the political outlook would be completely different. For now, though, Amsterdam is in many ways still a segregated city, with stark divides between many neighbourhoods and communities. In the Overtoomse Veld the average income is less than €26,000 a year, compared to €80,000 in the Museumkwartier.[38] Amsterdam remains a city that is unusually welcoming to immigrants and many newcomers (like me) feel very much at home here. But you could sit on the Keizersgracht or Muntplein for hours without seeing a single hijab.

The brisk walk from the coffeeshop has sobered me up, and with a new spring in my step, I continue walking west along the Robert Fruinlaan. I'm now in the neighbourhood called Slotervaart, which forms a small part of the area of Amsterdam known as Nieuw-West, a large segment of the city that was mostly built after World War II. The scenery here is pleasant but unremarkable: wide streets, wide red bike lanes, and wide post-war apartment blocks lining the road like discarded cereal boxes. I remember that this area used to be known as the home of the Dutch statesman Wim Kok, who served as prime minister from 1994 to 2002 and lived for many years close to the Antoni van Leeuwenhoek hospital. He was famous in the Slotervaart for going by bicycle to do his own shopping — not something you'd see former presidents or prime ministers doing in many other countries.

The settlement of Sloten (south of where I'm now walking) is older than Amsterdam itself — correspondence from the Bishop of Utrecht in 1063 refers to people living in 'Scloten'. Well into the 20th century, much of this area was rural. That began to change after the General Expansion Plan (AUP) of

1935 decreed that thousands of new homes should be built here. In 1951, the Dutch housing minister personally drove the first pile for thousands of new homes and by the 1970s, a huge area had been added to the west of the city.

For Amsterdammers looking for improved housing, the new developments were a boon, but for farmers who had lived in the area for years, they were a disaster. The writer Marja van der Veldt once published in *Ons Amsterdam* some extracts from the diary of 'the last farmer on the Zomerlust farm', Jan Rijnierse, who had his home forcibly purchased by the state. 'Today Moortje, my last dairy cow at Zomerlust, was milked for the last time,' Rijnierse wrote in April 1954 ...

> Since 1862, our family has kept and milked cows at
> Zomerlust and it is now like this due to the urban
> expansion ... we farmers have to make way for the
> big city ... [The architects] are so proud that they
> thought of everything when constructing Nieuw
> West: good homes, houses for the elderly, spacious
> schools, beautiful parks, sports fields and so on.
> They only forget to mention one thing: they chase the
> owners and tenants off their property, they have to
> fend for themselves.[39]

He died a couple of months later.

I keep walking east until the path runs out and I find myself facing an enormous body of water. This is, I quickly realise, the Sloterplas — a huge lake, roughly a mile and a half long and four miles round, which was partly created when thousands of tons of sand were extracted for housebuilding. The layout was inspired by the Maschsee in Hannover. I've never been here before but have heard good things about it from friends, and I can see why: after the crowded, slightly scruffy streets of the Overtoomse Veld and the Slotervaart, the lakeside offers a welcome sense of space. It's autumn and most of the trees have already turned from green to yellow, and the ground is littered with mustard-coloured leaves. There aren't many people about, but a young couple canoodle happily on a bench, and a woman jogs past in running clothes and a tight Lycra headscarf, looking overheated. Despite the chilly weather, I can also see someone swimming a long way from the shore. I wonder if it might be the celebrity swimmer Wim Hof, who once lived near the Sloterplas and swam in it nearly every day, before converting his love of cold water into a lucrative public speaking business. Running a *Rondje Sloterplas* (circuit of the Sloterplas) is a popular pursuit for local athletes, who sometimes proudly announce their intention to '*een plasje doen*'.*

It's getting colder, and as evening approaches, I look forward to getting back to the bustle of the city centre. I round the northern edge of the lake and then catch a rattly tram back to Central Station, sitting next to a young man wearing a green baseball cap bearing the words 'Lehman Brothers Risk Management Dept'. It's almost six o'clock by the time we arrive, and night has already fallen — short days in winter are something anyone living in this part of the world has to get used to. As I walk south along the Damrak from the station, the city looks wonderfully atmospheric, with the illuminated tower of Westerkerk peeking over the top of the handsomely lit old buildings on the Warmoesstraat. At the end of the harbour I turn left, onto the Oudebrugsteeg, on the

*   This is a pun. A *plasje* can be either a small lake or a pee, so saying you're going to 'do a *plasje*' has a cheeky double meaning.

edge of the Red Light District. I have a flashback to a night when I stayed in a youth hostel very close to here, about a decade and a half ago. Stranded when a snowstorm cancelled my flight, I called a young woman I knew slightly to see if she wanted to go for a drink and ended up happily married to her.

I turn east and reach a canal — the Oudezijds Voorburgwal. The café terraces are filled with drinkers, almost all of whom are under the age of forty, and the air smells strongly of cannabis. Café Emmelot, knowing its customer base well, is serving beers in English pint glasses rather than little Dutch ones. As I pass, a man drops a full glass of beer on the table, smashing it and sending lager flooding into his female companion's lap. 'Jesus Christ, Jerry!' she shouts, 'Not again!'

I walk a short distance south to the Oude Kerk, which looms in the darkness like an obsidian mountain. Just before the church, I see my first red-lit windows: a row of about ten glass doors with ruby lamps angled above them like patio heaters. It's still early in the evening, so many are not open for business yet, but a blonde woman behind one window catches my eye and waves a flirty greeting, which I awkwardly acknowledge with a little wave. I see someone tidying café chairs away, just as smiling bikini-clad women begin appearing behind more windows. Amsterdam's day shift is ending, and the night is taking over.

Tucked in behind the Oude Kerk is the Red Light Information Centre, which a reporter from the *Guardian* once memorably described as 'the kind of place where you can ask for a third slice of apple tart or the local rate for a blow job in the same breath'.[40] The centre is closed now but I've visited it before and found it fascinating. The big front window is filled with colourful printed posters in Dutch and English:

DON'T TAKE THE CHARM AWAY! THE RED
LIGHT DISTRICT IS HERE TO STAY

DON'T SAVE US, SAVE OUR WINDOWS!

RESPECT SEX WORKERS

GEEN WALLEN IN ZUID EN NOORD! MAAR IN
HET CENTRUM WAAR HET THUISHOORT (No
Wallen in South and North! But in the centre where it
belongs)*

I've come at an interesting moment in the Red Light District's
history. Sex work in Amsterdam goes back a long way. In
1413, one of the city's first by-laws decreed that:

> Because whores are necessary in big cities and
> especially in cities of commerce such as ours – indeed
> it is far better to have these women than not to have
> them – and also because the holy church tolerates
> whores on good grounds, for these reasons the court
> and sheriff of Amsterdam shall not entirely forbid the
> keeping of brothels.[41]

During the boom years of the 17th century, sex workers
in Amsterdam inevitably did a lively trade, with travellers,
sailors and merchants crowding into so-called *speelhuizen*,
which were ostensibly music halls but were in fact somewhere

---

* 'The Wallen' is the Dutch name for the neighbourhood where the
Red Light District sits; I use both names interchangeably.

men could pay for sex. Brothels were largely tolerated by the authorities: in 1688 the English consul reported that if they weren't, sailors would be 'so mad for women that if they had not such houses to bait in, they would force the very citizens' wives and daughters'.[42] One visitor claimed if you set out to drink a glass of wine in each of Amsterdam's sordid 'music' houses and whorehouses, you'd be kept busy for two months.[43]

In the early 1900s, prostitution was criminalised, but the law wasn't fully enforced, and as tourist numbers grew, so did the sex trade. The cheerful Dutch whore who enjoyed her work even became something of a cultural trope, with the ageing sisters Martine and Louise Fokkens becoming minor celebrities and publishing a memoir of the years they spent working in the Wallen, under the bracingly direct title *Ouwehoeren*, or *Old Whores*. For foreign tourists, Amsterdam's red-lit windows are now as much of an attraction as the Van Gogh Museum or the canals.

As with the drugs trade, however, Amsterdam's sex industry has some seriously dark undercurrents. The real problems began in the 1980s, when the Dutch women who worked in the Wallen began to be replaced by immigrants from poorer parts of the world, some of whom hadn't chosen to be here. As heroin became more popular, addicts also started offering sexual services in cars or in doorways, and the HIV/AIDS epidemic raised fears of a public health crisis. After an intense political debate, in 2000 the Dutch government legalised the sex trade, believing that a regulated industry could better protect women and combat exploitation. On the Dutch government's website, there's even a page with an English-language description of the administrative steps a budding entrepreneur needs to take before 'starting as a self-employed sex worker in the Netherlands'. Estimates of the number of women involved vary wildly, but in 2009 a study suggested there were 5,150 to 7,660 sex workers in Amsterdam.[44] Another survey found that about one in seven Dutch men had visited a sex worker at least once in their life — or at least were willing to admit doing so.[45]

Various unions and advocacy groups are keen to argue that most sex workers have chosen the world's oldest profession voluntarily. However, the sad truth is that at least some of the women working in Amsterdam have been coerced or trafficked by criminal gangs, and are essentially raped dozens of times a day. The National Rapporteur on Human Trafficking and Sexual Violence against Children estimates that between 5,000 and 7,000 people in the Netherlands are victims of human trafficking every year, with Amsterdam taking the lion's share.[46] Not all these victims are entangled in the sex trade, but experts have said the Netherlands is in the top five countries in the world for human trafficking;[47] an astonishing achievement — if one can call it that — for a small and wealthy country. In 2020, the oldest victim of trafficking in this country was sixty-eight years old. The youngest victim was two. In a report on their website, the European Centre for Law and Justice tells the harrowing story of one young Romanian woman:

> At the age of 17, someone she thought of as her
> boyfriend lured her from Romania to London where
> she believed she would have a good paying job as
> a hairstylist. Soon after getting to London she was
> sold and forced to go work in an Amsterdam brothel
> ... According to her, 'The man who brought me to

England and then to Holland used me like a piece
of meat ... When I saw the brothels with all the girls
in the windows, I cried. I cried very hard because
they looked horrible, and I knew what was coming
to me'. She was forced to work 12 hours a day and
only received £9 a day for food. After being sexually
exploited for five years, she was finally able to escape
with the help of a support agency. She explains
perfectly the problem of legalised prostitution: 'The
problem is that once I was in that brothel, everybody
just walked past smiling and waving, or glaring
and laughing, including some of the police, because
everything was perfectly legal'.[48]

Partly in response to such stories, the city has been
making a concerted effort to clean up the Wallen. Starting in
2007, an initiative known as Project 1012 (after the area's
postcode) set out to close brothels and replace them with
fashionable boutiques and cafés. The project was arguably a
success: well over a hundred sex workers' windows closed,
and some streets in and around the Wallen have noticeably
gentrified, with funky little vintage stores springing up where
there were once only brothels. However, the 1012 project
was also controversial, with some critics angry at the way the
government had effectively made large cash grants to brothel
owners while stripping sex workers of their livelihoods. In the
words of one reporter: 'The only people who didn't get land,
money or new opportunities were the women working in the
windows — the very people Project 1012's anti-trafficking
initiative was supposed to benefit.'[49] Others also argued that
by closing the brothels, the city was just forcing women to

work in other parts of town where there were fewer police. 'Sex work is constantly conflated with human trafficking,' Velvet December, a memorably named coordinator for the sex workers' alliance Proud once told a journalist. 'This, and the dichotomy attached to it for categories of sex workers — the "happy hooker" and the "poor victim" — leaves no room for the realities we face and to address the problems we see.'[50]

At the time of my visit, the city government's latest wheeze is a plan to relocate the Red Light District entirely, moving all the brothels and sex workers to a new *Erotisch Centrum* (Erotic Centre) outside the city centre. Most sex workers are outraged by the suggestion that they should relocate, with one memorably calling the proposed establishment 'an erotic prison'.[51] The plan might, I suppose, be successful in bringing house prices at NDSM under control, but to me it seems bizarre. Moving sex work to a different location presumably won't do much to tackle human trafficking, and probably won't deter many tourists from visiting the city and misbehaving. Moving brothels to the other end of a tram line is unlikely to magically transform Amsterdam into Delft. But the mayor seems determined, and by the time you read this, it may actually have happened. Or, knowing Amsterdam, it may not have happened, and everyone will spend another decade debating the issue instead. Whatever happens, I suspect that, like the coffeeshops, Amsterdam's brothels will be with us in some form for many years to come.

Group tours of the Red Light District are meant to be forbidden these days, but as I study the posters in the window of the Red Light Information Centre, I'm nearly swept off my feet by a stampede of Spaniards coming round the corner, led by a confident man in a yellow cap who's telling them all about *prostitución y drogas*. Some rules are still being followed: when one of the group raises his phone to take a photo of the red-lit windows, he has his hand slapped down by the guide. In this part of town, live sex shows are ten a penny and dildos are easier to buy than newspapers, but taking a photo of a woman at work is considered a terrible breach of protocol.

I follow the road curving round the back of the Oude Kerk, where there's an Irish pub. The weed has almost completely worn off by now, and I can't resist popping in for a restorative drink. I'm rudely awakened from my happy stupor by the price: nearly nine euros for a pint of Guinness. I drink it quickly, muttering darkly to myself about bloody tourists and bloody inflation. Back outside after my drink, I look around at the street names and realise with a start that the last time I came here was several years ago, during one of the COVID lockdowns. For someone like me, who deeply admires many things about the way the Netherlands is run, the pandemic of 2020–2022 was a disconcerting experience. In an emergency situation, a political system based on finding consensus proved incapable of making decisions swiftly or doing things that were unpopular, even if they could have saved lives. A strong tradition of free speech also meant misinformation and conspiracy theories spread rapidly, including inside Parliament. Unable or unwilling to take decisive action, the authorities veered around like a broken shopping trolley, imposing almost no restrictions one minute and extremely strict ones the next, including two Christmases under strict lockdown. The periods of no restrictions were popular with the public — no one likes being told they can't go out and have fun — but also led to the Netherlands having the highest COVID infection rate in Europe, and the slowest vaccination campaign. Thousands of people died.

In Amsterdam, as in most places, the pandemic was an unsettling time. Even during strict lockdowns, I often passed through the city centre for medical appointments, and found it completely deserted. I'll never forget standing on the Rembrandtplein at about eight o'clock one Friday evening just before Christmas, at a time when it would usually be jammed with revellers, and going a good five minutes without seeing another soul. The bars were shuttered, the big square was empty and even the bike lanes were deserted. I felt as if I was somehow starring in an apocalyptic horror movie made real, which in a way I suppose I was.

Once the pandemic ended, I was pleasantly surprised by the speed with which the city returned to normality. Pundits had spent much of 2020 and 2021 telling us that the age of the big city was over, and in the future everyone would work from home in Idaho or Somerset or the Veluwe, but when the pandemic ended, everyone seemed to love urban life just as much as they had before. There was little room for commemoration or reflection, as if everyone had agreed that COVID was an embarrassing secret which we'd never mention again. However, the pandemic did have at least one long-term effect: it helped change the way Amsterdammers see tourists.

Mass tourism in Amsterdam is nothing new. According to the academic Roos Gerritsma, the first official canal cruise in Amsterdam took place in 1914 and the city opened its first tourist office in the same year.[52] By 1956, dozens of cruise ships were regularly visiting Amsterdam and tourist numbers had hit an impressive 1.5 million a year.[53] By the late

1950s, Amsterdam had a kosher hotel, a hotel for ministers with seven altars in it, and a hotel for women only, situated in 'a marvelously feminine and proper canal building' with 'a 10-girl dormitory'. [54] For parents, there was also a hotel a short drive outside the city which was exclusively for children, where adults could 'house their children in a junior resort while they continue their trips throughout the rest of Europe'.[55]

As tourist numbers rose through the seventies, eighties and nineties, most of the city's leaders saw it as a very good thing. For a mercantile city that had grown rich trading with outsiders, inviting them home seemed a natural next step, and some parts of the city (such as the Zeedijk) visibly gentrified and grew safer as tourists flooded in. Amsterdam saw itself as in competition with cities like Berlin and Madrid, and Amsterdam's promoters were not shy about marketing it as the perfect place for stag parties and rowdy weekends away. In the 2000s, European integration and cheap flights made it easier than ever for foreigners to visit. According to calculations by SEO Economic Research, between 2005 and 2016, the number of tourists visiting Amsterdam grew by more than 50 per cent.[56] By 2019, on the eve of the COVID-19 pandemic, a city with a population of roughly 800,000 people was receiving about twenty million visitors a year.[57] A tourism consultant calculated that Disney World in Florida, the world's most popular theme park, had fewer guests per square metre than Amsterdam.

All that changed, however, with COVID-19. Almost overnight, the city went from receiving tens of thousands of visitors a day to receiving almost none. For Amsterdammers who made their living from tourism, it was disastrous. Many local residents, however, enjoyed having the city to themselves for the first time in years. 'I haven't seen a single tourist in weeks!' one friend in the city told me in late 2020. 'It's wonderful!'

When the pandemic ended, many Amsterdammers concluded they didn't actually want things to go back to how they were before. A petition calling for the number of visitors to be cut back to 2014 levels gathered tens of thousands of signatures, and the city council declared, 'We do not want to go back to what we saw before the pandemic'.[58] Overtourism is not a problem unique to Amsterdam. Venice, Barcelona, Santorini, Dubrovnik, and many other places in Europe have grown exasperated with the problems which mass tourism creates. What's perhaps different about the Dutch capital, though, is that so many tourists come here with the explicit aim of doing things which they wouldn't be allowed to do at home. As a Dutch politician once brilliantly put it, this is a place where many people go 'on holiday from their morals'.[59] Part of the problem is perhaps due to the way foreigners often overestimate the extent to which Dutch people are liberal. Yes, gay marriage was legalised here a long time ago, and smoking weed and bedding sex workers are tolerated. But this is, in many ways, a rather right-wing country: every government of the last twenty-plus years has been conservative, and in national elections well over half of people typically vote for right-leaning parties. To foreign visitors the Wallen may seem like the epitome of Dutch liberalism, but to many Dutch people, it feels like the antithesis of the tidy, cautious, neighbourly values that their country holds dear. If you want a quick way of finding out a Dutch person's political leanings, just ask what they think of Amsterdam. Leftwingers will generally say they love it while rightwingers think it's the worst thing since cold sores.*

Before the Covid pandemic the authorities had already been taking cautious steps to curb certain types of tourism. In practice, this meant trying to disperse tourists to other destinations such as Zandvoort, a beach resort eighteen miles from the city that has been boldly rebranded as 'Amsterdam Beach' in an attempt to lure day-trippers. Between about 2010 and the early 2020s, almost every month seemed to bring a new policy aimed at controlling tourism. There were stricter rules on who could visit coffeeshops, a ban on tour guides in the Red Light District, a ban on 'beer bikes' with bicycle seats arranged around a mobile bar, a ban on coffeeshops near secondary schools, and restrictions on how often homeowners could sublet via Airbnb. Tourist taxes were ramped up and large cruise ships were restricted — with plans to ban them entirely by 2035. In 2018, the city even dismantled the iconic 'I amsterdam' text from the Museumplein. These giant upright Hollywood-style letters had been a major tourist attraction since 2006, and were tagged on Instagram well over a million times, but once the authorities decided they had become too popular, they were gone. (With typical Amsterdam bravado, a local designer called Pauline Wiersema promptly replaced the missing sign with three new giant orange letters spelling 'HUH'. These were also removed.)** Other efforts to change tourism were more creative. One local group created a Marry an

---

* When I told one Rotterdammer who I know well that I was writing a book about Amsterdam, his reply was succinct: 'It'll be a short book, then. One page, one word: "Kut."' (vagina, but ruder).

** The original sign wasn't destroyed; you can still see it next to a bus stop at Schiphol Airport.

Amsterdammer scheme, where a local and a visitor held a fake wedding ceremony, complete with rings and vows, before spending their 'honeymoon' visiting less-well-known parts of the city. For those not keen on getting hitched to a stranger, there was an alternative: Weed Dating, where tourists and locals got to know one another while pulling out weeds at an urban farm or plucking and eating a city pigeon at a local artists' studio.

After the pandemic, efforts to curb tourism accelerated. 'Amsterdam is a world city,' deputy mayor Sofyan Mbarki told a reporter. 'But to keep our city liveable, we need to choose limits instead of irresponsible growth.'[60] The municipality banned smoking cannabis in the street, forced brothels to close earlier in the evening and pledged to enforce a ban on drinking in public.* An advertising campaign with the brazen title of 'Stay Away' was also launched, aiming to tell young British men that if they headed to Amsterdam for a 'messy night out and getting trashed',[61] they were liable to end up with a criminal record. City leaders seem proud of these campaigns but they haven't been hugely successful — in the first three years of the most recent campaign to cut tourist numbers, they went up by 10 per cent.[62] To me, the authorities' efforts always feel rather daft, after decades of encouraging people to come and have fun — a case of shutting the door after the horse has already bolted, done a line of coke, and thrown up in a canal.

---

* One unforgettable headline I saw not long ago: 'Decriminalise cocaine to beat crime, says Amsterdam mayor' (DutchNews.nl, 26 January 2024).

It's about seven o'clock by now; the time of day when you can feel the mood in the Wallen turning a bit darker. A woman vomits on a street corner, and a man shouts something unintelligible in my face, then goes to pee off a bridge. But as always in this city, there's no real sense of menace; just people enjoying themselves to excess. I buy a slice of pizza that costs almost as much as a whole pizza would in Tilburg. Glancing right down an alley (the Pijlsteeg), past an Argentinian restaurant,** I see the war memorial on Dam Square neatly framed between narrow walls. The name of the alley sounds familiar and when I check my notes, I remember why: in Rembrandt's time, the brothels on the Pijlsteeg provided female models for local artists' paintings. I look up again and realise I'm accidentally standing next to a drug deal. A Dutch man on a bike is halfway through selling a small bag of white powder to a nervous-looking male tourist in a tracksuit. Seeing me watching and tapping on my phone, the Dutchman eyes me suspiciously and then asks in English: 'Are we good here?' I assure him in Dutch that I'm not a cop and move on. Just along the street a young American woman is crying hysterically and wailing: 'I just didn't want to do this again. I'm sick of being your mother!' The man with her looks chastened, and stares at his shoes. 'But I thought you wanted to do shrooms,' he says quietly.

I zigzag up and down the Warmoesstraat, looking in shop windows and writing notes on my phone. This is one of the oldest streets in the old city, built when people first began settling along the banks of the IJ and Amstel, and some side streets still have a pronounced slope to them, confirming

** Last time I checked, there were at least ten Argentinian restaurants within five minutes' walk of the Oude Kerk. I've no idea why.

they were once part of a raised dike. Other than that incline, though, few signs of the city's ancient history remain. Outside a noisy Irish pub called Durty Nelly's, a burly doorman is carefully folding a paper napkin into an origami bird, while a young woman outside a tattoo shop is looking at a fresh bandage on her wrist and crying — whether from joy or sorrow, it's hard to tell. Nearby is the Condomerie, which specialises in exactly what you'd think. The window display includes contraceptives that look like an orange carrot, the Eiffel Tower, and an elephant's head. The Statue of Liberty one looks painful.

After wandering in circles for a while, I spy my final destination for the day, which has an entrance marked with a circular neon sign like a target to aim for. Depending on who you ask, the Bulldog coffeeshop is either a proud Amsterdam institution or one of the worst things to arrive in this city since the plague. One friend described it to me as 'the Planet Hollywood of coffeeshops', which wasn't meant to be a compliment.

The first Bulldog coffeeshop was started in the 1970s by a man called Henk de Vries, who apparently inherited a sex shop from his father (as you do) and promptly threw all the sex paraphernalia into a canal and converted the store into 'a living room for all to enjoy'.[63] To say the shop he founded became popular would be an understatement: the original Bulldog now sits at the heart of an empire to rival the VOC's, including five coffeeshops in Amsterdam, 'social clubs' in Ibiza and Barcelona, hotels in the Netherlands and Canada, and shops selling Bulldog-branded paraphernalia. There's even a coffeeshop in an old police station at the Leidseplein. You could feasibly spend a weekend in Amsterdam without ever needing to leave Bulldog outlets to eat, smoke and sleep — and some visitors probably do. The British comic creation Ali G once filmed a scene in a Bulldog, and the brand was name-checked by Van Halen in their song 'Amsterdam':

> Got a pocket full of money
> Got me a long night ahead
> Quick stop by the Bulldog
> Score me some Panama Red, yeah*

I've snobbishly assumed that I'll hate the Bulldog and its trashy English-speaking clientele. I'm surprised, therefore, to step inside and find that I actually like it a lot. The contrasts with Coffeeshop Ruthless are stark: here nearly half the customers are female, and the décor feels like a Dutch pub crossed with an American sports bar, with cosy corners and low stools covered in furry animal skins. A powerful fan system in the ceiling ensures smoke is whisked away as soon as it appears. Jurassic 5 plays on the speakers and a handful of young people in hoodies pass around chunky joints. Behind the bar, a big sign reads: 'SMOKING POT CAN LEAD TO ... UM ... AH ... I FORGET'.

I try to sit down, but an enthusiastic young man in a Bulldog jumper directs me downstairs, to a counter where the weed is sold from behind a plastic screen. Opposite it there's a framed picture of what I assume is the original Bulldog: a wrinkly, muscular-looking fellow called Joris. Next to it, a pair of men in beanies are having a loud video call with

---

* The band's lead singer, Eddie Van Halen, was born in Amsterdam and moved with his family to the US as a child. He once said his family left the Netherlands 'with $50 and a piano'.

someone. 'I'M WARNING YOU JAY, DON'T DO SPEED',
one of them says. Emboldened by my experience at the last
coffeeshop, I confidently choose a variety from the menu and
order a pre-rolled joint, as if I've been doing this all my life.
The lady behind the counter hands over another little plastic
cone with a joint in. The price is an unpleasant surprise this
time: €10, plus €2.50 for a lighter.

I go back upstairs and find a seat next to a man in a
Yankees cap who's watching Netflix on his phone. Snoop
Dogg — the patron saint of weed smokers — is on the stereo
now, and it's a warm, welcoming, chilled-out scene. To my
left, a French couple are having a marvellous time, and to my
right, a pair of Dutch women are patiently teaching a non-
Dutch friend the correct usage of the word 'zo'. (Depending
on the speed and intonation with which it's deployed 'zo' can
mean anything from 'wow, that's amazing, I'm impressed'
to 'I'm afraid it's time to leave' or 'oh my goodness, I'm so
sorry for your loss'.) On the table in front of me, a little tent-
shaped sign says, in English: 'NO TOBACCO'. Smoking is
encouraged here, but only if it's the right kind.

I light my joint, and puff happily on it while watching
people come and go. After a few minutes, the man in the
Yankees cap leaves, and his seat is taken by an African
American woman of about forty, wearing a black leather
jacket and jeans. We chat for a while. She's on holiday and
loving it. 'Just look at that! So great!' she says, gesturing out
of the front windows at the nicely lit houses across the canal.
'The people who live here don't have curtains, so they don't
have to pay taxes!' I'm not sure about her grasp of economic
policy but her enthusiasm is infectious. She's clearly having
the time of her life. 'I just love it here!' she gushes. 'Just look

at all the windows and the lights! It's so pretty! And everyone here is so nice! This is so great! It's really, like, the nicest city in the world! Just great!' And despite it all, I think she's probably right. I sink back in my seat and take another deep drag on my joint and think: I could get used to this.

CONCLUSION

The Dam to Bijlmer and IJburg

Climate change, plane crashes, and the future of Amsterdam

I've always loved Amsterdam Central Station. In an age when many big train stations feel like shopping malls, this one is still the real deal: a colossal building that looks like a cathedral from the outside and from the inside still evokes the golden age of travel. Departure boards list trains leaving for Paris, Brussels, and Köln, and people with suitcases stomp around talking in half a dozen different languages. If my train's delayed, I'm usually happy to spend half an hour admiring the hidden details that are tucked away throughout the building: the bronze plaque commemorating the war dead on platform 2b; the shiny golden gates to the old Royal Waiting Room; the old postbox which is taller than me and as red as a fire engine. It all feels pleasingly old-fashioned and glamorous, as if you've stepped into an Agatha Christie novel or are about to run into Harry and Ron on their way to Hogwarts.

Today is a Sunday, yet the station is even busier than usual. There's a big protest in town today, and the concourse in front of the station is crowded with protestors young and old, wrapped up warmly against the cold and carrying cardboard banners and colourful flags. I join them and am swept along the Damrak towards the city centre. On Dam Square it's even busier. The whole space between the tram tracks and the Royal Palace is packed with people, many of whom are holding placards. At the centre of the square, a big cardboard chimney pumps out white smoke, partly obscuring the view of the Nieuwe Kerk, as if the Provos have come back for one final smoke bomb protest. From time to time someone leads the crowd in a hearty chant, in English: 'What do we want? Climate justice! When do we want it? Now!'

A huge rolling cheer goes up, like an oral Mexican wave rippling through the crowd, and we all begin to move down the Rokin. Bemused tourists scurry out of the way, and then stop to take photos with their phones. As we pass the Ozymandian broken stone heads on the Rokin, a seven-piece jazz band plays jaunty tunes. Next to them, a bearded tourist with a neck tattoo shouts, 'Climate change isn't real!' but is swiftly drowned out by boos.

I had seen some things online that suggested the march today might be hijacked by the kind of people who eat tofu for breakfast and think Stalin was misunderstood. Thankfully, that doesn't seem to have happened (yet): the attendees are uniformly good-natured and politely outraged about global warming, and many have young children in tow. I, meanwhile, am distracted by the placards and posters they're brandishing. Some slogans are prescriptive: '*Bescherm Onze Natuur*' (Protect Our Nature); '*Ik wil schone lucht*' (I want clean air). Some are militant: 'Capitalist Greed Destroys the Earth'. And some are flirty: 'Make love not CO2'; 'Fuck Me, Not the

Planet'. A man in a woolly red hat who is accompanied by a young blonde woman carries a big sign which says: 'The Climate Is Hotter Than My Daughter'.

In many ways, Dam Square is an apt place to protest rising sea levels. Many of the marchers probably don't know it, but beneath their feet, roughly in the middle of the square, there's a round black stone that looks like a manhole cover. About 90 centimetres under this cap, a bronze bolt on a long wooden post marks the *Normaal Amsterdams Peil*, or NAP. This is the Amsterdam sea level against which all other water levels are measured; the prime meridian of elevation. If I want to know the water level in the river in my garden, I can look at the official ruling stick, which some public servant has stuck there, and see exactly how high the water is relative to this meridian in Amsterdam.

Sadly, all the evidence shows that this meridian might one day be far underwater. As I've learned from my walks, much of modern Amsterdam (including Diemen, Bijlmer, and Slotermeer) is built on ground that was, within living memory, at least partly underwater. Nationwide, perhaps a third of the Netherlands is below sea level,* and the country lies in what a journalist once unkindly called 'the gutter of Europe'[1] — the point where several major rivers drain into the North Sea. According to the national weather agency KNMI, in the worst-case scenario, the North Sea will rise by between one and two metres by 2100, and by three to five metres by

---

* No one seems to agree exactly how much of the country is below sea level, and almost every source gives a different proportion. But they all agree: it's a lot.

around 2150.[2] If carbon emissions are successfully cut, the rise would happen much more slowly, but even the best-case scenario forecasts more than forty centimetres of rise in the Netherlands by 2100.[3] And given how flat and low-lying the land is, that's enough to spell disaster. 'The question,' a Dutch meteorologist once wrote, 'is not *if* the Netherlands will disappear below sea level, but *when*.'[4]

The good news is that compared to pretty much everywhere else in the world, this country is well prepared to deal with climate change. After devastating flooding in 1953, much of the southern Netherlands was encased in a web of dams and dikes (known as the Delta Works) which means even major storm surges go largely unnoticed. Just outside Amsterdam, the huge *zeesluis* at IJmuiden is the biggest sea lock in the world,* and in the city itself an array of locks, sluices, and pumping stations enables excess rainwater to be cleanly flushed away like bathwater. Thanks to all this infrastructure, the government estimates that even a sea-level rise of three metres wouldn't necessarily spell disaster for the Netherlands. If you're already living a couple of metres under sea level what difference does another metre make? Dikes could be raised and widened, and bigger pumps installed to ensure big rivers could still empty smoothly into the sea. However, the cost would be extraordinary, and even then it might not be enough. Not long before today's march, flooding expert Professor Maarten Kleinhans told the broadcaster NOS: 'If the sea level rises more than one and a half to two meters, we will no longer be able to survive in this country.'

---

* A couple of years ago, the *zeesluis* (lock) at IJmuiden went viral when a competition to settle on a new name for it was won by the bold, imaginative suggestion of Zeesluis IJmuiden.

Other experts have in recent years even begun to discuss the unthinkable: a future evacuation of the coastal areas of the Netherlands, including Amsterdam. 'We must consider a controlled withdrawal in the long term,' meteorologist Michiel van den Broeke told NOS.[5] A colleague of his agreed: 'Moving to Germany should be a topic of discussion.' Some claim these views are exaggerated, and they may be right. If anyone can survive a sea level rise, it's the wealthy and resourceful Dutch. But it's also clear that while in some parts of the world climate change feels like an abstract threat, in Amsterdam, it feels more imminent and real. Checking an app on my phone I see that as the climate protestors march along the Rokin, between all the shops and restaurants and people, they're already about two metres below sea level.

At the end of the Rokin, I break away from the crowd and walk southeast. I would have liked to have stayed longer, but I have other plans. From Waterlooplein I take the metro for about fifteen minutes south to Bijlmer Arena station, with plans to walk from there until I reach the beach. The Bijlmer is (you'll remember from Chapter 8) the great post-war housing project south of the city, It was planned as a leafy utopia but rapidly became a byword for urban decay, thanks to overcrowding, high crime rates, and widespread unemployment. I used to pass this way often but haven't been for a couple of years, and am curious to see what it's like now.

The area immediately around the Arena train station[**] is busy with bars, restaurants, and performance venues, but I

[**] Marketers have decreed that Arena station should be called 'ArenA', but I'm not doing that.

avoid all that and head east. I pass through a large shopping precinct and then into a residential area where many of the streets have charmless bureaucratic names: F-buurt (F-neighbourhood), G-buurt, H-buurt. A Muslim woman goes hands-free with a phone tucked under her headscarf, and a man struggles to balance three crates of beer on his bicycle. I've read that serious money is being pumped into this area as part of a wider regeneration plan, but there aren't many signs of it here. The area reminds me a lot of Tutti Frutti and the other post-war neighbourhoods I visited near NDSM — it has the same grey suburban semis and small apartment blocks arrayed along narrow drainage canals, and the same air of bland suburban domesticity. There's nothing particularly attractive about it, but nothing unpleasant either; I could easily be in any modern suburb of Brussels, Copenhagen, or Frankfurt. The public art is still unmistakably Dutch, though. At one point I walk under an overpass and see six life-sized figures painted in bright primary colours, each with a long jet of water spraying from their concrete penis in a celebration of urination. I don't dare google to find out what it cost.

About half an hour after leaving the train station, I find myself walking through a part of the Bijlmer where massive apartment blocks are arrayed at jaunty angles across a patch of grass. The apartments look quite scruffy, with graffiti on the ground floor walls and greenish water stains higher up. However, the roads and pathways between the towers contain the usual Dutch bustle of cyclists and pedestrians, and it doesn't feel particularly downtrodden or depressing. There are lakes and drainage canals everywhere, and each tower block is surrounded by a sizeable lawn and big willow, beech, and fir trees.

Reaching the mid-point of a large grassy area, I find a memorial. It's a rather ugly wall of concrete and steel, about as tall as I am and as long as a bus, adorned with clusters of dead flowers in coloured bottles. The floor around the structure is decorated with little rainbow mosaics and there's a pile of broken glass where one panel in the wall has been broken. It looks like a badly maintained tram stop. There is, however, a moving simplicity to the list of names displayed on the rear of the main panel, under the headline '*Ter nagedachtenis*' (in memoriam). There are about forty names in all, many of them pointing to heritage elsewhere: Ekow Annan, Farida Kiberu Nakiberu, Maybel Addo, Zahid Hussain. A few steps away, a big beech tree protrudes from between the concrete floor tiles. A sign at the base explains this is the famous '*boom die alles zag*' — 'the tree that saw it all'.

The accident known as the *Bijlmerramp* (Bijlmer Disaster) happened on 4 October 1992. A Boeing 747 operated by the Israeli airline El Al was carrying cargo from New York to Tel Aviv. The plane had just made a stopover in Amsterdam when, soon after takeoff from Schiphol, it suddenly lost power in the right wing. The pilot called the control tower: 'El Al 1862, Mayday, Mayday, we have an emergency'. In the dry words of the official investigation that followed 'the number 3 and 4 engines ... departed the right wing', and the plane lurched downwards, leaving a long plume of jet fuel behind it. The pilot tried desperately to turn back to Schiphol, but the plane lost altitude. As the pilot realised he wouldn't make it back to the airport, he broadcast his final words: 'going down 1862, going down, going down'.[6]

On the ground, it was a quiet Sunday evening and many of the residents of the Bijlmer were busy cooking dinner or sitting down to eat it. In an instant, domestic tranquillity was transformed into a hellish inferno. The plane plummeted nose-first into the point where two apartment buildings met in a corner, not far from where the memorial is now. Burning jet fuel sprayed across a wide area. A former soldier who lived nearby told reporters he heard an explosion and ran outside to see the building torn apart. 'People were jumping from the seventh-floor balcony in panic ... there were many more still trapped inside their homes. It was hopeless,' he said.[7] One survivor described people throwing small children into canals to save them from the flames. Another resident later recalled:

> We heard ... a terrible crash that caused the entire apartment to shake. Cracks appeared in the walls and all the windows were broken. Smoke came into the apartment and there was fire outside. At first we thought there was an earthquake. [Someone] told us to run. We then went outside and there was a terrible panic. People running and screaming everywhere. Smoke and fire everywhere ... We fled down the stairs. We finally made it outside. It was a terrible situation there. People were running and screaming back and forth everywhere. People jumped down [from windows]. I was afraid that [my relative] was dead. While we were walking around there, I came across [a neighbour]; she told me that three of her children were dead.[8]

Firefighters arriving at the site were greeted with an apocalyptic scene, with huge fires whipped up by a strong wind and helicopter search beams sweeping through thick black smoke. Initial reports estimated that well over a thousand people had been killed, so it was with some relief that a much lower death toll was later confirmed: 39 residents on the ground, plus three crew members from the jet and one passenger who was on her way to get married in Israel. The crash was Amsterdam's Grenfell Tower; a tragedy which helped expose some of the city's deepest inequalities.

In the days following the crash, a memorial march through the Bijlmer attracted some ten thousand people, and the wreckage was visited by the Queen. Many Bijlmer residents were not just shocked, but angry at what they perceived as a lack of accountability. 'No one called the Dutch government, El Al and Boeing to account for their lies and deceit,' a resident called Sonya van Zoest said during a later memorial service.[9] Conspiracy theories about the disaster spread fast, with many rumours inevitably centring on the fact that the plane had been Israeli. Locals and journalists swapped stories about men in white space suits who had allegedly taken items from the wreckage and then flown off in a helicopter. More plausible were claims that the true death toll was higher than the forty-three deaths reported, given the number of unregistered immigrants who were probably living in the towers. One expert who had been involved in the Lockerbie air disaster and also worked on the Bijlmer site said some of the dead could have been vaporised.[*]

More positively, the aftermath of the crash helped changed the way many people saw the Bijlmer and its residents. For

---

[*] An extensive investigation later found that the crash had been caused when defective pins broke, causing one engine to shear off and knock off a second engine and parts of the wing. No trace of the 'men in white suits' was ever found, and the plane's cargo was declared harmless.

some Amsterdammers, it felt as if a curtain had been pulled back to reveal how an ethnic minority underclass lived in their midst, largely unseen and unheard. A few days after the crash, a columnist for the *Nederlands Dagblad* wrote:

> Since Sunday evening, no one is ashamed to live in the Bijlmermeer ... The district is, of course, full of scary apartment buildings. But it is also a neighbourhood with people of flesh and blood ... We got to know them openly: the Surinamese, the Antilleans, the Arubans, and also the Ghanaians ... With all the sorrow and misery that arose in the Bijlmermeer on Sunday evening, we are also beginning to realise better what all those beautiful words about 'learning to live together' exactly mean in practice ... this tragedy has transformed 'us' and 'them' into 'we, together'.[10]

That assessment would turn out to be optimistic, but the crash certainly changed the Bijlmer in many ways. In the years that followed the accident, many of the original towers were knocked down and replaced by low-rise buildings. (The toilets from some homes were reportedly sent to Suriname for reuse.) New shopping centres, a theatre, churches, and a swimming pool were also built, along with a new arena which created hundreds of jobs. These days the area is home to some 50,000 people, a third of whom are of Surinamese descent, with about another third coming from other 'non-Western' backgrounds.[11] Many social and economic indicators don't look good: incomes in the Bijlmer average only about 20,000 euros per year, one of the lowest levels in the whole city, and less than a third of the level in parts of the city centre.[12] In one of the neighbourhoods surrounding the Bijlmerramp memorial, the K-buurt, about one in eight residents is physically disabled and one in six is seriously overweight. Forty per cent of adults have a limited education, and 55 per cent say they feel lonely.[13] De Pijp and the Vondelpark may be only about six miles from here, but they feel a world away.

Despite these problems, however, on my occasional visits to the Bijlmer, I find it rather likeable. Residents are not blind to the area's problems, and are exasperated by antisocial behaviour and crime. But they also still have some of the idealism of the area's designers, and view the Bijlmer as a fascinating, lively, welcoming place, which is as much part of Amsterdam's history as the Herengracht or Waterlooplein are. They are right, of course. This place might not feature on many tourist postcards, but it's still Amsterdam — and it's no French banlieue, Glaswegian housing estate or American housing project. As someone once said: a Dutch 'bad area' is not a bad place to be.

I leave the memorial and walk northeast, passing a running track, a mosque and a 'drum academy' in a purple shipping container. A group of about twenty small children passes happily by, walking somewhere with a couple of teachers. Not one of the group is white. I walk briskly through a big leafy park (the Bijlmerweide) and then over a high footbridge into another large area of parkland — the Diemerbos. The landscape here is low-lying and swampy, and within minutes I find myself wading through big puddles which stretch across the footpath. A sign explains some of the local wildlife which can be found here, including grass snakes and tree martens. Beyond the Diermerbos, a big harp-shaped bridge carries me over the massive Amsterdam Rhine canal, a steely grey channel wider than a motorway. An easyJet plane roars overhead, rocking like a galleon in the North Sea wind. The scenery is drab and industrial, and I start wondering if I should give up and go home. But then, quite suddenly, through a gap in the roadside foliage, I see a cluster of expensive-looking wood-fronted homes in the distance. They look like an architect's fantasy, arrayed along the edge of what seems to be an island. I cross a bridge towards the houses and see there's loads of them: dozens or perhaps hundreds of shiny new semi-detached homes and five-storey apartment buildings with big glass windows. I check my map to confirm where I am: IJburg, one of the newest neighbourhoods of Amsterdam, built on land recently reclaimed from the IJmeer. It looks as if a nice suburb of Stockholm has washed up on a random sandbank.

A couple of decades ago this area was nothing but marsh and water. However, in 1996 the council adopted a plan to build a new community known as IJburg here, and by 2008 the new suburb already had some ten thousand residents. The government currently aims to build homes here for some 50,000 people — the equivalent of building a new suburb half the size of Delft, from scratch, out in the middle of nowhere.[14] Under local planning rules, the height of many new homes is limited to two floors, but some have a third floor underwater.

At the time of my walk, IJburg remains a work in progress. I walk further inland and see that although some homes are occupied, many are unfinished. There is scaffolding everywhere, and the streets are busy with whistling builders, plumbers, and glaziers putting the finishing touches on dozens of new apartment buildings. I get lost for a few minutes, and belatedly realise that the street layout here doesn't match the one shown on Google Maps: these roads probably didn't exist a couple of months ago. The homes themselves are mostly quite nice, in an IKEA kind of way, but the overall effect of so many of them crammed into a small area is rather bleak. I see no shops, no churches, no bars, and nowhere to walk a dog or chat with an acquaintance. Like many new-build areas, this feels like a dormitory rather than a community.

I pull out my phone and check the house prices: about half a million euros for a maisonette which won't actually be built for another two years, plus another thirty thousand if you want a parking space. 'The completion [of the property] is not included', the advert reads. 'Consider the finishing of the floors and walls, the design of the bathroom and the installation of the kitchen [and] reserve some extra budget for that too.' It all feels mildly dystopian. I also can't help wondering what will happen to places like this when sea levels rise. It seems likely that Amsterdam's centre will be protected from the waves for several decades at least, perhaps with a costly new flood barrier like the one built in Venice. But places like this, on the waterfront six miles out of town? I wouldn't place bets on residents keeping their feet dry. At the moment, IJburg is a haven for the relatively well-off, but it's not hard to imagine a future in which the wealthy have retreated inland to hillier places like Het Gooi or the Utrechtse Heuvelrug, and places like this are given back to the fishes.

There is one lovely thing here, though. Leaving the new-builds behind, I walk along a quiet new road to my final destination: the beach. A long stretch of yellow sand curves into the distance, meeting a wide expanse of titanium water

— the Buiten IJ, which forms the link between the IJ and the huge lakes to Amsterdam's northeast. Three beach volleyball nets flap in the breeze, near a lifeguards' tower and a couple of small shops and bars. The only other person around is a woman walking along the waterline accompanied by no fewer than twelve dogs, which are literally running rings around her. Looking across the water I can see dozens more apartment buildings sprouting along the shorelines like mushrooms after a rainstorm. Somewhere behind them, about six miles to the northwest, is Amsterdam city centre.

I walk across the sand to a small shop and buy an iced tea, and then sit on the beach to soak up the scenery. I try to imagine how this place must have looked at different times in its history: when it was a sandy swamp speckled with primitive hunters and fishermen; when it was a sandbank on which great VOC galleons feared running aground; when it saw big steam ships roar past on their way to Scandinavia and Germany; when it saw massive British and American bombers turning in circles overhead after dropping their bombs on Amsterdam.

Completing the final stage of my final walk has put me in a pensive mood, and as I watch the cranes swinging around across the water, I can't help but reflect on what I've seen and learned in the past few months of walking the city.

Some of what I've seen has been sobering. The Dutch are generally a cheerful bunch, but if you talk to older Amsterdammers, or people who have lived here for a while, you'll often be told that the city isn't what it used to be, and they're thinking of moving out of town, probably to Haarlem. If one wanted to, it would be quite easy to put together an argument that Amsterdam is failing. Homelessness is up and prices are up. Dutch politics is polarised and public services are patchy. The precious Polder Model has sprung some serious leaks, as the Netherlands shifts towards an Anglo-Saxon model of cutthroat capitalism and flimsy social services. House prices have been growing at explosive rates and for many young people — and many older ones too — the idea of owning a home close to Amsterdam's centre feels about as attainable as joining the Olympic judo team. The Netherlands' expected Brexit dividend has not really materialised, and some big companies including Shell and Unilever have moved their headquarters abroad.* Tourists have colonised everything inside the Prinsengracht, and the Red Light District has become a seedy caricature of itself. Amsterdam grew fabulously rich as a trading and banking hub, but it's now liable to be left behind in the next industrial revolution, which will be steered by Silicon Valley and Shanghai rather than by cute little cities on the North Sea. With only tourism to fall back on, Amsterdam risks becoming Disneyland with live erotica and pancakes.

All these arguments are at least partly true. Amsterdam has, in the last decade or two, been dragged into the modern age in an often unsettling way. However, you could, I think, make similar complaints about most other big cities in Europe. And there are plenty of things that others do terribly, but which Amsterdam gets very right. Public transport here is excellent. Schools are generally excellent. Healthcare is generally excellent. Infrastructure, like roads and bridges, is superb, and the cycling infrastructure is probably the best in

---

* Amsterdam did successfully lure the European Medicines Agency away from London after Brexit — but only after agreeing to spend a reported €250 million on new offices for them.

the world. (The Dutch language doesn't really have a word for 'pothole' — they don't exist here.) The Netherlands is still incredibly wealthy — Dutch GDP per capita is roughly 20 per cent higher than Britain, France or Germany's and nearly double Saudi Arabia's.[15] Amsterdam itself is one of the richest cities in the OECD,[16] with an economy bigger than that of Ghana or Croatia.[17] Yet the fact that political and royal power is concentrated in the Hague means Amsterdam has not grown to dominate or skew the national economy in the way that London or Paris have. There are few of the plutocrats and oligarchs who prance around London or Paris. Unemployment here is low and the state still provides a reasonable safety net for those who need it. The cultural life — not just big museums and art galleries but also dance music parties, orchestras, pop-up theatres, and film festivals — is superb. The bookshops are excellent. The food is ... edible. Taxes are high, but lower than in Belgium and Scandinavia.[18] Despite headlines about divisive politics, political diversity is widely tolerated: only 38 per cent of Dutch people think it's difficult to get on with people who support different political parties, compared with 90 per cent of Americans.[19] Life expectancies are high, and child mortality is low.[20] Crime rates are low and falling,[21] and prisons are literally closing because there are not enough convicts to fill them.[22] Amsterdam has as many murders in a year[23] as London does in a month.[24] (Yes, the population is smaller.) An incredible 48 per cent of Dutch people work part time,[25] and Dutch children are (according to numerous surveys) among the happiest in the world.[26] According to the OECD, the average Dutch person works about 20 per cent fewer hours per week than the average Brit,[27] but earns about twenty per cent more.[28]

Perhaps most importantly, Amsterdam also has a sparky, eccentric, innovative quality that makes most other cities look Swiss by comparison. 'We don't just sit around in the dark and the snow here,' one young Dutch woman explained to me. 'We go out all night and do drugs and have fun.' For all its faults, Amsterdam is better organised than Berlin, more entertaining than Copenhagen, more laid back than London, more lively than Brussels, and more modern than Paris. As Johnny Jordaan sang years ago: 'Better to live in Mokum without money, than in Paris with a million.'

At the time of writing, the city's biggest problem is perhaps one of identity. Amsterdam spent much of the late 20th century and early 21st century aggressively promoting itself as the kind of holiday vacation that makes Bangkok look like a nunnery. But now, like a playboy who finally grows up and settles down with a family, it finds itself slightly sickened by the antics of many of its visiting friends. At the time of writing, the city receives around sixty thousand visitors *per day*,[29] and Schiphol handles well over a thousand flights daily.[30] Few think this is sustainable. And so Amsterdam still finds itself struggling to choose which it loves more: its safety and tranquillity, or the revenues it earns from tourism. As a friend once said to me: 'The only thing worse than being a city which everyone wants to visit is being a city which no one wants to visit.'

Amsterdam has reinvented itself more times than Madonna, and it seems we may now be on the cusp of another reinvention, as the city seeks to pivot away from being a tourist hotspot known for rowdy behaviour into something else. What? Well, Amsterdam never seems quite sure. At the time of writing, Western Europe faces daunting challenges. Things we thought we'd consigned to another century — pandemics, tank invasions, pogroms, rampant inflation, waves of refugees fleeing to Europe — have returned to haunt us again. However, as I sit on the beach in IJburg, watching a new neighbourhood being conjured from the sand, I feel confident that if anyone can weather the coming storms, it's the placid, sensible, consensual, hardworking Dutch. If any city can thrive in an era of mobile labour and capital and global competition, it's this one.

I finish my tea and watch a dog chasing seagulls across the sand. IJburg is an odd place at the moment, half-built and largely unpopulated. But I can well imagine that in a few years it will have grown and thrived just as Slotermeer and Diemen and Tuindorp Ostzaan did before it. On sunny days, the café bike racks will be full, and the beach will be crowded with families enjoying the sand and water. Amsterdam will have spread to swallow this place whole, like an ink stain spreading across a tablecloth, and it will be all the richer and happier for it.

I gather my things and begin the long walk home.

ACKNOWLEDGEMENTS

I am deeply grateful to all the Amsterdammers (and others) who showed me interesting bits of the city, told me their tales of city life, or grumbled about how it is changing.

I'm also very grateful to the excellent team at Scribe who helped turn a bulging, error-strewn manuscript into the (hopefully) sleek and readable book you're now holding. Laura Ali in particular did a great job of editing the text, providing some sharp insights into the structure and suggesting numerous improvements; this would be a much worse book without her. Francine Brody and Vimbai Shire also did a fine job of copyediting and proofreading the book; many thanks to them for their help. Simon Wright no longer works at Scribe but saw the potential of the idea early and helped get the project off the ground.

More personally, I would also like to thank my parents, who sparked a very slow-burning fire somewhere inside me when they brought me to Amsterdam as a child. It's hard to believe that more than twenty-five years after sulking my way around the city, I've now written a book about it. I guess you were right after all, mum: it is very nice here. Eva and Max slowed the writing process down considerably but also made it all more worthwhile. Finally, the biggest thanks must go to Kim, for whom the phrase 'long-suffering' could have been invented. She is my best friend and I couldn't do it without her.

ENDNOTES

Introduction: Miracle City

1   https://onderzoek.amsterdam.nl/artikel/prognose-
    bevolking-2023-2050
2   https://www.amsterdam.nl/verkeer-vervoer/fiets/parkeren/
    amsterdam-centraal/#h28398ad5-8519-4a04-9007-77bd46a1a1ff
3   https://www.bloomberg.com/news/articles/2023-04-20/how-the-
    dutch-investment-in-bike-parking-paid-off

Chapter One: Pride, the Prinsengracht, and the Old City Centre

1   Pew Global Attitudes Survey, 2020: https://www.pewresearch.
    org/global/2020/06/25/global-divide-on-homosexuality-persists/
2   *Algemeen Dagblad*, 'Hoogste generaal voor het eerst bij
    botenparade Pride', 2022
3   Gemeente Amsterdam, 'Diversiteit en inclusiviteit in Amsterdam',
    2022
4   CBS, '20 jaar na invoering homohuwelijk 20 duizend homo-
    echtparen in Nederland', 2021
5   Thomas Macaulay, 'The History of England from the Accession
    of James II', 1861
6   World Bank, 'Population Density: People per square kilometre of
    land area', 2020
7   Geoffrey Cotterell, *Amsterdam: the life of a city*, Little, Brown
    1972
8   Geert Mak, *Amsterdam: a brief life of the city*, Harvill Press, 1999
9   Lodovico Guicciardini, *The description of the Low countreys and
    of the prouinces thereof*, 1581

10 Deric Regin, *Traders, Artists, Burghers: a cultural history of Amsterdam*, Van Gorcum, 1976

11 G.P. van de Ven (editor), *Man-made lowlands: history of water management and land reclamation in the Netherlands*, Uitgeverij Matrijs, 2004

12 Johan Huizinga, *The Autumn of the Middle Ages*, University of Chicago Press, 1996

13 John Howard Hinton, *A Tour in Holland and North Germany*, Houlston and Stoneman, 1851

14 Geoffrey Cotterell, *Amsterdam*

15 Anthony Bailey, *Rembrandt's House*, Littlehampton Book Services, 1978

16 G. Parker, *The Dutch Revolt*, Cornell University Press, 1977

17 Martyn Rady, *The Netherlands: revolt and independence, 1550–1660*, Hodder Arnold H&S, 1987

18 Geoffrey Cotterell, *Amsterdam*

19 Adam Hopkins, *Holland: its History, paintings and people*, Faber & Faber, 1988

20 ibid.

21 Geoffrey Cotterell, *Amsterdam*

22 William Carlos Martyn, *The Dutch Reformation: a history of the struggle in the Netherlands for civil and religious liberty in the sixteenth century*, American Tract Society, 1868

23 Deric Regin, *Traders, Artists, Burghers*

24 Martyn Rady, *The Netherlands*

25 Geoffrey Cotterell, *Amsterdam*

26 M. Hageman, *Het A'dam boek: 1275–2003*, Thoth, 2003

27 Charles Wilson, *The Dutch Republic and the Civilisation of the Seventeenth Century*, McGraw-Hill, 1968

28 ibid.

29 Michael Pye, *Antwerp: the glory years*, Allen Lane, 2021

30 Hubert Meeus, *Integratie van Zuidnederlandse schrijvers in de Republiek*, Belgisch Historisch Instituut te Rome, 1995

31 Violet Barbour, *Capitalism in Amsterdam in the 17th Century*, University of Michigan Press, 1950

32 Timothy Brook, *Vermeer's Hat: the seventeenth century and the dawn of the global world*, Bloomsbury, 2009

Chapter Two: The Zuiderkerk, Entrepotdok, and the Eastern Docklands

1 Zbigniew Herbert, *Still Life with a Bridle*, Notting Hill Editions, 2012
2 Deric Regin, *Traders, Artists, Burghers*
3 Paul F. State, *A Brief History of the Netherlands*, Facts on File Inc., 2008
4 Jack Turner, *Spice: the history of a temptation*, Harper Perennial, 2005
5 Stephen Bown, *Merchant Kings: when companies ruled the world, 1600–1900*, St Martin's Press, 2010
6 Jack Turner, *Spice...*
7 Giles Milton, *Nathaniel's Nutmeg: how one man's courage changed the course of history*, John Murray Press, 2000
8 Stephen Bown, *Merchant Kings...*
9 Ibid.
10 Giles Milton, *Nathaniel's Nutmeg ...*
11 Roger Crowley, *Conquerors: how Portugal forged the first global empire*, 2016
12 Lodovico Guicciardini, *The description ...*
13 Jan Huyghen van Linschoten, *Itinerario*, 1596
14 Richard Hakluyt, *The Principal Navigations, Voyages, Traffiques and Discoveries*, 1589
15 Giles Milton, *Nathaniel's Nutmeg...*
16 Ian Burnet, *Spice Islands: the history, romance and adventure of the spice trade over 2000 years*, Rosenberg Publishing, 2013
17 M. Hageman, *Het A'dam boek*
18 Giles Milton, *Nathaniel's Nutmeg*
19 M.C. Ricklefs, *A History of Modern Indonesia since c.1300*, Stanford University Press, 1993
20 Deric Regin, *Traders, Artists, Burghers*
21 Mike Dash, *Batavia's Graveyard: the true story of the mad heretic who led history's bloodiest mutiny*, Crown, 2003
22 Ian Burnet, *East Indies: the 200 year struggle between the Portuguese Crown, the Dutch East India Company and the English East India Company for supremacy in the Eastern seas*, Rosenberg Publishing, 2013
23 https://www.rtl.nl/economie/beurs/artikel/3762251/onze-voc-was-het-allergrootste-beursfonds-ooit

24 Ron Harris, 'A new understanding of the history of limited liability: an invitation for theoretical reframing', *Journal of Institutional Economics*, 2020

25 *New York Times*, 'No Accounting Skills? No Moral Reckoning', 2014

26 Mike Dash, *Batavia's Graveyard*

27 *The New Yorker*, 'A Dutch Architect's Vision of Cities That Float on Water', 2024

28 https://www.nemosciencemuseum.nl/en/about-nemo/organization/nemosciencemuseum/building/

29 CBS, 'Nederland in cijfers; Hoeveel musea zijn er?', 2022

30 Display in Scheepvaartmuseum, 2024

31 ibid.

32 Violet Barbour, *Capitalism in Amsterdam in the 17th Century*, University of Michigan Press, 1950

33 Andrew Pettegree and Arthur der Weduwen, *The Bookshop of the World*, Yale University Press, 2019

34 John J. Murray, *Amsterdam in the Age of Rembrandt*, University of Oklahoma, 1967

35 Richter Roegholt, *A Short History of Amsterdam*, Bekking, 2006

36 John F. Richards, *The Unending Frontier: an environmental history of the early modern world*, University of California Press, 2003

37 Display at Scheepvaartmuseum, 2024

38 Charles Wilson, *The Dutch Republic and the Civilisation of the Seventeenth Century*, McGraw-Hill, 1968

39 William Temple, *Observations Upon the United Provinces of the Netherlands*, 1747

40 Elizabeth Staffell, 'The Horrible Tail-Man and the Anglo-Dutch Wars', Journal of the Warburg and Courtauld Institutes, 2000

41 Anon, 'Strange newes from Holland being a true character of the country and people', 1672

42 Lars de Bruin, *Defaming the Dutch: the discourse of Hollandophobia in early modern England*, Leiden University, 2018

43 David Rooney, *About Time: a history of civilization in twelve clocks*, W.W. Norton & Company, 2021

44 Deric Regin, *Traders, Artists, Burghers*

45 John J. Murray, *Amsterdam in the Age of Rembrandt*

46 ibid.
47 William Temple, *Observations Upon ...*
48 Sir John Carr, *A Tour Through Holland*, 1807
49 Geoffrey Cotterell, *Amsterdam*
50 Frans-Willem Korsten, *A Dutch Republican Baroque*, Amsterdam University Press, 2018
51 Deirdre Nansen, *The Bourgeois Virtues: ethics for an age of commerce*, University of Chicago Press, 2006
52 Lindsey Hughes, *Peter the Great: a biography*, Yale University Press, 2008
53 Daniel Brook, *A History of Future Cities*, W.W. Norton & Company, 2014
54 Lindsey Hughes, *Peter the Great*
55 Fred Feddes and Marjolein de Lange, *Bike City Amsterdam: how Amsterdam became the cycling capital of the world*, Lubberhuizen, 2019
56 AT5, 'Steeds meer lokale brouwerijen: hoe Amsterdam weer een bierstad werd', 4 September 2022

Chapter Three: Garden-hopping from the Grachtengordel to the Jordaan

1 Frances Hodgson Burnett, *The Secret Garden*, Heinemann, 1911
2 C.D. van Strien, *Voltaire in Holland, 1736–1745*, Editions Peeters, 2011
3 Geert Mak, *The Angel of Amsterdam: seven city stories*, Atlas Contact, 2014
4 Geoffrey Cotterell, *Amsterdam*
5 *Newsweek*, 'Cees Nooteboom Reflects on Amsterdam', 28 November 2011
6 Conor Cruise O'Brien, *Camus*, Faber & Faber, 2015
7 Bernard MacLaverty, *Midwinter Break*, Jonathan Cape, 2017
8 https://www.guinnessworldrecords.com/world-records/637317-most-bicycles-recovered-from-waterways-city
9 ibid.
10 HuntingBond.com, 'Bridges at Tiffany's', 22 May 2016
11 John J. Murray, *Amsterdam in the Age of Rembrandt*
12 ibid.
13 Renée Kistemaker and Roelof van Gelder, *Amsterdam: the*

Golden Age, 1275–1795, Abbeville Press, 1983
14   William Temple, *Observations Upon* …
15   Alain de Botton, *The Art of Travel*, Vintage, 2003
16   Anne Goldgar, *Tulipmania: money, honor, and knowledge in the Dutch Golden Age*, University of Chicago Press, 2008
17   Anna Pavord, *The Tulip: the story of a flower that has made men mad*, Bloomsbury, 2001
18   ibid.
19   Zbigniew Herbert, *Still Life with a Bridle*
20   Deric Regin, *Traders, Artists, Burghers*
21   Anthony Bailey, *Rembrandt's House*
22   Anne Goldgar, *Tulipmania*
23   Willy Alberti, 'O mooie Westertoren'
24   Elizabeth Sanderson Haldane, *Descartes: his life and times*, Hardpress Publishing, 1966
25   Jack Rochford Vrooman, *René Descartes: a biography*, G.P. Putnam's Sons, 1970
26   M. Hageman, *Het A'dam boek*
27   Cees Nooteboom, *Labyrint Europa*, De Bezige Bij, 2010
28   RTL Nieuws, 'Scheldende Holleeder in de rechtszaal', 2018
29   Manfred Wolf, *Amsterdam: a traveler's literary companion*, Whereabouts Press, 2001
30   NOS, 'Bruin café wordt zeldzamer', 2023

Chapter Four: Along the Amstel from Ouderkerk to Rembrandt's House

1   M. Hageman, *Het A'dam boek*
2   Eva Johanna Holmberg, *Jews in the Early Modern English Imagination: a scattered nation*, Routledge, 2012
3   https://www.bethhaim.nl/english/
4   Zbigniew Herbert, *Still Life* …
5   Deric Regin, *Traders, Artists, Burghers*
6   Zbigniew Herbert, *Still Life* …
7   Laura Cumming, *Thunderclap*, Scribner, 2023
8   Michael North, *Art and Commerce in the Dutch Golden Age*, Yale University Press, 1999
9   Charles L. Mee, *Rembrandt: a life*, CreateSpace Independent Publishing, 2016

10 Sir Joshua Reynolds, *The Complete Works*, 1824

11 Elise van Nederveen Meerkerk and Ariadne Schmidt, 'Between Wage Labor and Vocation: Child Labor in Dutch Urban Industry 1600–1800', Journal Of Social History, 2008

12 Harriet Gunn, *Letters Written During a Four-days' Tour in Holland in 1834*, 1834

13 Nieuwe Haarlemsche Courant, 'Een kijkje van de groote drukte bij den Omval', 1938

14 *Het Parool*, 'Hausse in hozen', 9 September 1947

15 Charles L. Mee, *Rembrandt: a life*

16 ibid.

17 https://www.rijksmuseum.nl/en/rijksstudio/artists/rembrandt-van-rijn

18 Derek Blyth, *Amsterdam, Rotterdam & The Hague*, Mitchell Beazley, 1992

19 Bernard Hulsman, 'Herzien', *NRC*, 5 February,1998

20 *Multatuli, Max Havelaar, 1860*

21 Anthony Bailey, *Rembrandt's House*

22 Zbigniew Herbert, *Still Life with a Bridle*

23 Deric Regin, *Traders, Artists, Burghers*

24 Anthony Bailey, *Rembrandt's House*

25 Deric Regin, *Traders, Artists, Burghers*

26 John J. Murray, *Amsterdam in the Age of Rembrandt*

27 Deric Regin, *Traders, Artists, Burghers*

28 Anthony Bailey, *Rembrandt's House*

29 John J. Murray, *Amsterdam in the Age of Rembrandt*

30 Timothy Raylor, *Philosophy, Rhetoric, and Thomas Hobbes*, Oxford University Press, 2018

31 Adrien Delmas, *Written Culture in a Colonial Context: Africa and the Americas, 1500–1900*, University of Cape Town Press, 2013

32 Matthew Stewart, *The Courtier and the Heretic: Leibniz, Spinoza, and the fate of God in the modern world*, W.W. Norton & Company, 2007

33 Charles L. Mee, *Rembrandt: a life*

34 Willem van Focquenbroch, Op Amsterdam, quoted in Manjusha Kuruppath, 'Dutch drama and the company's Orient', Universiteit Leiden, 2014

35 Michiel van Groesen, *Amsterdam's Atlantic: print culture and the making of Dutch Brazil*, University of Pennsylvania Press, 2016
36 Charles L. Mee, *Rembrandt: a life*
37 Anthony Bailey, *Rembrandt's House*
38 Charles L. Mee, *Rembrandt: a life*
39 Letter to Theo van Gogh, 10 October 1885

Chapter Five: The Oosterpark to Multatuli's House and the Royal Palace

1   Travel Channel, *Anthony Bourdain's Amsterdam Travel Tips*
2   E.E. Rich and C.H. Wilson, *The Cambridge Economic History of Europe*, Cambridge University Press, 1967
3   Jonathan Israel, *Dutch Primacy in World Trade 1585–1740*, Oxford University Press, 1990
4   ibid.
5   Johannes M. Postma, *The Dutch in the Atlantic Slave Trade, 1600–1815*, Cambridge University Press, 2008
6   Jonathan Israel, *Dutch Primacy*
7   *New York Times*, 'Telling Stories of Slavery, One Person at a Time', 11 June 2021
8   Johannes M. Postma, *The Dutch in the Atlantic Slave Trade*
9   Eveline Sint Nicolaas, *Slavery*, Atlas Contact, 2021
10 Kwame Nimako and Glenn Willemsen, *The Dutch Atlantic: slavery, abolition and emancipation*, Pluto Press, 2011
11 *Het Parool*, 'Amsterdam's involvement in slavery was much greater than many people realise', 7 October 2020
12 Geert Wilders tweet, 3 November 2022
13 Human Rights Watch, 'Dutch Apology on Slavery Only First Step', 15 December 2022
14 *BBC News*, 'Amsterdam mayor apologises for city's role in slave trade', 1 July 2021
15 YouGov, 'How unique are British attitudes to empire?', 11 March 2020
16 *Algemeen Dagblad*, 'Balkenende gelooft nog steeds in VOC-mentaliteit', 31 October 2016
17 *Eenvandaag*, 'Vertrouwen in Koningshuis Blijft Laag', 20 April 2024

18 https://www.nationalgeographic.com/traveler/deals/
    toptenshoppingstreets.html
19 Albert Camus, *The Fall*, Penguin Books, 1956
20 Helena Enders, 'The Role of Children in Seventeenth Century
    Dutch Paintings', Senior Independent Study Theses, 2018
21 Multatuli, *Max Havelaar*
22 ibid.
23 D.H. Lawrence, introduction to *Max Havelaar*, Alfred A. Knopf
    edition of 1927
24 Tracy C. Davis and Stefka Mihaylova, *Uncle Tom's Cabins: the
    transnational history of America's most mutable book*, University
    of Michigan Press, 2020
25 Lennox A. Mills, *Ceylon Under British Rule 1795–1932*,
    Routledge, 1964
26 Anthony Bailey, *Rembrandt's House*
27 Samuel Smiles, *James Brindley and the early Engineers*,
    Salzwasser-Verlag, 1864
28 ibid.
29 Charles Wilson, *The Dutch Republic* ...
30 ibid.
31 ibid.
32 Ralph Fell, *A Tour through the Batavian Republic during the
    latter part of the year 1800*, 1801
33 Display in Royal Palace, 2023
34 William Temple, *Observations Upon* ...
35 Charles Ralph Boxer, *The Dutch Seaborne Empire, 1600–1800*,
    Penguin Books, 1965
36 James Boswell, edited by Frederick A. Pottle, *Boswell in Holland,
    1763–1764*, McGraw-Hill, 1956
37 John Adams, *The Letters of John and Abigail Adams*, Penguin
    Books, 2003
38 John Adams, *The Works of John Adams Vol. 7*, Little, Brown,
    1852
39 Graeme Callister, Napoleon and the Netherlands: a country
    misunderstood, Napoleonica, 2022
40 Laura Cruz and Willem Frijhoff, Myth in History, History in
    Myth, Proceedings of the Third International Conference of the
    Society for Netherlandic History, 2006

41 ibid.
42 *Historisch Nieuwsblad*, 'Nederladers juichen voor Napoleon', 30 March 2011
43 Stadsarchief Amsterdam, 'Stadhuis wordt Paleis', 23 April 2019
44 *Historisch Nieuwsblad*, 'Nederladers juichen voor Napoleon', 30 March 2011
45 ibid.
46 Lotte Jensen (ed.), *Napoleons nalatenschap: Sporen in de Nederlandse samenleving*, De Bezige Bij, 2020
47 Sir John Carr, *A tour ...*
48 *Encyclopedia Britannica*, 'Netherlands', 2024
49 Richter Roegholt, *A Short History ...*

Chapter Six: De Pijp, Museumplein, and the Amsterdamse Bos

1   Marielle Hageman, *Heineken: the brewery in Amsterdam*, Bekking & Blitz, 2013
2   ibid.
3   ibid.
4   ibid.
5   Robert C. Allen, *Global Economic History: a very short introduction*, Oxford University Press, 2011
6   Geoffrey Cotterell, *Amsterdam ...*
7   Herman Beliën and Monique van Hoogstraten, *Dutch history in a nutshell*, Prometheus, 2016
8   *Rotterdamsche Courant*, 18 May 1816
9   *The New York Herald*, 'Important Enterprise at Amsterdam', 10 June 1853
10 *Chicago Daily Tribune*, 'The city of Amsterdam - Its Appearance and Wealth', 15 August 1874
11 Justus van Maurik, *Toen ik nog jong was*, Van Holkema & Warendorf, 1901
12 *The Coolidge Examiner*, 'The Code of the North', 19 January 1934
13 ibid.
14 *Ons Amsterdam*, 'Hoeveel IJ houden we over?', 2 February 2009
15 Dubravka Ugrešić, *The Ministry of Pain*, Ecco Press, 2005
16 Tim Verlaan and Aimée Albers, 'From hippies to yuppies: marginal gentrification in Amsterdam's Jordaan and De Pijp neighbourhoods 1960–1990', City, 2022

17 Hans Janssen, *Piet Mondrian: a life*, ACC Art Books, 2022

18 ibid.

19 Geoffrey Cotterell, *Amsterdam* ...

20 *iAmsterdam*, 'De Pijp then and now', 24 January 2024

21 https://www.iamsterdam.com/en/explore/neighbourhoods/de-pijp

22 H. M. van den Brink, *On the Water*, Grove Atlantic, 2001

23 *Het Vaderland*, 2 May 1883

24 *Ons Amsterdam*, 'Hier gebeurde het... Museumplein, 26 december 1887', 17 December 2010

25 Steven Naifeh and Gregory White Smith, *Van Gogh: the life*, Random House, 2012

26 ibid.

27 ibid.

28 Letter to Theo van Gogh, 19 May 1877

29 ibid., 2 March 1884.

30 ibid., 10 October 1885

31 ibid.

32 Steven Naifeh and Gregory White Smith, *Van Gogh* ...

33 Marjolein de Lange, 'De Onderdoorgang van het Rijksmuseum: een nader onderzoek naar de doorstroming en verblijfskwaliteit', Fietsersbond Amsterdam, 2011

34 Michael Pye, *The Edge of the World: how the North Sea made us who we are*, Viking, 2014

35 *De Tijd*, 15 July 1885

36 Steven Naifeh and Gregory White Smith, *Van Gogh* ...

37 ibid.

38 ibid.

39 ibid.

40 Letter to Theo van Gogh, 10 October 1885

41 Concertgebouw.nl, 'Historie', 2021

42 Richter Roegholt, *A Short History* ...

43 Steven Naifeh and Gregory White Smith, *Van Gogh* ...

44 Charles George Harper, *On the road in Holland*, C. Palmer, 1922

45 *Algemeen Handelsblad*, 'Het Nieuwe Wandelpark', 28 February 1866

46 *De Tijd*, 'Het Nieuwe Park', 17 June 1865

47 Barry Eichengreen and T.J. Hatton (editors), *Interwar Unemployment in International Perspective*, Springer Dordrecht, 1988

48   *Ons Amsterdam*, 'Het Amsterdamse Bos', 1 June 2019
49   Patricia F. Wessels, *De wensdagen: een jeugd in de Jordaan*,
     Luitingh-Sijthoff, 2016
50   Johan Cruijff, *Mijn Verhaal*, Nieuw Amsterdam, 2016

Chapter Seven: The Jewish Quarter, the Plantage, and the Holocaust
Monuments
1   Martin Mulsow and Richard Henry Popkin (eds), *Secret*
     conversions to Judaism in early modern Europe, Brill Academic
     Publishing, 2004
2   Display at Jewish Museum, 2023
3   *The Day Book*, 'A Thousand Homeless Antwerp Babies Will
     Never See Their Mothers Again', 1914
4   Joseph Roth, *A Life in Letters*, W.W. Norton & Company, 2012
5   https://www.annefrank.org/en/anne-frank/the-timeline/#64
6   ibid.
7   Francine Prose, *Anne Frank: the book, the life, the afterlife*,
     Harper Perennial, 2009
8   Adam Hopkins, *Holland* ...
9   Teade Sysling, *A Boy From Amsterdam*, Lulu.com, 2012
10   Jan L. van Zanden, *The Economic History of the Netherlands*
     1914–1995, Routledge, 2005
11   Jacob Presser, *Ashes in the Wind: the Destruction of Dutch*
     Jewry, Wayne State University Press, 1988
12   Anne Frank, *The Diary of a Young Girl*, Doubleday, 1952
13   ibid.
14   ibid.
15   The Wiener Holocaust Library, 'Persecution of gay people in
     Nazi Germany', 2023
16   D. van Galen Last and Rolf Wolfswinkel, *Anne Frank and After*,
     Amsterdam University Press, 1996
17   Katja Happe, Barbara Lambauer and Clemens Maier-Wolthausen
     (eds), *Western and Northern Europe June 1942–1945*, De
     Gruyter Oldenbourg, 2022
18   Teade Sysling, *A Boy* ...
19   Geert Mak, *In Europe: travels through the twentieth century*,
     Vintage, 2012
20   Jacob Presser, *Ashes in the Wind* ...

21 *The New Yorker*, 'The Last Trial', 9 February 2015
22 Frank van Vree, Hetty Berg and David Duindam (eds), *Site of Deportation, Site of Memory: the Amsterdam Hollandsche Schouwburg and the Holocaust*, Amsterdam University Press, 2017
23 Miep Gies, *Anne Frank Remembered: the story of the woman who helped to hide the Frank family*, Simon & Schuster, 2012
24 Peter Longerich, *Wannsee: the road to the final solution*, Oxford University Press, 2021
25 Anne Frank, *The Diary* ...
26 The Bezalel Narkiss Index of Jewish Art, https://cja.huji.ac.il
27 Anne Frank, *The Diary* ...
28 Otto Frank interview with *Life* magazine, 18 August 1958
29 Francine Prose, *Anne Frank* ...
30 ibid.
31 ibid.
32 *The New Yorker*, 'Who Owns Anne Frank?', 28 September 1997
33 Frank van Vree, Hetty Berg and David Duindam (eds), *Site of Deportation* ...
34 ibid.
35 ibid.
36 Henri van der Zee, *The Hunger Winter: occupied Holland, 1944–1945*, University of Nebraska Press, 1998
37 *Ons Amsterdam*, 'Honger eiste in de winter van 1944/45 5000 doden', 2010
38 Geert Mak, *Een kleine geschiedenis van Amsterdam*, Olympus, 2012
39 *The New Yorker*, 'Letter from Amsterdam', 15 February 1947
40 Ingrid de Zwarte, *The Hunger Winter: fighting famine in the occupied Netherlands*, Cambridge University Press, 2020
41 Harry Mulisch, *The Assault*, Pantheon Books, 1982
42 *Ons Amsterdam*, 'Hier gebeurde het... Museumplein, 26 januari 1953', 2006
43 Hannah Arendt, *Eichmann in Jerusalem: a report on the banality of evil*, Penguin Books, 1963
44 *The New York Times*, 'Holocaust Memorial Is Closer to Reality in Amsterdam', 16 December 2016
45 Ian Buruma, *Murder in Amsterdam*, Penguin Books, 2014

46 Tony Judt, *Postwar: a history of Europe since 1945*, Penguin Books, 2005

47 Keith Lowe, *Prisoners of History: what monuments to the Second World War tell us about our history and ourselves*, William Collins, 2020

48 Simon Kuper, *Ajax, The Dutch, The War: football in Europe during the Second World War*, Orion Publishing, 2011

49 NRC, 'Bernhard had het bewijs voor zijn lidmaatschap van de NSDAP in zijn eigen archief', 3 October 2023

50 *De Volkskrant*, 'De prins is dood, de prins spreekt', 14 December 2004

51 Tony Judt, *Postwar* …

52 Keith Lowe, *Savage Continent: Europe in the aftermath of World War II*, Picador, 2012

53 Documentary film *Anne Frank Remembered*, 1995

54 Francine Prose, *Anne Frank* …

55 https://www.annefrank.org/annes-wereld/the-return-of-otto-frank

56 Anne Frank Fonds, *Anne Frank: the collected works*, Bloomsbury Continuum, 2019

57 Francine Prose, *Anne Frank* …

58 Dara Horn, *People Love Dead Jews*, W.W. Norton & Company, 2021

59 Francine Prose, *Anne Frank* …

60 *The Jerusalem Post*, 'Israel and Anne Frank's Jewishness', 12 April 2018

61 *The New Yorker*, 'Who Owns Anne Frank?', 28 September 1997

62 Roxane van Iperen, *The Sisters of Auschwitz: the true story of two Jewish sisters' resistance in the heart of Nazi territory*, Seven Dials, 2019

63 The *Guardian*, 'The Evenings by Gerard Reve review – a masterpiece, translated at long last', 9 November 2016

Chapter Eight: NDSM, the North, and the River IJ

1 Rijnmond, 'Rotterdams schip vaart door Amsterdamse tunnel', 21 November 2015

2 https://www.eyefilm.nl/en/about-eye/discover-our-buildings

3 *Het Financieele Dagblad*, 'Wat is Nederlandse architectuur?', 1 May 2019

4 NOS, 'Duurste penthouse van Nederland verkocht', 18 januari 2016

5 *Het Financieele Dagblad*, 'Won Yip, de horecatycoon van Amsterdam', 27 October 2017

6 Stichting NDSM-Herleeft, 'Bloei en ondergang van een Amsterdamse werf'

7 N.F.R. Crafts and Gianni Toniolo (eds), *Economic Growth in Europe Since 1945*, Cambridge University Press, 1996

8 *The New Yorker*, 'Letter from Amsterdam', 15 February 1947

9 Eelco N. van Kleffens, 'If the Nazis Flood Holland', Foreign Affairs, 1 July 1944

10 P. Lieftinck, *The Post-War Financial Rehabilitation of The Netherlands*, Springer, 2012

11 CBS, 'Natural gas revenues almost 417 billion euros' 28 May 2019

12 N.F.R. Crafts and Gianni Toniolo (eds), *Economic Growth ...*

13 *The Economist*, 'How Australia broke the record for economic growth', 6 September 2017

14 World Bank, GDP per capita (current US$), 1960–2022

15 ibid.

16 OECD, 'Average Annual Wages', 2022

17 *Ons Amsterdam*, 'De Baanderij: oud-scheepsbouwers praten na', 1 September 2000

18 ibid.

19 ibid.

20 Raquel Varela, Hugh Murphy and Marcel van der Linden (eds), *Shipbuilding and Ship Repair Workers Around the World: case studies 1950–2010*, Amsterdam University Press, 2017

21 *Het Parool*, 'Nasmaak faillissement nog altijd bitter', 30 August 1994

22 *Ons Amsterdam*, 'De Baanderij ...'

23 https://allecijfers.nl/wijk/tuindorp-buiksloot-amsterdam/

24 *Biografisch Woordenboek van het Socialisme en de Arbeidersbeweging in Nederland*, International Institute of Social History, 2023

25 ibid.

26 *Dagblad van Zuidholland en 's Gravenhage*, Residentie Nieuws, 13 September 1872

27 *Omaha Daily Bee*, 6 July 1917

28 *Ons Amsterdam*, 'De windvlaag des doods', 24 juli 2018

29 *De Telegraaf*, 'Meer Levensvreugd, meer rust', 27 July 1926

30 *Ons Amsterdam*, 'Een wandeling door Tuindorp Nieuwendam', 16 May 2002

31 Richter Roegholt, *A Short History* ...

32 H.M. van den Brink, *On the Water*

33 F. Wassenberg, *Large Housing Estates: ideas, rise, fall and recovery — the Bijlmermeer and beyond*, TU Delft, 2013

34 *Nederlands Dagblad*, 'Bijlmermeer krijgt bosachtig karakter', 19 January 1968

35 *Algemeen Dagblad*, 'Eerste bewoner in Bijlmermeer', 29 November 1968

36 Cor Wagenaar, *Happy: cities and public happiness in post-war Europe*, NAi, 2004

37 Eline Westra, Saskia Bonjour and Floris Vermeulen, 'Claiming a postcolonial differential citizenship', Migration Studies, 2023

38 F. Wassenberg, *Large Housing Estates*

39 ibid.

40 Uriel Rosenthal, *Complexity in Urban Crisis Management: Amsterdam's response to the Bijlmer air disaster*, Routledge, 1994

41 H. Entzinger, *A Tale of Two Cities: Rotterdam, Amsterdam and their immigrants*, Springer, 2019

42 Gemeente Amsterdam, 'Bevolking in cijfers', 2023

43 ibid.

44 Patricia, *Ethnic Amsterdam: a complete guide to the city's faces, places and cultures*, Vassallucci Amsterdam, 2001

45 Frank van Tubergen and Matthijs Kalmijn, 'Language Proficiency and Usage Among Immigrants in the Netherlands: Incentives or Opportunities?', European Sociological Review, 2009

46 Patricia Gosling, *Ethnic Amsterdam* ...

47 *De Kanttekening*, 'Minder Tweede Kamerleden met een migratieachtergrond', 4 December 2023

48 The *Guardian*, 'Liberal culture under threat in Dutch religious and ethnic crisis', 11 November 2004

49 Gemeente Amsterdam, 'Theo van Gogh: 23 juli 1957 – 2 November 2004', 2 November 2023

50 Simon Cottee, 'We Need to Talk About Mohammad:

Criminology, Theistic Violence and the Murder of Theo Van Gogh', The British Journal of Criminology, 10 June 2014

51 *Ons Amsterdam*, 'Annexaties 1921. Landhonger. 28 December 1920. Amsterdam wordt vier keer zo groot', 1 December 2020

52 ibid.

53 *Het Parool*, 'Noord een der fraaiste delen van hoofdstad', 26 March 1966

54 ibid.

55 NOS, 'Weesp is nu een stukje Amsterdam', 24 March 2022

56 Kimberley Kinder, *The Politics of Urban Water: changing waterscapes in Amsterdam*, University of Georgia Press, 2015

57 ibid.

58 *Ons Amsterdam*, 'Hier gebeurde het... Surinamekade 3 September 1988', 1 November 2008

59 Bloomberg, 'Amsterdam's Development Boom Runs Up Against Rising Seas', 14 October 2022

60 Kimberley Kinder, *The Politics of Urban Water ...*

Chapter Nine: West, the Sloterplas, and the Red Light District

1   Nu.nl, 'Cannabis van 4200 jaar oud in graf Hanzelijn',10 April 2012

2   Joanna Bourke, 'Enjoying the high life—drugs in history and culture', The Lancet, 27 November 2010

3   Jean-Paul C Grund and Joost J. Breeksema, *Drug Policy in The Netherlands*, Routledge, 2017

4   Tony Judt, ...

5   ibid.

6   CBS, 'Baby Boomers in the Netherlands', 2012

7   ibid.

8   Derek Taylor, *Fifty Years Adrift*, 1984

9   Beata Labuhn, 'From Het Lieverdje to NDSM. Historical Background of Amsterdam's Countercultural Places', Global Built Environment Review, 2019

10 Rob van Scheers, translated by Aletta Stevens, *Paul Verhoeven*, Faber & Faber, 1997

11 *Nieuwsblad van het Noorden*, 'Rel rond rijksmuseum loopt met sisser af', 12 June 1969

12 Beata Labuhn, 'From Het Lieverdje ...'

13 https://www.government.nl/topics/drugs

14 Gemeente Amsterdam, 'Coffeeshops, prostitutie en tourisme in het Singel/Wallengebied', 2019

15 *DutchNews.nl*, 'Dutch murder rate stable and is one of the lowest in Europe', 28 September 2022

16 Trimbos Instituut, 'Netherlands National Drug Monitor', 2010

17 *New York Times*, 'Solving the Dutch Pot Paradox', 25 March 2018

18 *De Volkskrant*, 'Auteur maffiaboek Gomorra: De maffia in Amsterdam is erger dan in Napels', 27 September 2019

19 Gemeente Amsterdam, 'De achterkant van Amsterdam', 2019

20 The *Guardian*, 'Severed head found outside Amsterdam cafe linked to drugs gang war', 2016

21 *EenVandaag*, 'Reconstructie: vier direct betrokkenen vertellen over de eerste uren na de moordaanslag op misdaadjournalist Peter R. de Vries', 16 October 2021

22 *BBC News*, 'Is the Netherlands becoming a narco-state?', 19 December 2019

23 *Time Out*, '40 Coolest Neighbourhoods in the World Right Now', 17 Oct 2023

24 *Ons Amsterdam*, 'Amsterdam als fietsstad: "Verkeer per rijwiel is noodig en gemakkelijk"', 28 February 2000

25 Fred Feddes and Marjolein de Lange, *Bike City Amsterdam*

26 ibid.

27 ibid.

28 *De Groene Amsterdammer*, 'Het Algemeen Belang', 23 February 2011

29 *Ons Amsterdam*, 'Amsterdam als fietsstad: "Verkeer per rijwiel is noodig en gemakkelijk"', 28 February 2000

30 Gemeente Amsterdam, 'Monitor Autoluw', 2023

31 European Commission, 'Quality of life in European cities', 2023

32 The *Guardian*, 'How Amsterdam became the bicycle capital of the world', 5 May 2015

33 Allecijfers.nl

34 Kiesraad, Databank Verkiezinguitslagen

35 Pew Research Center, 'European Public Opinion Three Decades After the Fall of Communism', 2019

36 Pew Research Center, 'Diversity and Division in Advanced Economies', 2021

37 Gemeente Amsterdam, 'Bevolking in cijfers', 2023

38 Allecijfers.nl

39 *Ons Amsterdam*, 'Opgeslokt door Nieuw-West', 10 March 2003

40 The *Guardian*, 'Amsterdam's sex workers: the unlikely victims of gentrification', 15 January 2016

41 Chrisje Brants, 'The Fine Art of Regulated Tolerance: Prostitution in Amsterdam', Journal of Law and Society, 1998

42 Anthony Bailey, *Rembrandt's House*

43 Lotte van de Pol, *The Burgher and the Whore: prostitution in early modern Amsterdam*, Oxford University Press, 2011

44 Joyce Outshoorn, 'Policy Change in Prostitution in the Netherlands: from Legalization to Strict Control', Sexuality Research and Social Policy, 2012

45 NPO Radio 1: 'Feit of fictie: 1 op de 7 mannen betaalt weleens voor seks', 24 October 2019

46 *Metro*, 'Nederland eindigt hoog op lijst mensenhandel: 'Speelt in verborgene af", 18 October 2022

47 ibid.

48 ECLJ, 'Legal prostitution and human trafficking in the Netherlands', 2022

49 The *Guardian*, 'Amsterdam's sex workers: the unlikely victims of gentrification', 15 January 2016

50 *Foreign Policy*, 'It's Legal to Sell Sex in Amsterdam, But Don't Expect the Same Rights As Other Workers', 19 February 2019

51 *DutchNews.nl*, '"An erotic prison": sex workers oppose plans for mega brothel', 1 February 2024

52 Roos Gerritsma, 'Overcrowded Amsterdam: Striving for a Balance Between Trade, Tolerance and Tourism', in book Overtourism: excesses, discontents and measures in travel and tourism, 2019

53 ibid.

54 Arthur Frommer, *Europe on Five Dollars a Day*, Frommer's, 1957

55 ibid.

56 Gemeente Amsterdam, 'De achterkant van Amsterdam', 2019

57 Gemeente Amsterdam, 'Bezoekersaantallen Amsterdam 2018–2021', 2022

58 CNN, '"Don't come to Amsterdam." Dutch capital tells rowdy tourists to stay away', 30 June 2021

59   *UnHerd*, 'The drug trade has wrecked Amsterdam', 24 October
     2022
60   *Forbes*, 'Amsterdam Wants Foreign Tourists To "Stay Away"
     From Drugs, Alcohol, And Sex', 19 December 2022
61   *Euronews*, 'See Amsterdam's newest campaign urging drunken
     British tourists to "stay away"', 29 March 2023
62   *Het Parool*, 'Nog nooit zoveel bezoekers in Amsterdam als in
     2023', 31 May 2024
63   https://thebulldog.com/weed/the-history-of-the-bulldog/

Conclusion: The Dam to Bijlmer and IJburg

1   *The New York Times*, 'The Dutch Have Solutions to Rising Seas',
     15 June 2017
2   KNMI, 'Nieuwe KNMI-klimaatscenario's: "Nederland moet zich
     voorbereiden op zwaardere weersextremen"' 9 October 2023
3   ibid.
4   University of Utrecht/NRC, 'The question is not if the
     Netherlands will disappear below sea level, but when', 13 July
     2018
5   NOS, 'Kustlijn opgeven en het hogerop zoeken, dat is een plan B
     bij zeespiegelstijging', 9 February 2019
6   Nederlands Aviation Safety Board, 'Aircraft Accident Report
     92-1 1: El Al 1862', 1994
7   *BBC News*, 'El Al jumbo crashes in Amsterdam', 4 October 1992
8   J.M. van de Laar, chapter in 'Aansprakelijkheid en schadeverhaal
     bij rampen', Vrije Universiteit Amsterdam, 2002
9   *The Times of Israel*, '20 years on, El Al crash in Amsterdam still
     spawns conspiracy theories', 15 October 2012
10   *Nederlands Dagblad*, 'Nederland misschien kleurrijker na
     Bijlmerramp', 10 October 1992
11   CBS, 'Vijftig jaar Bijlmer', 13 December 2016
12   https://allecijfers.nl/ranglijst/hoogste-en-laagste-inkomen-per-
     wijk-in-de-gemeente-amsterdam/
13   RIVM, 'Gezondheidsmonitor Volwassenen en Ouderen', 2020
14   Gemeente Amsterdam, 'IJburg: nieuwe eilanden en woningbouw',
     2023
15   World Bank, 'GDP per capita: current $US', 2023
16   OECD, 'Regions and Cities at a Glance: The Netherlands', 2020

17 Oxford Economics, 'Global Cities', 2023 and World Bank, GDP, 2023

18 OECD, 'Tax-to-GDP ratios', 2021

19 Pew Research Center, 'Diversity and Division in Advanced Economies', 2021

20 World Bank Open Data, 2023

21 *DutchNews.nl*, 'Dutch murder rate continues to fall', 2024

22 NOS, 'Kabinet sluit gevangenissen Almere, Zeist, Zoetermeer en Zwaag', 22 June 2018

23 NOS, 'Rotterdam moordhoofdstad van Nederland', 29 August 2023

24 Metropolitan Police, 'Murders in London 2021 by age, gender and race', 2022

25 CBS, 'Wie werken het vaakst in deeltijd?', 2022

26 UNICEF, 'Worlds of Influence: Understanding what shapes child well-being in rich countries', 2020

27 OECD, 'Average usual weekly hours worked on the main job', 2022

28 OECD, 'Average annual wages', 2022

29 Gemeente Amsterdam, 'Hoeveel toeristen komen er naar Amsterdam en regio, en waar verblijven zij?', 2023

30 Schiphol Annual Traffic Review, 'Persistent growth of passenger air movements globally', 2024